Speech Communities

What makes a speech community? How do they evolve? How are speech communities identified? Speech communities are central to our understanding of how language and interactions occur in societies around the world and in this book readers will find an overview of the main concepts and critical arguments surrounding how language and communication styles distinguish and identify groups.

Speech communities are not organized around linguistic facts but around people who want to share their opinions and identities; the language we use constructs, represents, and embodies meaningful participation in society. This book focuses on a range of speech communities, including those that have developed from an increasingly technological world in which migration and global interactions are common. Essential reading for graduate students and researchers in linguistic anthropology, sociolinguistics, and applied linguistics.

MARCYLIENA H. MORGAN is Professor of African and African American Studies at Harvard University.

KEY TOPICS IN LINGUISTIC ANTHROPOLOGY

'Key Topics in Linguistic Anthropology' focuses on the main topics of study
and research in linguistic anthropology today. It consists of accessible yet
challenging accounts of the most important concepts, phenomena and
questions to consider when examining the relationship between language
and culture. Some topics have been the subject of study for many years,
and are re-examined in the light of new developments in the field; others
are issues of growing importance that have not so far been given a
sustained treatment. Written by leading experts, and designed to bridge
the gap between textbooks and primary literature, the books in the series
can either be used on courses and seminars, or as succinct one-stop guides
to a particular topic for individual students and researchers.

Forthcoming titles:

Language Socialization by Garrett

Language Endangerment by Bradley and Bradley

Language as Social Action by Ahearn

Speech Communities

MARCYLIENA H. MORGAN

CAMBRIDGE
UNIVERSITY PRESS

CAMBRIDGE
UNIVERSITY PRESS

University Printing House, Cambridge CB2 8BS, United Kingdom

Published in the United States of America by Cambridge University Press, New York

Cambridge University Press is part of the University of Cambridge.

It furthers the University's mission by disseminating knowledge in the pursuit of education, learning and research at the highest international levels of excellence.

www.cambridge.org
Information on this title: www.cambridge.org/9781107678149

© Marcyliena H. Morgan 2014

First published 2014

Printed in the United Kingdom by CPI Group Ltd, Croydon CR0 4YY

A catalogue record for this publication is available from the British Library

Library of Congress Cataloging in Publication data
Morgan, Marcyliena H.
Speech Communities / Marcyliena Morgan.
pages cm. – (Key topics in linguistic anthropology)
Includes bibliographical references and index.
ISBN 978-1-107-02350-5 (hardback) – ISBN 978-1-107-67814-9 (paperback)
1. Languages in contact. 2. Speech – Social aspects. 3. Communities – Social aspects.
4. Intercultural communication. 5. Speech and social status. 6. Sociolinguistics. I. Title.
P40.5.L38M68 2013
306.44 – dc23 2013028340

ISBN 978-1-107-02350-5 Hardback
ISBN 978-1-107-67814-9 Paperback

Contents

Acknowledgments

Research on speech communities is a collaborative process involving numerous contexts and competing ideologies. Many people have influenced this book and have been generous in their discussions of their own language socialization and their interest in discourse in general. My editors at Cambridge University Press, Helena Dowson and Andrew Winnard, have been especially patient and helpful throughout this process. Students in my Urban Speech Community classes and Digital/Blacks Online Communities classes at Stanford University and Harvard University have played a special role in my understanding of the complexity of speech communities and how youth experience their identities through language and discourse as everyday life in their multicultural and complicated political and social world. I am grateful for the colleagues who have shared their insightful observations and comments over the years. They include Dionne Bennett, Nicole Hodges Perseley, Lisa Thompson, Theodore Miller, Schuyler Polk, Jenigh Garrett, Jessica Norwood, Dorinne Kondo, Jamaica Kincaid, Lorene Cary, Sumeeya Mujahid, Kris Guitierrez and Prudence Carter. I especially want to thank the anonymous reviewer for his or her thoughtful and often revealing comments, which raised important observations and arguments that helped every aspect of this book. Alvin Carter has been extremely helpful with the collection of references and wrestling with the new technology.

I am indebted to Alessandro Duranti who first encouraged me to write about speech communities and helped me realize that most of my work has been about what it means to share language ideologies and the excruciating situations that can develop when they are in conflict. I owe a special gratitude to Evelyn Higginbotham, Henry Louis Gates Jr. and the faculty of African American Studies at Harvard University who encouraged me throughout this project. Dionne Bennett shared her insight and participated in many discussions about the theoretical and social aspects of speech communities and read and edited the entire manuscript. Her passion and intellect are reflected throughout this work. Special thanks go to my husband, Larry Bobo, and the amazing friends, social networks and speech communities that have participated in countless conversations and shared their insight about what they think about language and discourse and the ways in which it matters in their lives.

Finally, I would also like to recognize my early teachers who encouraged me to hear, observe and listen: Claudia Mitchell Kernan, Geneva Smitherman, Beryl Bailey, Grace Holt, Thomas Kochman, Gillian Sankoff, Shirley Brice Heath, Erving Goffman, Dell Hymes and William Labov. Any shortcomings that remain, of course, are my own.

Transcription Conventions

CAPITAL LETTERS indicate some form of emphasis which may be signaled by changes in pitch or amplitude.

BOLD CAPITAL LETTERS indicate loud-talking.

Italics indicate a change in the quality of speech.

.   A period indicates a stopping fall in tone, not necessarily the end of a sentence.

,   A comma indicates a continuing intonation, not necessarily between clauses of sentences.

:   Colons indicate that the sound just before the colon has been lengthened.

?   A question mark indicates a rising inflection, not necessarily a question.

!   An exclamation point indicates an animated tone, not necessarily an exclamation.

-   A single dash can indicate a (1) short untimed pause, (2) halting, abrupt cutoff, or, when multiple dashes hyphenate the syllables of a word or connect strings of words, the stream of talk so marked has (3) a stammering quality.

[All overlapping utterances, including those which start simultaneously are marked with a single left bracket.

]   The point where overlap stops is marked with a single right bracket.

=   When there is no interval between adjacent utterances, the second being latched immediately to the first, the utterances are linked together with equal signs. They are also used to link different parts of a single speaker's utterance when those parts constitute a continuous flow of speech that has been carried over to another line to accommodate an intervening interruption.

(.)   A period within parenthesis indicates a one second pause.

( )   When intervals in the stream of talk occur, they are timed in tenths of a second and inserted within parentheses either within an utterance or between.

(())   Double parentheses in italics provide description of quality of talk and activity related to talk.

1 What are speech communities?

The study of speech communities is central to the understanding of human language and meaning. Speech communities are groups that share values and attitudes about language use, varieties and practices. These communities develop through prolonged interaction among those who operate within these shared and recognized beliefs and value systems regarding forms and styles of communication. While we are born with the ability to learn language, we do so within cultures and societies that frame the process of learning how to talk to others. This framing once exclusively occurred as face-to-face interactions within communities of speakers. Constant relocation, mass migration, transmigration, ever-evolving technology and globalization have transformed many societies and increased the need to provide more detailed descriptions and theories regarding the nature of speech communities. The importance of our growing understanding of speech communities remains one of the most significant projects faced by those interested in language, discourse and interaction. This chapter defines and identifies types of speech communities, provides the history of the term and examines its importance to the study of language and discourse in general.

The concept of speech community does not simply focus on groups that speak the same language. Rather, the concept takes as fact that language represents, embodies, constructs and constitutes meaningful participation in society and culture. It also assumes that a mutually intelligible symbolic and ideological communicative system must be at play among those who share knowledge and practices about how one is meaningful across social contexts.[1] Thus as peoples relocate away from their families and home communities and build others, relationships and interactions continue and change, and are sustained through the

---

[1] Of course concepts like mutual intelligibility and meaning are complex in and of themselves. The point here is that speech communities are also political and historical sites where social meaning is intrinsic in talk.

use of evolving technology and media that enhances, recognizes and re-creates communities. These interactions constitute the substance of human contact and the importance of language, discourse and verbal styles in the representation and negotiation of the relationships that ensue. It is within speech communities that identity, ideology and agency are actualized in society.[2]

1.1 SPEECH COMMUNITIES

A group of people is not necessarily a community unless they share a common view, activity, belief etc. Speech is not simply sounds that come from a person's mouth. Social actors recognize the significance of innate human sounds such as screams, moans, cries etc. without learning and being socialized into a system of meaning. In contrast, the act of turning human sound into symbols that are recognizable as speech and particular to a group of people requires an agreement of some sort regarding the system of symbols in circulation. That agreement can vary within a language and among various languages. Members must be socialized to learn the language symbols of that community and how and when to use them.

Communities can be defined and identified in terms of space, place, affiliation, practices and any combination of these terms. For example, while the term "community" is generally used in reference to a social unit larger than a household, it can also refer to a national and international group. Online communities can exist where members are in the thousands and there may be no physical, visual or auditory contact among members. Anthony Cohen believes that communities can be understood by their boundaries, since they are identified by both their uniqueness and difference. He argues that "a reasonable interpretation of the word's use would seem to imply two related suggestions: that the members of a group of people (a) have something in common with each other, which (b) distinguishes them in a significant way from members of other putative groups" (1985: 12). What is fundamental to both speech and community is that a system of interaction and symbols is shared, learned and taught, and that participants and members are aware they share this system. This is why speech communities are one way that language ideologies and social identities are constructed.

[2] See Bucholtz and Hall 2004, Duranti 2004 and Kroskrity 2004.

While there are many social and political forms a speech community may take – from nation-states to chat rooms dedicated to extraterrestrial sightings – speech communities are recognized as distinctive in relation to other speech communities. That is, they come into collective consciousness when there is a crisis of some sort and their existence is highlighted in relation to other communities. This is also triggered when hegemonic powers consider what the speech community is doing and saying to be a problem, or when researchers highlight speech community distinctiveness in some way and rely on them as a unit of study.[3] Thus, while speech community is a fundamental concept, it is also the object of unremitting critique. In fact, speech communities have been blamed for poor literary skills, epidemics, unemployment, increases in crime and so on.[4]

Many of the critical arguments surrounding speech communities concern two contrasting perspectives on how to define language and discourse. The first focuses on the analysis and description of linguistic, semantic and conversational features that are gathered from a group and are in turn deemed to be stable indicators of that speech community. The second perspective refers to the notion of language and discourse as a way of representing social life (Foucault 1972; Hall 1996a). In this case the focus is on how language is used to represent ideology, construct relationships, identity and so on. Although these perspectives can be complementary, they are often in contention with each other. The choice of perspective can have far-reaching implications for the speech community in question as well as the concept in general.

1.2 EARLY DEFINITIONS OF SPEECH COMMUNITY

In 1933 Leonard Bloomfield wrote: "A group of people who use the same set of speech signals is a *speech-community*" (1933: 29). This definition reflects a common belief of the time, that monolingualism – one language, one nation-state – is the canonical example of speech community (e.g. Anderson 1983). It focuses on the analysis and description of linguistic, semantic and conversational features that are identified by language authorities as belonging to a defined group. In this

---

[3] See Mercer (1994) and Bucholtz and Hall 2004 for discussion of identity coming into question when it is in crisis.

[4] This is true for the 1997 "Ebonics" case in the US, as well as arguments among sociologists that participation in the speech community leads to unemployment (e.g. Massey and Denton 1993 and Wilson 1987, 1996).

case, a community is considered to be a "social group of any size who reside in a specific locality, share government, and have a common cultural and historical heritage" (Random House Dictionary). During this period, the field of linguistics was mainly concerned with describing languages and the historical relationships of language families (R. A. Hudson 1980; Lyons 1981). Language itself was viewed as the product of history and politics but not integral to and entangled in it – and therefore not as an aspect of historicity and the context of politics and social life.[5]

Within the confines of descriptive and structural linguistics, it is best to think of language as a system of arbitrary symbols that exists at interconnecting levels that are devoid of meaning and significance beyond their function (see also Duranti 1997). Thus phonemes and sounds can be combined into meaningful morphemes that can become words, phrases, sentences and so on. Predictably, for traditional linguistics, the study of various aspects of languages was highly compartmentalized, so that the abstract and social aspects of language were not the subjects of study. While linguists are fond of saying "all grammars leak"[6] to acknowledge that there are exceptions to most linguistic rules, less attention has been paid to the outpouring of creativity and complexity that lead to these *leaks* and how, when and why speakers of languages find their system of symbols a subject of interest.

Of course, discovering the history of and describing the world's languages is very important business, and, in many respects, early definitions corresponded to Western arrogance and assumed the responsibility to "represent the world correctly" – with itself as the reference point. As Edward Said argued: "Every empire, however, tells itself and the world that it is unlike all other empires, that its mission is not to plunder and control but to educate and liberate."[7] From this perspective, it is not surprising that while Bloomfield considered the speech community to be the most important kind of social group, his evaluation of contact situations only recognized the most perceptible characteristics of speech communities. It did not assume that various sectors of society interacted with each other in a complementary way.[8] Instead, communities that arose out of European aggression and cultural hegemony

---

[5] This omission comes back to haunt the term, since sociolinguists' notion of context began to differ greatly from that of anthropology (see below).

[6] This quotation is generally attributed to Edward Sapir (1921: 39).

[7] *Los Angeles Times*, July 20, 2003.

[8] Of course I do not mean to suggest that Bloomfield was at fault here. Until as late as the 1960s, many linguists assumed that the contact situation that resulted from the Atlantic slave trade meant there was no mutual intelligibility among captives.

were regulated to supplemental status. Unfortunately, the notion that viable speech communities could not exist under such circumstances suggests that the great cultural, linguistic and social restructuring and reconstitution accomplished by colonized and conquered people were inconsequential in light of the enormity of the catastrophic events that they endured. This perspective also greatly affected earlier linguistic descriptions of speech communities that developed within plantation slavery in the Americas. Whether in relation to the language spoken throughout slave communities in the US or the Caribbean, earlier linguistic studies argued that African languages had minimal influence on language development (see below). As the later work of many sociolinguists and creolists proved, they were mistaken.

Bloomfield's conception of the homogeneous speech community represented the canon in linguistic anthropology until Noam Chomsky (1965) began to challenge the concept's utility. Chomsky's work critiqued descriptive and structural analyses of language and introduced a theoretical approach that explored the human capacity to produce language rather than language as a social construct. In *Aspects of the Theory of Syntax*, Chomsky (1965) introduced the distinction between competence and performance, and abandoned the model that incorporated the speech community as the focus of linguistic analysis. The possibility of discovering human linguistic capacity was found in the individual: the cognitive, psychological self that develops irrespective of where performance of that knowledge resided – the speech community. Instead of resolving the conflict between whether the speech community establishes language and discourse norms or whether it is constituted through linguistic descriptions, Chomsky insistently argued that the essence of language resides in discovering the mechanism and theory behind the human ability to produce language. By regulating people's actual use of language to descriptions of linguistic problems (e.g. false starts, errors, etc.) the speech community suddenly was at risk of becoming the garbage dump for linguistic debris – what remains after theoretical analysis of linguistic capacity is complete.

As Chomsky's theories began to attack the concept's foundations, new generations of linguistic anthropologists began to offer more evidence of its importance for both members of speech communities and theorists who sought to develop analyses of language and discourse in groups. However, the most difficult tasks remained. Those were to determine: the role of cultural hegemony, the construction and re-construction of values, norms and standards in speech community representation, and why group differences do not destroy speech communities.

1.3 LANGUAGE, DISCOURSE AND REPRESENTATION

The linguistic analysis – disregarding speakers' beliefs, politics and social life – is often considered to be the "objective" and accurate description of speech community from the perspective of the dominant culture. Thus a national language can be proclaimed, even if it is only spoken by an elite few, and one dialect can be declared the prestige variety. At the same time, members of speech communities may, also, recognize that they can incorporate and act on, discursively and literally, the cultural hegemony that the dominant culture sustains, enforces and reproduces in ways that highlight representations of others who reside outside its boundaries (see Gramsci 1971 and Bourdieu 1991). That is to say, membership in a speech community includes local knowledge of the way language choice, variation and discourse represents identity, generation, occupation, politics, social relationships and more. This point is illustrated in the writer Jamaica Kincaid's description of the effect of colonization on Antigua and the complexity of using the language of the colonizer as the speech community's language:

> [W]hat I see is the millions of people, of whom I am just one, made orphans: no motherland, no fatherland, no gods, no mounds of earth for holy ground, no excess of love which might lead to the things that an excess of love sometimes brings and worst and most painful of all, no tongue. (For isn't it odd that the only language I have in which to speak of this crime is the language of the criminal who committed the crime?) And what can that really mean? For the language of the criminal can contain only the goodness of the criminal's deed. (Kincaid 1988: 31)

Throughout the social sciences, there has been a growing awareness of the importance of language and discourse in the representation of local knowledge, culture, identity and politics. This is especially true in the works of cultural anthropologists whose ethnographies are situated within communities whose members are aware of intra-community social and cultural differences and where transmigration, social identity and memory of imagined and experienced notions of *home* are part of the cultural fabric. In speech communities where there are multiple sites of contact across social class, status and sometimes national origin, local ideologies of language often reflect heteroglossia (Bakhtin 1981), the diversity and shifting of styles or linguistic codes that exist within and often among communities. For example, Deborah A. Thomas' ethnography of Jamaican identity includes the rural community Mango Mount, where social classes interact on a regular basis. Although the groups communicate with each other, Thomas reports that "it is often clear which sector of the Mango Mount community the speaker belongs to by their language" (2004: 24). Dorinne Kondo (1997) explores the power of discourse in the representation of the lives of Asian Americans through the analysis of Asian American playwrights' and actors' performance of identity as a manifestation of their community norm of mediating multiple language ideologies and heteroglossia. Language and discourse are also integral to Kesha Fikes' (2009) work on Cape Verdeans in Cape Verde and Portugal. Fikes explores how transnationals rely on African language usage and referents to frame membership in multiple speech communities that represent both resistance to and inclusion of an African Diasporan speech community, and how they use these same referents to index the Portuguese metropole in contrast to rural Cape Verde as well.

As the preceding cases suggest, describing speech communities is no simple matter; nor should it be. Speech communities cannot be defined solely through linguistic analysis and description or by static physical location, since membership can be experienced as part of a nation-state, neighborhood, village, club, compound, online chat room, religious institution and so on. Moreover, unless they are members of highly stratified societies, adults often experience multiple communities. One's initial socialization into a speech community may occur within a culture with communicative values that differ from other cultures and communities that one encounters later in life.

Speech communities are often recognizable by the circulation of discourse and the repetition of activities and beliefs and values about these topics which are constantly discussed, evaluated, corroborated, mediated and reconstituted by its members. One's awareness of these issues is determined by whether and to what degree speech communities are in crisis. For some, awareness is ingrained in the cultural fabric and thus represents unmarked usage that encompasses the community's historicity, politics, ideology, representation and so on. Although these values are agreed upon, that does not necessarily mean that there is complete consensus about the implementation of these principles. Rather, what is at stake is knowledge of the symbolic, market and exchange value of varieties and styles within and across speech communities.

An earlier ethnography of the Vaupés Indians of southeastern Colombia by Jean Jackson (1974, 1983) revealed the complex intersection of culture, language, variation, ideology and society that may constitute speech communities. The Vaupés occupy a tropical rainforest that covers the countries of Colombia and Brazil. Whereas early reports described the languages of the region as mutually unintelligible, Jackson discovered a decidedly different situation.[9] She found that the area was mainly a multilingual community where, with few exceptions, "all semi-sedentary Indians in Vaupés are multilingual speaking Tukanoan, Arawak, and Carib language families. All speak fluently at least three languages . . . some as many as ten" (1974: 55). Her analysis challenged many widely held linguistic theories about the overall effects of multilingualism in societies and the formation of speech communities. Moreover, although everyone was multilingual, language difference did not distinguish rank and other forms of social differentiation. In fact she found that "all Vaupés share a strikingly homogeneous culture" (53). They all share cultural and religious practices about how language should be used in daily life and the same rule of speech, "even though some Indians' verbal repertoires do not overlap" (55). She goes on to say that lack of overlap is rare because of the use of Tukano as a lingua franca.

The Vaupés lived in communities comprised of longhouses with patrilineal descent groups based on the language of the father. While the longhouses are multilingual, the main rule of marriage is "linguistic exogamy" – that the person marries outside the father's language aggregate. These aggregates do not occupy discrete territories and are not corporate groups, and most interactions are between aggregates. The use of the father's language reflects one's social identity. As Jackson states: "Membership is permanent and public; the one fact which will be known about an Indian before anything else will be his language-aggregate membership. If he marries a woman from far away, this is often the only information some of his relatives will have about her" (1974: 53).

Because of the complexity of the multilingual dynamics, Jackson suggested that the region be defined as a speech area and the longhouses be described as a speech community. Hymes (1974a) refers to Neustupny's interpretation of the Prague School notion of sharing ways of speaking across language boundaries – Sprechbund – to describe a "speech area" rather than a speech community to distinguish the phenomenon of shared ways of speaking, although people may not share languages (also see Romaine 1994). Yet it is not clear that this distinction is necessary to claim a speech community.[10] As Hymes has argued: "To participate in a speech community is not quite the same as to be a member of it . . . A

---

[9] Jackson reports that members from the Summer Institute of Linguistics which maintained fieldworkers in the region held this opinion; also Sorensen 1967.

[10] "Speech area" in some ways minimizes the importance of language ideology in distinguishing speech communities. This is especially important when media and technology are considered and groups form that share communicative norms and values but not necessarily native competence in the same language.

speech community is defined ... as a community sharing knowledge of rules of conduct and interpretation of speech. Such sharing comprises knowledge of at least one form of speech, and knowledge also of its patterns of use" (1974: 50–51).

As examined in the following sections, the notion of language that binds the speech community concept is constructed around several major theories regarding language as a social construct. These include the disciplinary perspectives of linguistic anthropology, the perspectives of sociolinguistics and the perspective of theorists who focus on language ideology and attitudes about language use, varieties and practices.

1.4 RETRIEVING THE SPEECH COMMUNITY

The work of John Gumperz (1968, 1972, 1982a) revived the concept of the speech community by considering it a social construct. He defined verbal interaction as "a social process in which utterances are selected in accordance with socially recognized norms and expectations" (1972: 219). Instead of focusing on a single language model, he defined the speech community as "any human aggregate characterized by regular and frequent interaction by means of a shared body of verbal signs and set off from similar aggregates by significant differences in language usage" (219).[11] Gumperz focused on interface communication and determined that the notion of consistent, repetitive and predictable interactions and contact is necessary for a speech community to exist. He argued that regardless of the linguistic similarities and differences, "the speech varieties employed within a speech community form a system because they are related to a shared set of social norms" (220). This formulation could incorporate the sociolinguistic research that was occurring in cities at the time (see below) and reconstituted the notion of speech community to include not only languages and language boundaries, but also values, attitudes and ideologies about language. Thus, while the concept of the speech community initially focused on language systems, relationships and boundaries, it expanded to include the notion of social representation and norms in the form of attitudes, values, beliefs and practices – and the notion that members of speech communities work their languages as social and cultural products.

---

[11] This is reprinted from his 1968 contribution. The Speech Community, in the *International Encyclopedia of the Social Sciences*.

Many direct and indirect efforts to reclaim the integrity of speech community that complemented Gumperz's interpretation emerged. In particular, Dell Hymes described the speech community as a "fundamental concept for the relation between language, speech, and social structure" (1964: 385). He considered the question of boundaries essential in order to recognize that communities are not, by definition, fixed units. In fact, Dell Hymes' model of ethnographies of communication and speaking argued for the importance of communicative competence – the knowledge a speaker must have to function as a member of a social group. Communicative competence is based on language use and socialization within cultures, and one becomes knowledgeable of both grammar and appropriateness across speech acts and events that are evaluated and corroborated by others. Hymes' argument that competence was "the interrelationship of language with the other code of communicative conduct" (1972: 277–278) replaced the notion that a language constitutes a speech community with the recognition that speech community, also, requires a code of beliefs and behaviors about language and discourse and knowledge of how to use them.

The influence of John Gumperz and Dell Hymes on the understanding of speech communities and language and discourse cannot be overstated. Their analyses and contributions are discussed throughout this text.

1.5 SOCIOLINGUISTS AND SOCIAL ACTORS

One of the greatest challenges to the reformulated concept of speech community described above actually came from the field of sociolinguistics and creole language studies. This is not surprising, since sociolinguistics is the study of language variation and the identification of features that systematically differ from other varieties. Similarly, creole language studies, which examines how multiple languages combine to form new language systems, must shift through contact language systems in order to determine whether one is distinct enough from all other languages present to be called a language in and of itself.[12] Thus both areas focus on the differences among and within speech communities that often resulted from discrimination in terms of class, gender and race and colonial conquest. In a field notorious for proclaiming that the difference between a language and dialect is who controls the army,

---

[12] This is to say nothing of the complex arguments necessary to assign pidgin, creole, semi-creole and dialect designations to languages that arose from plantation contact situations.

one could predict that the social, cultural and political parameters of speech communities would encroach on sociolinguistic methodologies that claim to be apolitical.

William Labov's (1980) definition of speech community addressed the question of methodological strategies and focused on the relationship of sociological categories like race, class and gender to variation in language use. Labov contrasted speech community attitudes toward linguistic variables and corroborated Hymes' depiction when he wrote, "The speech community is not defined by any marked agreement in the use of language elements, so much as by participation in a set of shared norms" (120–121). Moreover, he found that though these norms were often at odds with prestige standards, it did not mean that speakers within and outside of speech communities did not use them. Instead, it is necessary to consider their value within social contexts. As Gregory Guy explains:

> One reason that shared norms form part of the definition of the speech community is that they are required to account for one of the principal sociolinguistic findings regarding variation by class and style, namely that the same linguistic variables are involved in the differentiation of social classes and speech styles. (Guy 1989: 50)

In contrast, Milroy and Milroy, who conducted research in Belfast and Philadelphia, believe that contrasts in attitudes toward varieties within and between speech communities were embedded in the researcher's methodology rather than the social stratification of speech communities themselves. They argued that in Labov's notion of the sociolinguistic speech community, the shared norms of evaluation were also the very linguistic norms that symbolize the divisions between them. Rather than reflecting a shared belief, they assert that Labov's findings "are more readily interpretable as evidence of conflict and sharp divisions in society than as evidence of consensus" (1992: 3).

But speech communities can indeed have a consensus about divisions and use the same symbols to reflect complex and diverse opinions about divisions and to bring about consensus. That is, it is possible to represent views about variable choice through some form of consensus, and variables can have different values depending on the social and cultural context without representing conflict. For example, the African American speech community considers it ludicrous to think that a professional would use vernacular African American English (AAE) in formal settings unless it was done intentionally to make a point.[13] Moreover,

---

[13] Comedian Chris Rock's 1996 HBO television special, "Bring the Pain", includes a hilariously angry routine regarding non-African Americans' repeated mention

conversations among middle-class members often include imitations of speakers using AAE in formal settings to signify that listeners outside of the African American speech community are bigoted. Zentella makes a similar argument for Spanish and English code-switching in New York: "Relationships among language, setting and meaning are not fixed. Switching into Spanish in public or into English at home does not necessarily communicate intimacy or distance, respectively" (1997: 3).

Labov interpreted speech community values that recognize social differentiation within and between communities by contrasting dominant and overt norms with what he calls covert norms (1980: 249). While he described covert norms as a preference for the social dialect irrespective of the role of standard varieties, the question of how these norms function and whether they are, in fact, covert in the same way to all members of the speech community still remains.[14]

While members of speech communities may value many language varieties, speakers and theorists sometimes have different agendas about how to view these varieties. Theorists are, generally, concerned with variation as it relates to norms and linguistic patterns, while members of speech communities may be concerned with variation as a form of representation that is not fixed but fluid within multiple interactions.[15] As Eckert explains, "The claim that the social unit that defines one's sociolinguistic sample constitutes a speech community, then, is above all a way of placing the study itself rather than the speakers" (2000: 33).

For the most part, sociolinguistic training focuses on the identification and analysis of linguistic variation compared with sociological variables such as ethnicity, class, age and gender. The difficulty is in incorporating attitudes about language and the notion of shared and corroborated beliefs into the analysis of linguistic practices. If speech community members are not aware of these forms, linguists often argue that they are not aware of what constitutes their speech

---

that Colin Powell, a Black army general and later attorney general of the US, spoke clearly.

[14] See Patrick (2002) and Rampton (1998) for further discussion.

[15] Labov's first basic principle of social judgments is "social attitudes toward language are extremely uniform throughout a speech community" (1972b: 248). He includes the footnote: "In fact it seems plausible to define a speech community as a group of speakers who share a set of social attitudes towards language" (fn. 40 p. 248). The argument here is that this is probable within the scope of the linguistic study. As I have argued elsewhere (Morgan 1994b), varying attitudes may be a norm in some speech communities even though a particular methodology may not capture it.

community. But John Rickford (1985) argues that sociolinguistics must also pay attention to what speakers actually believe about how their language practices reflect their social lives. He investigated ethnicity as a sociolinguistic boundary by comparing linguistic variation between a Black and a White speaker on the South Carolina Sea Islands. While he found that social differentiation between speakers was marked at the morphosyntactic level, he argued that Sea Islanders were well aware of the function of the norms of their speech community, in spite of the contrasts.[16]

In this case, the definition of community and social context creates a dichotomy between the knowledge developed by theorists versus the abstract communicative and linguistic knowledge of speakers involved in everyday interactions. In fact, one of the more persistent challenges in creole language studies and sociolinguistics in general is to determine the extent to and ways in which information or linguistic facts gathered from a particular speech community can, in some way, benefit that community (Labov 1980, 1982). In creole language studies, this challenge often comes in the form of questions about power and hegemony when discussing historical linguistics and European colonization. Modern creole language situations have arisen mainly from European conceived and controlled plantation systems that brought together people of different nations, cultures and languages to serve as either indentured workers or slaves (M. C. Alleyne 1980). While the situations from which creole languages have emerged can be described merely as examples of language contact, that denotation is hardly sufficient if one considers the complex ways in which these communities of speakers currently use language to mediate and substantiate the multiple realities that constitute their world. These situations also provide an opportunity to illuminate the sites of contention in which creole language speakers and descendants negotiate and seek power. How linguists address these questions is as important to the speech community under study as the linguistic information that has been assembled.

1.6 LANGUAGE IDEOLOGY

In examining speech communities, "one must take into consideration how cultures reflect and express their ideological foundations . . . Thus,

---

[16] Rickford's respondents were a Black woman and White male. He argues that gender differences were not as important as race in this case.

the language ideology not only recognizes but relies on the knowledge that language varieties exist and represent different positions of power, politics, and history" (Morgan 2002: 37–38). Language ideologies are complex and textured in that, as cultural beliefs and practices, they are reproductions and representations, as well as tools to examine, reflect, subvert and exalt those representations. Mikhail Bakhtin, a Russian philosopher and literary critic, was well aware of this problem and argued that the notion of linguistic homogeneity is tied to the development of the European states and efforts to establish a national identity through a national language. As we can see above, such a notion may not be related to how people use language. In speech communities where there is multiple contact across social class, status and sometimes national origin, local ideologies of language often reflect heteroglossia, the shifting of styles or linguistic codes that exist within and often among communities (Bakhtin 1981). Bakhtin considered linguistic variation to be a continuous tension between centripetal (centralizing and unifying) and centrifugal (decentralizing and disunifying) forces of language. He was interested in language in context and argued, "At any given time, in any given place, there will be a set of conditions – social, historical, meteorological, physiological – that will insure that a word uttered in that place and at that time will have a meaning different than it would have under any other conditions" (428).

Communication under ideal circumstances (e.g. all channels are open and clear and most interpretations are shared) can still be confusing. Part of the communication process is determining the intentions of the speakers and interactions. When multiple languages and language ideologies are added, the determination of why variation is occurring is both more complex and more important. In this regard, the writer Junot Diaz explains why he includes Dominican Spanish in his novels written largely in English:

> I assume any gaps in a story and words people don't understand, whether it's the nerdish stuff, whether it's the Elvish, whether it's the character going on about Dungeons and Dragons, whether it's the Dominican Spanish, whether it's the sort of high level graduate language, I assume if people don't get it that this is not an attempt for the writer to be aggressive. This is an attempt for the writer to encourage the reader to build community, to go out and ask somebody else.[17]

---

[17] Responding to a moderator at the Sydney Writers Festival in 2008 (video) about the Spanish words in his book.

Often knowledge about events that are not directly discussed is necessary to understand what people are saying and intend to say. Use of words, names, expressions, linguistic variation, etc. can represent a speaker and speech community's critical attitude toward a situation or topic. Indexicality provides a method to identify when and how identity is constituted, as well as indicating when an interaction has been framed around referential symbols (C. S. Peirce 1960a). Indexicality incorporates all aspects of social and political context in order to construct referential systems of signs and symbolism – the core ingredients for ambiguity and indirection. It is the muscle that regulates the language and discourse of speech communities, and it enforces its boundaries. This is because when a symbol is indexed, it brings social and cultural significance to what is being communicated. Through indexicality we manage to understand what is being said within a contextual framework of the social, cultural, local, political, imagined and artistic world within which communication occurs. Thus indexicality may not only reveal and display cultural knowledge, beliefs and practices, but may also serve as an endorsement to cultural insiders that a particular set of interpretive beliefs and practices are in play. Silverstein (1979, 2003) elaborates on Peirce's analysis and suggests that there is an indexical order (or levels) that defines the tension within ideologies. The first order is associated with what Silverstein refers to as noticing, while the next order introduces the ideology of the relationship identified. As Woolard explains:

> At this second level, actors rationalize, explain, and thus inevitably naturalize and ideologize the sociolinguistic associations (indexical relations) that they have registered at the first order. Both local and social categories can be indexed including familial relationships and institutions like schools. That is, in picking such associative or indexical relations out of the flow of social life and talk, actors – both analysts and community members – do not simply perceive but actually in a sense create and re-create categories of speaking and speakers as well as types of sociolinguistic variables. (Woolard 2008: 437)

1.7 CONCLUSION

This chapter has explored the theoretical arguments involved in identifying speech communities and reviewed ways in which speech communities have been studied and represented. Although it has included

analysis and critique of the methods and findings of sociolinguistics and linguistic anthropology notions of speech communities, the
interest is in how particular communities engage, represent and think
about the language varieties available to them. Recognizing these relationships and dynamics is an important aspect of understanding how
social actors move within and between their speech communities. As
Alessandro Duranti explains, "any notion of language variety presup-
poses a community of speakers. Such a community is a point of reference for the individuals who use a given variety as much as for the
researcher who is interested in documenting such usage" (1997: 72).

Early formal linguistic definitions of speech communities were based
on theories about language structure rather than considering language
as culture. In fact, As Romaine states: "Modern linguistics has generally
taken for granted that grammars are unrelated to the social lives of
their speakers" (2000: ix). Although linguists may have represented language as an object outside of social influence, it is not. The question of
when a language is a dialect and whether there is mutual intelligibility
between languages is often a social question and one of language ideology. Speech communities may be marginal and contested, some are
part of a dominant culture and others may result from an event, activity,
etc. I have introduced some of the intricacies inherent in each example of speech community to demonstrate that members actively engage
these complexities of language and representation. Dell Hymes (1974a)
considered diversity to be the starting-point in the study of speech communities. Yet he warns: "The great stumbling block is that the kinds
of organization most developed by linguists presuppose the grammar
as their frame of reference" (433). He argues that whereas linguistic
models, intuitions and theories may result in elegant analyses, those
findings may not be fundamental to understanding speech communities and what is important to those whose lives are lived as members.
"Where community members find patterns natural, we do not want to
have to make them out to be unnatural" (433).

DISCUSSION QUESTIONS

1. What is the difference between a group and a community? Why
   is it important?
2. Discuss some speech communities of which you are a participant.
   What are the characteristics of the speech community?
3. Why is language ideology important?

4. Do you think people will always look for and form speech communities? Why? Why not?
5. Explain what is meant by interaction as a social practice.

FURTHER READING

Gumperz, J. (1968). The Speech Community. In David L. Sills and Robert K. Merton (eds.), *International Encyclopedia of the Social Sciences* (pp. 381–386). New York: Macmillan.

Hymes, D. (1972). On Communicative Competence. In J. B. Pride and J. Holmes (eds.), *Sociolinguistics* (pp. 269–293). Harmondsworth: Penguin Press.

Labov, W. (1980). Is There a Creole Speech Community? In A. Valdman and A. Highfield (eds.), *Theoretical Orientations in Creole Study* (pp. 369–388). New York: Academic Press.

Morgan, M. (2004b). Speech Community. In Duranti (ed.), 2004, pp. 3–22.

2 Representing speech communities

Oppressive language does more than represent violence; it is violence;
does more than represent the limits of knowledge; it limits knowledge.
Whether it is obscuring state language or the faux-language of
mindless media; whether it is the proud but calcified language of the
academy or the commodity driven language of science; whether it is
the malign language of law-without-ethics, or language designed for
the estrangement of minorities, hiding its racist plunder in its literary
cheek – it must be rejected, altered and exposed. It is the language that
drinks blood, laps vulnerabilities, tucks its fascist boots under
crinolines of respectability and patriotism as it moves relentlessly
toward the bottom line and the bottomed-out mind. Sexist language,
racist language, theistic language – all are typical of the policing
languages of mastery, and cannot, do not permit new knowledge or
encourage the mutual exchange of ideas. (Morrison 1994: 15)

Irrespective of when nations are formed, their emergence as a speech
community and their establishment and enforcement of a national language occur as acts of sacrifice, loss and gain. This chapter considers the
question of what frames and characterizes speech communities that
come together as the result of domination, mutual endeavor, personal
ties and collective identities. The importance of this analysis is at the
heart of Toni Morrison's 1993 Lecture for the Nobel Prize in Literature
(published the following year). While all social actors belong to speech
communities, every interaction is not based on membership in one community or another. Speech communities are not organized around linguistic facts but around people who want to share their opinions, identities, thoughts and solidarities, and generally communicate with their
evolving social world. Although many people operate within multiple
speech communities, they do so in order to participate in the "mutual
exchange of words and ideas" and to represent their identity(ies) as full
social actors. Speech communities may develop as the result of force and
political contact where language ideology is promoted and imposed by
those in power.

2.1 IMAGINED SPEECH COMMUNITIES AND CONTACT ZONES

Awareness of systems of privilege and rules of interaction in societies does not mean that one can easily abandon identities, roles and communities. While communicating with others is part of the social human experience, the actual building of communities is not straightforward. Benedict Anderson introduced the term "imagined community" to explain how people may see themselves as part of a nation even if they do not participate in everyday, face-to-face interaction between its members. Instead, as Anderson explains, members hold in their minds a mental image of their affinity – for example, the nationhood one feels when your "imagined community" participates in an international event or when the nation is attacked by adversaries from outside of the nation. He argues that a nation:

> is imagined because the members of even the smallest nation will never know most of their fellow-members, meet them, or even hear of them, yet in the minds of each lives the image of their communion . . . regardless of the dissent and inequalities within the nation, the imagined alliance among people of the same imagined nation is so strong as to drive men to heroic deaths in nationalistic sacrifice. (Anderson 1983: 7).

In fact, citizenship allows people to imagine boundaries, even though they may not physically exist, and, as boundaries are imagined, they include "the partition of culture, ethnicity and social structure" (Anderson 1983: 7).

For speech communities, especially at the level of the nation, there is also recognition of a system of language and interaction that recognizes and often tolerates diverse segments of the population. Speech community norms may incorporate webs of meanings, meaning potentials, values, etc. that are constructed and recognized through a process of indexicality. As discussed in Chapter 1, indexicality is the linguistic and discourse process that indicates that an interaction is framed around referential symbols and specifiable contexts (Peirce 1960a). Since it brings social and cultural significance to what is being communicated, indexicality is always in play and can indicate and imply the presence of genres, styles, etc. as well as views on social class, gender, ethnicity, race, power and so on. That is why the concept of imaginations is important and refers to both the symbols and references of past and present events, as well as the social, psychological and linguistic processes that guide the attachment of these symbols by social actors. Milani and Johnson (2010) refer to the ways that groups attach meaning to language use and

variation as *sociolinguistic imagination* or "the process of naming, signifying and valorizing sociolinguistic practices" (4). These sociolinguistic
imaginations reflect particular ideologies about who is a member and
who is in power that have real-life consequences.

Contact situations are often catastrophic events and include con-
querors and the conquered, oppressors and the oppressed, intermedi-
aries, onlookers and many, many, more actors. Mary Louise Pratt refers
to these situations as contact zones where "the space in which peoples
geographically and historically separated come into contact with each
other and establish ongoing relations, usually involving conditions of
coercion, radical inequality, and intractable conflict" (1992: 6). The fact
is that when two or more languages come together, two or more peoples
have come together, and the result is often some sort of resolution of
which language and dialect become the ultimate symbol of who has the
power. Any student of historical linguistics can become immersed in
language family trees as they trace the development of the world's languages. Yet whether language families are Indo-European, Sino-Tibetan,
Afro-Asiatic, Niger-Congo, Austronesian or other, the language histories
that led to English, Chinese, Arabic, Yoruba, Malay, were a partner to
and proof of the presence of movement, cultures and the political history of different peoples. This reality is the basis of many of the epic
stories about power and good and evil created and imagined in literature and folktales.[1] In fact, some of the more epochal tales are based on
historical fact like that of the development of the English language.

The story of the English language is one of conquest, war, dominance,
insurgency and more. English did not exist before the West Germanic
tribes (Angles, Jutes and Saxons) settled in Britain. Although the history
of the English language really begins with the three Germanic tribes in
the fifth century AD, the Romans had invaded in 55 BC and again in AD
43, occupying Britain until AD 436. The culture of the majority indigenous population that those Germanic tribes encountered was Celtic. In
the centuries following their arrival, the Celtic languages and associated culture retreated ever westwards, to what is now Scotland, Wales,
Ireland and the far southwest of England (Cornwall).[2] From around AD
850, Vikings or Norsemen made a significant impact on the English language by importing many North Germanic words into the language.[3]

---

[1] For example, *Beowulf,* the *Lord of the Rings* and the Harry Potter novels, to name a
few where conquests and peoples were identified by language and other customs.

[2] The modern languages of Welsh, Irish and Scots Gaelic descend from the Celtic
languages spoken in Britain in those earlier times.

[3] They added basic words such as "they" and "them," and also may have been responsible for some of the morphological simplification of Old English, including the
loss of grammatical gender and cases (Bragg 2004).

These tribes, along with the English language, may well have been wiped out altogether by Viking raiders if not for King Alfred the Great. After defeating the Vikings, who threatened both the English way of life and its language, Alfred encouraged English literacy throughout his kingdom (McCrum, MacNeil and Cran, 1986). In the ninth century, King Alfred began a series of textual translations from Latin into Old English. One such book that he translated with the help of some clerical scholars was Pope Gregory I's *Liber Pastoralis Curae* (*Pastoral Care*). It became one of the most important ecclesiastical texts in early medieval Europe. He added a Preface that argued that England was in a state of moral and cultural decline, and outlined a program for educational reform. This reform included an argument for an English language-speaking nation that could unite the kingdom.

The Old English period ended with the Norman Conquest, when the French-speaking Normans influenced the language to an even greater extent. The Normans transformed England, both culturally and linguistically. For over 300 years French was the language spoken by the most powerful people – royalty, aristocrats and high-powered officials – some of whom could not speak English at all. French was used in political documents, in administration and in literature. Latin was still the language of the church and of scholars, but most of the general population spoke some form of English in their everyday lives. In subsequent centuries, British colonialism and imperialism created new contact zones throughout the world in which the English language took on an increasingly powerful, and widely contested, global significance that affects the way millions of people speak today.

Although in today's world it may be difficult to recall the story of the prolonged and turbulent development of English, it is important to realize that issues of language development, representation, loyalty, etc. remain in Great Britain and most of the world. Not surprisingly, the concept of who belongs and where one speaks and congregates means that space and place are often understood in relation to nation and community – and can be real or imagined, claimed, occupied and contested. Architects, urban planners, politicians and real-estate owners may construct spaces to privilege some communities and discourse styles over others. The claim of space may result in a conflict over power and authority, and representation.

As Keating and Sunakawa (2010) explain, social scientists and philosophers have long been interested in how space and place are viewed in societies. For example, the access to speech is often compared to the notion of a public sphere (Habermas 1991, 1992), where private people get together as a public, articulating the needs of the society with the state. In many cities written language can become a powerful way of literally labeling the public sphere – as the language used on signs and businesses can become symbols of linguistic, cultural and economic authority. In the public sphere, people use spaces that are physical, online and sometimes organized to represent their interests and for them to be heard. Of concern is access to spaces where policy and public speech occur. As borders and boundaries change, grow and collapse, the urge to claim and reclaim spaces and places does not subside. Yet the representation of public space can result in the process of "othering," emphasizing perceived differences of marginalized groups as a way to stress the alleged strength of those in positions of power (cf. Said 1978). Susan Ruddick argues that how "certain others are represented in public spaces is not simply a byproduct of other structures of inequality; it is deeply constitutive of our sense of community – who is allowed in, who is excluded, and what roles should be ascribed to 'insiders' and 'outsiders'" (1996: 146).[4] An example of the political nature of public space for communicating, especially in urban areas, occurred in Brazil.

The absence of public space for Black Brazilians in São Paulo, Brazil, led to the politicization of public spaces in the city and the rise of a Black consciousness movement. According to Teresa Caldeira (2000), a division between wealthy and poor Brazilians occurred when the poor and largely Black population was moved to the suburbs on illegal land without basic infrastructure such as hospitals, schools, security, asphalt, electricity, sanitation, water treatment, etc. This move was interpreted as an attempt to silence Black voices critical of the government. Meanwhile, the middle class and the rich had their homes furnished with funding from public institutions, in structured regions. This context created the structural and geographical distance between the different social classes in São Paulo. Santos (2012) reports that, in response, Black youth who lived in different regions of São Paulo occupied the same downtown space for public discourse. She writes: "Especially on Fridays, they . . . keep São Paulo as a space for identification and reference, where they can exchange information about Black scenarios, and come back to their houses to share this information in their communities through images and symbols" (Santos 2012: 5).

The insistence of São Paulo's Black population to occupy a space for public discourse and political discussion eventually led to the public recognition of the need to address housing, employment and educational issues. Black youth in Brazil represented a marginalized

---

[4] Her argument is in relation to a shooting in a coffee shop named "Just Desserts" in Toronto in 1994.

speech community that was transported from the suburbs of São Paulo to the city in order to make their community and social situation visible.

2.2 LANGUAGE AND SYMBOLS: INDEXING IDEOLOGIES

As Hymes has argued, irrespective of how and why communities come together, they develop and share ideologies around the "knowledge of rules of conduct and interpretation of speech [as well as] knowledge of at least one form of speech, and knowledge also of its patterns of use" (1974a: 50–51). There is often a wide range of views about the role that language and variation may play in a speech community. While the role of the linguist is to focus on what people are actually doing, developing an analysis can be very complicated. There are particular challenges in determining and interpreting what is going on or, as Michael Halliday (1978) says, "how people mean." Indexicality incorporates contextual layers that invoke related contexts and ideologies and belief systems about language so that those who know the indexed reference can manage to understand what is being said. Linguistic anthropologists explore and analyze conversational practices that incorporate both general and local attitudes concerning variants of norms and rules of interaction specific to a speech community. In this regard, Paul Grice's (1975) concern with what is not spoken, yet understood as being meant, is a useful starting-point. Grice proposed that conventional signs and conversational maxims guide interactions as words are used in contexts that we understand and agree on at some level. These maxims include cooperative principles of quality (be honest), quantity (give sufficient information), relevance (be relevant) and manner (be lucid and brief) (Grice 1975). Grice's principles address the idea that speakers require and expect a certain type of information in interactions. As Brown and Levinson (1987) argue, however, not all utterances need to meet the conditions introduced by Grice.

In some speech communities the meaning of utterances are considered a part of the meaning and intention of a speaker, but not the entire story. In *The Presentation of Self in Everyday Life* (1959), Goffman argues that in order to participate in interactions, we make inferences about what people mean in those interactions (1959: 2–3). He considers it a basic principle that people can be calculating – and they can miscalculate – and our role in these interactions is to figure out these intentions. Consequently, intentions may not be transparent across domains and social contexts.

"Indirectness" occurs when someone intentionally says something that can also mean something else and when participants and witnesses (to use Goffman's term) indirectly refer to contexts that represent group membership/knowledge in some way. It is an act of language and power where people launch and deploy multiple meanings within culturally and historically specific discursive fields. In this case indirectness is a conversational strategy that can both index alternative meanings and references and also serve to save social face in conversation. Goffman (1967) identifies two types of social face: positive face, which focuses on the desire for appreciation and approval by others, and negative face, which is the desire not to be imposed on by others. Of course, within the act of discourse the real-life activity of representation and social standing are witnessed, scrutinized, maintained and constructed. This is even more apparent when personal and political discourse is delivered through media and technology – where to speak reflects both truth and theater (see Hill 2000) and is endlessly evaluated. Public interactions and comments, especially those witnessed by audiences and pundits, can involve pitfalls and pratfalls where one's social face and sense of oneself are potentially in jeopardy. Yet even these public discourses are influenced by norms and conventions of public and private discourse. An example of this occurred following the disaster of Hurricane Katrina in the Gulf of the US in 2005.

The indecisive government response to Hurricane Katrina had devastating consequences for the lives of those in the Gulf and led to numerous instances of indirect representations of American cultural and societal beliefs and policies about race and social class. These cases required collaboration, indexing of local knowledge and other discursive strategies. When, during a televised fundraiser, Kanye West, a popular hiphop artist, made an unscripted and heart-felt statement about the president of the US – "George Bush doesn't care about Black people" – it resulted in a public uproar in the form of concerned querying of numerous Black entertainers and professionals. "Do you agree with Kanye? Do you think it's fair to say that? How could he believe that?" These constant questions led to many interactions that revealed how the African American speech community in particular understood the intention of the question "What do you really think?" In fact, comedian Dave Chapelle commented on Kanye West's statement during his Las Vegas show: "I don't know if you agree with him or not, but give it up for him. I've got a lot of respect for him – and I'm going to miss him ... I'm not risking my entire career to tell White people obvious things."[5] This view was

---

[5] Dave Itzkoff, 2005: Dave Chappelle is Alive and Well (and Playing Las Vegas). *New York Times*. November 27.

also presented by Alberta Roberts during an interview by anthropologist John Langston Gwaltney for his classic book *Drylongso* (1993). Alberta Roberts explained to Gwaltney that "Play is pretending that what's out here is not really out here. If you are Black you just cannot make it like that because we can't buy our way out of things or make somebody say square is round" (1993: 106). I suppose when you're accustomed to having power and then that grip starts to weaken, it's harder to keep track of when "you're playing." She concluded by remarking that "Now, the biggest difference between [Black people] and White people is that we *know* when we are playing" (105).

The notion that indexicality is the muscle of speech communities is highlighted in hiphop culture, where members incorporate several stages of indexicality to demonstrate creative skill and recognize segments of the speech community. The emcee (MC) and lyricist incorporate and manipulate local and national languages and dialects, name and re-name places and spaces, streets, popular culture events, etc. (See Chapter 5 for further discussion.) For example, in 2001 Aceyalone – one of the lead MCs from Project Blowed, an underground hiphop group from Los Angeles – conveyed his support for his neighborhood, city and hiphop by referencing several locations that were considered to be crime-ridden sections of South Central LA, the center of the 1992 Rodney King riot. He recasts his neighborhood as a sacred place on earth:

> I was born in the *Jungle*, the concrete slab . . .
> It started at the *Good Life*, house of the first sightin'
> We snatched raps out of their mouths when they were *biting*
> There was nothing more exciting then *to serve* and perform
> On *Crenshaw and Exposition* god was born
> He said *"please pass the mic* to whomever is tight"
> Me and the *Fellowship* took it and we held it for dear life
> The *Inner City Griots*, the *wild, the style, the crew*
> The ones they got their styles from, but claimed
> They never knew. (Aceyalone, Project Blowed. 2001. Accepted Eclectic music label)

As reported in Morgan (2009c), the above excerpt is deeply indexical, with references to general and local knowledge. It is designed to send casual followers and witnesses of hiphop scrambling to understand the references, while recognizing and giving "shout-outs" to local speech community members and groups who support Project Blowed artists.[6] The **Jungle** is the local name for an area in Los Angeles where there is a concrete low-income housing area, drug addiction, poverty and crime.

---

[6] These include the group Freestyle Fellowship and their popular 1993 album, *Inner City Griots.*

The **Good Life** was a healthfood store that became a venue for impro-
visational/freestyle lyrical style. **Biting** refers to copying and stealing
someone else's lyrics. The MC also represents the hiphop speech community through the space and location of Project Blowed, as well as
recognition of where they and god were born – at the **Good Life** –
their first underground venue on **Crenshaw** Avenue near **Exposition**
Boulevard.[7] The **Inner City Griots** refers to a hiphop group that some
Project Blowed members belonged to and **wild, the style** is a reference to
both the movie *Wildstyle* (1983) and the graffiti writing style of the same
name. While this version of the neighborhood may be viewed by outsiders as counter-hegemonic and a critique of the dominant discourse,
it is still their neighborhood, their corner, their home and where their
families and friends live, die, love and dream.

In this case, indexicality incorporates contextual layers that invoke
related contexts and ideologies so that those who know the reference
can manage to understand what is being said in the present and in
a refreshed framework of the hiphop social, cultural, local, political,
imagined and artistic world (Peirce 1960b; Hanks 1996; Silverstein 2003).
Indexicality may not only reveal and display cultural knowledge, beliefs
and practices: it may also serve as an endorsement to cultural insiders
that a particular set of interpretive beliefs and practices is in play.
In terms of "ideal" middle-class American city dreams, Crenshaw and
Exposition is not where "god was born" or where the "house of the first
sighting" stood, as Acey claims. It is only the ghetto.

2.3 LANGUAGE, IDENTITY AND STEREOTYPE

> DIRECTOR: I'm sorry to tell you that yours is not the only part ... I
> too am well aware of the fact that everyone has his own interior life
> which he would like to bring out into the open. But the difficulty is
> precisely this: to bring out into the open only what is important in
> reference to the others; and at the same time reveal through that
> little bit all of that unrevealed interior life! Ah, it would be too easy
> if a character could in a nice monologue or ... better yet ... in a lecture
> dish it out to the public all that is boiling in his part. (Pirandello
> 1995: 49)

The question "Who are you – *really*?" is at the foundation of anthropological inquiry. Questions of identity are questions about culture,

---

[7] In this case, "god" refers to the 5 Percent Nation reference to the Black man discussed in detail in Chapter 5 below.

society, individuality, recognition, representation, ideology, meaning, taste, etc. As Edwards explains, "it is clear that identity is at the heart of a person, and the group, and the connective tissue that links them. People need psycho-social 'anchors': it is as simple as that" (2009: 2).

People who at times interact and use language that is viewed as marked in terms of race, ethnicity, social class and gender identities may use the language styles of the larger speech community as well. In contexts where interpretations of what is said are contested, speakers may be challenged to reconcile what they think they meant with how the social actors/speakers/audiences/interlocutors/overhearers and other speech community members understand what they said means. They must not only become aware of what they habitually do: "speakers are made accountable for something that they may claim to be an unconscious, unquestioned and unquestionable way of communicating" (Duranti 2011: 163). Although all kinds of speaking act can be subjected to evaluation, some of the most visible in the current public sphere are those that are thought to reflect a person's or a group's prejudice, racism, or gender bias (cf. Kulick 2003; Hill 2008; Lippi-Green 1997). For example, the habitual intentionality associated with referencing symbols that are stereotypical of African Americans in a "natural, common" conversation is the focus of the comedian David Chapelle's (2000) exploration into the complexity of determining intentionality when he asks the questions "When is someone being racist? How do you know what someone really thinks?"[8] Chapelle displays the complex symbols embedded in interpreting intentionality through a bitingly indirect narrative about a service encounter.[9]

> Have you ever had something happen that was sooo racist, that you didn't even get mad? You was just like: **"Goddamn! That was – that was racist!"** I mean, it was sooo blatant you were just like – **"Wow !"** Like – it's almost like it didn't happen to you? It was like a fuc**ing movie? Like you was watching *Mississippi Burning*? **"Wow!"** (*audience laughs*).[10]

According to Chapelle's account, his experience was so racist that he had to check with himself to make sure it was both an extreme act and that it actually happened. While Chapelle may be a genius at representing

---

[8] Dave Chapelle often performs with hiphop artists and demonstrates the layers of local knowledge and symbols in discourse about racism in his stand-up comedy special *'Killin' Them Softly*, 2000, HBO.

[9] This analysis is revised from Morgan 2009b.

[10] See Morgan (2009c) for further analysis of this routine.

the everyday life aspect of these encounters, they are also widely discussed within an ironic and satirical framework. In fact, the nationally
syndicated Tom Joyner radio show had an occasional segment named
"Was it racist – or someone just having a bad day?" He weaves through
many levels of local and popular knowledge as he develops a recursive
routine where one act produces another and also turns into itself as
he reflects on it. He successfully requires the audience to corroborate
with him using three rhetorical questions about the endemic yet subtle
nature of racism: "Isn't it crazy?" "Am I crazy?" "Did something crazy
just happen?" Yet the consequences can be devastating.

In *Stories in the Time of Cholera*, Briggs and Mantini-Briggs (2004) provide
a shattering analysis and critique of how speech community ideology
and prejudice can affect how one responds to urgent situations. They
chronicle the cholera epidemic in the Amacuro Delta of Venezuela in
1992 and 1993, where hundreds of Warao villagers died in a matter of
months as modes of discourse framed and incited the ongoing tragedy.
Although cholera can kill an adult through dehydration in half a day,
it is easily treated. They argue that health officials succumbed to and
perpetrated a narrative based on widely circulated and ingrained cultural and racial stereotypes rather than scientific data. Their analysis
of the intersection and conflict between indigenous and clinical narratives about disease, race and power is a cautionary tale of complex societies. Briggs and Mantini-Briggs use the term "medical profiling" to critique the racialized public and professional narratives about the mostly
indigenous "victims" of the Venezuelan epidemic. The book documents
the role of official public health authorities and of the media in dividing
the public into "sanitary citizens," with complex identities and nationality intact, and "unsanitary subjects," whose identity became reduced
to stereotypes of race or class and associated with a predictable package
of cultural beliefs and behaviors (33). Their notion that the racialized
discourse that circulated was particular to that speech community may
not have been considered seriously by outside health workers, and thus
adversely affected the response of the healthcare community to the
epidemic, resulting in hundreds of preventable deaths. In a cautionary
note to anthropologists, Briggs and Mantini-Briggs lay out the pitfalls
of what they call "cultural reasoning," in which the notion of culture
becomes decontextualized and invoked in explaining complex issues.
Such explanations risk becoming objectified as common knowledge and
appropriated in institutional ideologies. Used in this way, they warn,
"cultural reasoning" acquires a "liberal patina [which] helps disguise
timeworn stereotypes and institutional agendas" (318) and provides a
framework for racial profiling.

2.4 REPRESENTATION, KNOWLEDGE AND DIVERSITY

While speech communities may be evaluated and stereotyped, this does not mean that members of the speech community accept these designations and the ideology from those outside of its borders. Proficiency in a common language is a significant component of many speech communities, yet proficiency need not be in relation to a standard dialect or norm, or even a single language (Wodak et al. 1999; Romaine 2000). Irrespective of whether the speech community is based on a common activity and practice, is marginalized, or incorporates dominant ideology or is in resistance to it, its members must have communicative competence in relation to discourse about how language and/or language variety function in specific contexts and constitute the speech community. Consequently, discourse may focus on linguistic practices that are indicative of the variety or language, are in contrast to it or are dialogic with other dialects and languages. Ana Celia Zentella (1997) explores the necessity and expectation that speech community members share knowledge in her description of the New York Puerto Rican (NYPR) speech community where:

> interactions rely on shared linguistic and cultural knowledge of standard and non-standard Puerto Rican Spanish, Puerto Rican English, African American Vernacular English, Hispanized English, and standard NYC English, among other dialects. Speakers understand the overt and covert messages of fellow community members because they can follow varied linguistic moves and fill in the gaps for other speakers or translate for themselves. In the process they ratify each other's membership in the community and contribute to the re-shaping of NYPR identity. (Zentella 1997: 3)

The Pulitzer Prize-winning author Junot Diaz further illustrates the normalcy of diversity in speech communities in his quest to simultaneously embrace, fade and erase the borders of the multiple speech communities of his life in order to represent how he experiences his social world:

> I guess what strikes me at first is that language is a funny thing to attempt to nationalize or to put a stamp on. Language eludes any attempt anyone has to corral it. So, it's always weird when people feel that there's this sense of ownership in a language and that people use it to victimize other people, because language just doesn't work that way, so I always think about the way young people in any neighborhood or particular spot will immediately work the language to their experience, to their little anecdotes. One of the things about having childhood friends is you don't just have childhood friendships or relationships and physical proximities – you have your own

goddamn idiom. You just create this entire language, and in some
ways it holds you together – that idiom holds you together – longer
than even your physical presence. So, you're able to hang out with
people and say one thing and they all just start laughing. And I think
of that, in a sense, in the same way it happens for anyone who's
attempting to use language in an artistic enterprise, the same way that
we use language to forge a reality among our youthful friends – we're
going to attempt to use it to try to particularize that experience,
because there's no exchange rate of language-to-experience that ever
holds steady. Every experience of every moment seems to require some
new way of saying it, and every artist seems to provoke an attempt to
say something that might even be mundane, say, in an original way.
(Celayo and Shook 2008)

As Diaz, who was born in the Dominican Republic, demonstrates,
awareness of these issues and values is determined by whether and
to what degree speech communities are in crisis. For some, awareness
is ingrained in the cultural fabric and thus represents unmarked usage
that encompasses the community's historicity, politics, ideology, representation and so on. Although members of a speech community may
agree on the existence of these values, that does not necessarily mean
that there is complete consensus about the implementation of these
principles. Rather, what is at stake is knowledge of the symbolic, market and exchange value of varieties and styles within and across speech
communities.

Discourse about which linguistic features represent the speech community may come from linguistic study and from the communities
themselves. For example, in Morgan (1994b, 2002), I argue that while
sociolinguistic descriptions of the African American speech community
have yielded tremendous insight into the dialect, these analyses have
also prompted educators, social scientists and some linguists to argue
that it is the main cause of educational and economic inequities. In
fact, the African American speech community operates according to
an elaborate integration of language norms and values associated with
the symbolic and practical functions of African American English (AAE)
and General English (GE).[11] One outcome is what I have called **reading
dialect** (Morgan 2002), a code-shifting practice that occurs "when
members of the African American community contrast or otherwise

---

[11] The distinction here is similar to Labov's (1998) comparison of African American
vernacular English and General English components. Here, AAE includes usage
across social class and other interactions, and discourses where speakers use both
dialects. GE refers to prestige, and not White working-class, usage unless otherwise
indicated.

highlight what they consider to be obvious contrasting features of AAE and GE in an unsubtle and unambiguous manner to make a point" (2002: 74). This produces an environment where both varieties symbolize ideologies regarding African American cultural practices. In terms of language choice, GE is the only variety that one can *choose* to speak, since it is often learned in formal settings outside of the home and from those who are not members of the speech community. On the other hand, AAE is a variety that one may choose *not* to speak, since it is the language through which one is socialized into the speech community. That is, in the African American speech community, both AAE and GE function as the language of home, community, history and culture. For families that use both varieties, one is not necessarily valued over the other, although one may be considered more contextually appropriate. Within this system AAE is not only what one may hear and speak at home and in the community, but also the variety that delivers formal and informal knowledge, as well as local knowledge and wisdom. It is the language of both the profound and the profane.

On the other hand GE, rather than AAE, has a context-free exchange value outside of the speech community.[12] Within the dominant cultural system, GE usage represents hegemony, is considered "normal" and indexes intelligence, compliance and so on. Although speakers may not be aware of all the grammatical relationships and systems in their repertoire, by the time they are adults they know that AAE usage may be stigmatized within dominant cultural systems and may be considered deviant and index ignorance. Even when members are aware of the values, attitudes and norms of discourse of a speech community, their positive standing is not always guaranteed, especially when regular travel and transmigration are the norm. Instead, membership in and across speech communities requires the negotiation of languages, dialects, discourse styles and symbolic systems as part of normal practice.

2.5 STYLE AND STYLING IN SPEECH COMMUNITIES

Language style refers to the occurrence of linguistic variation that may have social meaning. A linguistic style is not a fixed attribute of a speaker. Rather, depending on context, a speaker may use different styles and multiple styles in their speech. Speech styles, as Irvine (2001) points out, have some of the characteristics of clothing styles, in that

---

[12] American advertising uses AAE linguistic and verbal expressions to represent urban sophistication as well as all social classes.

they can be put on to suit both an occasion and the situation. Instead of dressing the body, speech becomes the embodiment of a person's identity in play at that moment by identifying the person's group membership, what the person intends, how secure they are in that speech community. In this sense, speech styles can index and contrast and dispute an identity. As Giddens argues, "In the post-traditional order of modernity and against the backdrop of new forms of mediated experience, self identity becomes a reflexively organized endeavor ... (T)he more daily life is reconstituted in terms of the dialectical interplay of the local and global the more individuals are forced to negotiate lifestyle choices among a diversity of options" (1991: 5). From Gidden's perspective, these options and choices lead to numerous risks of social face. As Gumperz and Cook-Gumperz reveal, "speech styles also gain durability as they come to index an identity: though open to frequent revision they remain part of an individual's self presentation" (1982: 540). What's more, adults often participate in multiple communities, and one's initial socialization into a speech community may occur within a culture with communicative values that differ from cultures and speech communities one encounters later in life.

As discussed in Chapter 1, William Labov's (1972b) definition of speech community contrasted attitudes toward linguistic variables and the extent to which members participate in a set of shared norms. In sociolinguistic variation across class and race he focused on when speakers paid attention to speech (formal) and when they did not (vernacular), and found that although these norms were often at odds with prestige standards, it did not mean that speakers within and outside of speech communities did not use them. Instead, it is necessary to consider their value within social contexts, because "the same linguistic variables are involved in the differentiation of social classes and speech styles" (Guy 1989: 50). Bucholtz (2009: 146) argues that while style has been considered a unidimensional continuum between vernacular and standard based on the degree of speaker self-monitoring, it is more productive to view it as "a multimodal and multidimensional cluster of linguistic and other semiotic practices for the display of identity in interaction"; style shifts depend on the speaker's ideology and their representation and negotiation of identities in interactions.

Giles introduces the notion of Communication Accommodation Theory (CAT) to explain style-shifting in terms of two processes: convergence, in which the speaker attempts to shift their speech to match that of the interlocutor in order to gain social approval, and divergence, in which the speaker attempts to distance themselves from the interlocutor by shifting their speech away from that of the interlocutor. Two specific shortcomings of this basic form of CAT include its inability to explain situations in which convergence occurs when the motivation is clearly not social approval (e.g. in arguments) and the fact that non-convergent speech is often used to maintain social distance in asymmetric relationships (e.g. employer–employee). Another model developed to understand speech styles is the Audience Design Model or ADM (Bell). It is very similar to CAT but with an added component: ADM proposes the existence of non-present reference groups with which a speaker may converge or from which he or she may diverge. In this theory, a speaker is constantly negotiating his or her relationship not only with the audience, but also with other non-present people/groups that come up in the discourse.

Style-shifting can be a creative process in which the speaker shapes his or her speech in order to associate themselves with or disassociate themselves from specific social groups. Furthermore, a speaker does not have an underlying style. Rather, the casual speech style that some sociolinguists consider to be somehow fundamental is no more fundamental than any other style.

2.6 SOCIAL NETWORKING

Because of the widespread use of the Internet, social networking has become a focus of importance to understand social relationships, the spread of information and values, and the organization of collective action. Barnes (1954) introduced the idea of social network in the social sciences as an analytical concept in his description of the order of social relationships between inhabitants of a Norwegian village. Blom and Gumperz (1972) first introduced the notion of linguistic social networks, while Milroy and Milroy (1992) popularized the concept when they conducted research in both Belfast and Philadelphia. They argued that in Labov's notion of sociolinguistic speech community the importance of "attention paid to speech" and shared norms of evaluation did not reflect the range of choices available to be identified in speech communities. Rather than reflecting a shared belief about language variety, they assert that the findings of Labov and Harris (1986) were also the very linguistic norms that symbolize the divisions between speech community members and "are more readily interpretable as evidence of conflict and sharp divisions in society than as evidence of consensus" (Milroy and Milroy 1992: 3).

Data regarding social class is typically collected as the result of large-scale studies designed to elucidate social, political and economic structures and processes. In contrast, social network relates to the community and interpersonal level of social organization. Milroy and

Milroy (1992: 2) identify two types of personal network characteristic that are generally distinguished by anthropologists: structural, which pertains to the shape and pattern of the network, and interactional, which pertains to the content of the ties (5). They found that contrasts in attitudes toward linguistic varieties within and between speech communities were embedded in social class methodology that identified social categories – and then found them. They defined social networks as "a mechanism both for exchanging goods and services and for imposing obligations and conferring corresponding rights upon its members" (Milroy 1987: 47)

Milroy classed social networks into order zones: first order zone, second order zone, third order zone and so on. According to Milroy "the first order network is a bounded group" (1987: 53) containing personal friends on whom you can call at any time. The second order zone is a "friend of a friend," people who are known through someone else. Members of a second order zone have a very important social function according to Milroy, in that they extend the range of services and goods which the first order zone are able to provide. Milroy says that because of this important social function a "friend of a friend" will easily be integrated into the network and the exchanges that go on within it. The third order zone is a friend of a friend of a friend, and so it continues.

Milroy and Milroy's theory of social networks focused on face-to-face interactions and demonstrated that people respond more positively and in a more natural manner when they are among friends and people they know. Their concern is both the linguistic and communicative consequences of the nature of the contact between individuals and the resulting interrelationships and networks. With the introduction of the Internet, social networking often takes on a different character, and some of the principles introduced by Milroy and Milroy, especially regarding order zones, are reconfigured. In fact, online interaction of speech communities suggests that networks often elude social class designation and can be based on shared friendship, personal connection, etc., but also incorporate interests, goals, etc. (See Chapter 7.)

2.7 CONCLUSION

Speech communities occur for many reasons. When communities are formed because of force, conquest, etc. the language and style of usage are the clearest evidence of what happened, but it is only a small part of the entire story. It is this stage where language variety and prestige and standards are institutionalized. The second, which may result from the first, is when multiple and alternative language ideologies are enacted by people who are forced together or *end up* in proximity and develop into a speech community with diverse but coexistent ideologies about language or social life in general. A third type of speech community is formed intentionally around identity, activities, practices and sometimes communication itself.

Identity and ideologies about language are important to members of speech communities, especially at a time of crisis. Members of speech communities represent themselves, and others represent them. They are capable of defending their linguistic selves, as well as conceding some level of defeat in the face of overwhelming change. Yet at the most basic level, individual speakers and groups of speakers demonstrate that their existence must be substantiated with a system of interaction that represents their beliefs – even as they change. As the novelist Toni Morrison stated during her Nobel Prize Lecture: "We die. That may be the meaning of life. But we do language. That may be the measure of our lives" (1994: 15).

DISCUSSION QUESTIONS

1. Describe the sort of contacts that can lead to new speech communities.
2. What types of language situation develop from contact?
3. Describe the language varieties in your family and neighborhood.
4. In order to avoid future tragedies, suggest ways that Venezuelans can work to understand other members of their speech community.

FURTHER READING

Anderson, B. (1983). *Imagined Communities: Reflections on the Origin and Spread of Nationalism*. New York: Schocken Press.

Briggs, C. and Mantini-Briggs, C. (2004). *Stories in the Time of Cholera: Racial Profiling during a Medical Nightmare*. Berkeley: University of California Press.

Goffman, E. (2002). *Interaction Ritual – Essays in Face-to-Face Behavior*. New York: Pantheon.

3   Constructing speech communities

This chapter introduces some of the language and discourse styles and social factors that help define and identify specific speech communities. As we have seen in previous chapters, there are numerous activities and interactions within and between members of speech communities that can be ongoing and involve multiple participants. There are also numerous speech events and verbal genres that are framed and sequenced and determined by role and status of participants, norms of interactions, expectation of content, etc. At issue here is not only how people form speech communities and learn how to function competently as members, but also where they form their communities.

Participating in speech communities requires "learning how to mean" (cf. Halliday 1978) according to norms and details of language, discourse and ideology, and rules and goals of engagement. As discussed in Chapter 2, when speech communities are viewed as having physical boundaries, there may be disputes and claims to public spaces and places that signify power and full membership in society. There may also be claims to spaces that are imagined (cf. Anderson 1983), such as online communities that are constructed around and include many of the same social issues found in the physical world. In either case we understand that speech communities exist through participation and as a result of socialization about how to be a member of a social group. In order to participate fully one must develop "communicative competence" in the use of conventions, practices and ideologies of specific speech communities in order to navigate the social world and all its complexities.

3.1 COMMUNICATIVE COMPETENCE AND CONTEXTUALIZATION CUES

Because speech communities need not be conterminous with language communities, skill in applying the norms, values and rules of language use is fundamental to successful participation. As discussed in

Chapter 1, communicative competence is the knowledge a speaker must have to function as a member of a social group and is based on language use and socialization within cultures. Thus one becomes knowledgeable of both grammar and appropriateness across speech acts and events that are evaluated and corroborated by others. Yet competence is not about rules but about how in speech communities rules, norms and expectations are used, employed and manipulated. The truth of this statement, as well as its paradox, is suggested in a common statement made to children by caregivers in the US: "Do what I say, not what I do." The modification to this statement is really "Do what I say, and pay attention to what I do." As Romaine reminds us, "Speakers who speak the same language do not always understand each other because they do not necessarily share the same conventions for interpreting each other's speech or use speech in the same way" (2000: 24).

A somewhat perplexing example of the importance of competently sharing conventions occurred in March 2013 when pop star Beyoncé released a song titled *Bow Down/I Been On*. The song includes the lyrics: "I took some time to live my life, but don't think I'm just his little wife... Don't get it twisted, get it twisted, this (is) my sh**t, bow down b**tches!" Of course Beyoncé's millions of followers and speech community members understood her references and the situations she indexed. Many of them know that she is married to a successful businessman and entertainer. They know that "bow down" is in reference to Ice Cube's (1996) song *Bow Down*, where he claims his position as a stellar MC from Los Angeles and says:

> Bow down when you come to my town
> Bow down when we west-ward[1] bound (be)cause
> We ain't no haters[2] like you
> Bow Down to some n**gga's that's greater than you!

Beyoncé's speech community also know that "twisted" means "stupidly wrong" and that she is telling the haters who are envious – and her fans – that she has earned her celebrity and is proud that she has maintained her identity.

Conservative radio host Rush Limbaugh's interpretation of the lyrics suggests that he is from another speech community – from far, far away:[3]

---

[1] Westward is a reference to California and Los Angeles.
[2] A hater is an envious person.
[3] "Rush Limbaugh is Perhaps not The Most Reliable Source of Beyoncé Analysis," *The Huffington Post*, by the editors, posted 20 March, 2013, 4:07 pm EDT.

"She's done a total 180," "Beyonce's now saying 'Go ahead and put up with it!'... She's going to call herself Mrs. Carter on the 'Bow Down B – s' tour."

He added, "She got married, she married the rich guy, she now understands. She now understands that it's worth it to bow down. And she's passing on that advice."

Limbaugh seems to have missed the contextualization cues that would have helped him realize that she is using a different system of interpretation. Gumperz argues that understanding utterances requires knowledge of the use of contextualization cues that are relevant for the speech community. For instance, Gumperz observes that contextualization relies on cues that operate at the level of prosody in terms of intonation, stress, pitch, etc., paralinguistic signs such as tempo, pausing, hesitation, etc., code choice in terms of dialect, language, etc. and choice of lexical forms or formulaic expressions (1982a: 231). Levinson considers contextualization cues of special interest because they often lead to examples of subtle miscommunications and can only be learned "by rich exposure to a communicative tradition, a deep immersion in social networks" (2002: 29). He argues that "In Gumperz's view, the smallest formal differences may carry with them a chasm of incomprehension, because contextualization cues invoke the essential interpretive background for the foregrounded message" (29).

Contextualization cues are part of the bundled packages of indexicality, indirection, etc. discussed in previous chapters. They suggest the level of immersion, learning, and trial and error necessary to function as a communicatively competent person in a speech community.

3.2 SOCIALIZATION INTO SPEECH COMMUNITIES

Although people must constantly deal with changes in language and communicative styles throughout their lives, it is still possible to participate in speech communities. One can learn how to identify and participate in speech communities through other members who provide information about communication norms and expectations. Socialization into speech communities can prepare members to participate in a variety of social and cultural contexts using language and discourse norms and standards. As Garrett and Baquedano-Lopez report: "Socialization, broadly defined, is the process through which a child or other novice acquires the knowledge, orientations, and practices that enable him or her to participate effectively and appropriately in the social life of a particular community" (2002: 339). Knowledgeable members may impart linguistic information, as well as information about the social world that novices must navigate. The process of socialization occurs throughout the development of a child and involves changing and developing interactions with the social world. Ochs and Schieffe-lin (1984) argue that language socialization occurs as a result of two significant aspects of cultural and social life:

1. The process of acquiring language is deeply affected by the process of becoming a competent member of society.
2. The process of becoming a competent member of society is realized to a large extent through language, by acquiring knowledge of its functions, social distribution, and interpretations in and across socially defined situations, i.e. through exchanges of language in particular social situations. (Ochs and Schieffelin 1984: 277)

For psychology, socialization may include the process of understand-ing who one is as an individual and in the social world with others. Jessica Benjamin (1997) believes that the development of intersubjectiv-ity is the most productive environment for learning how to become a competent member of society.

> The intersubjective view maintains that the individual grows in and through the relationship to other subjects. Most important, this perspective observes that the other whom the self meets is also a self, a subject in his or her own right. It assumes that we are able and need to recognize that other subject as different and yet alike, as another who is capable of sharing similar mental experience. Thus the idea of intersubjectivity reorients the conception of the psychic world from a subject's relations to its object toward a subject meeting another subject. (Benjamin 1997: 30)

Berger and Luckman argue that membership in a society requires internalization of socialization and participation in each other's shared/mutual being. The world of everyday life is not only taken for granted as reality by the ordinary members of society in the subjectively meaningful conduct of their lives. It is a world that originates in their thoughts and actions, and is maintained as real by these. It further presents itself as an intersubjective world. Membership is internalized through socialization – "comprehensive and consistent induction of an individual into the objective world of a society" (1966: 33). This is accom-plished by significant others who mediate and modify the world. It is important to note that significant others change throughout the life cycle and across speech communities, especially as adults. They become other experts and generalized others who then represent identification with society at large. Significant others such as caregivers are extremely important during childhood and "primary socialization" into culture and society. A child cannot choose the significant other who socializes him and her into society. It is during what Berger and Luckman call secondary socialization that a young person is introduced to other realities, sub-worlds, etc. Berger and Luckman (1966) also discuss unsuccessful socialization that results in counter-definitions and counter-realities that can become the new reality of the community. Through this socialization process one develops an identity, a sense of one's uniqueness and place in a world with others, and the dialectic of individuals and societies.

Children become linguistically and culturally competent through interactions with caregivers and other more competent members of their community (Ochs and Schieffelin 1984; Schieffelin and Ochs 1986). However, diversity within speech communities can lead to forms of socialization that privilege some members and not others. In the case of childhood socialization, children may bring to school cultural ways of using language and participating in interactions that differ from those of mainstream school culture (Philips 1972; Heath 1983; Zentella 1997). These differences can lead schools to underestimate or misinterpret the competence of students. For instance, in some American households a child can learn that she should state her views and ideas to adults, while another child may learn to be silent in the presence of adults in other households. Children are taught how and when to speak by caregivers and significant others in their lives who want the child to be successful in the speech community.

Susan Philips (1972) identified the issue of addressing cultural differences in classroom participation for Native American children on a reservation in Oregon. She found that Warm Springs Indian children's culture preferred what she called "participation structures" that did not include speaking alone in front of other students and at a time dictated by a teacher for purposes that focused on demonstrating speaking ability rather than actually communicating with others:[4]

> [a] student's use of speech in the classroom during structured lesson sessions is a communicative performance in more than one sense of "performance." It involves demonstration of sociolinguistic competency . . . involving knowledge of when and in what style one must present one's utterances . . . In class, speaking is the first and primary mode for communicating competency in all of the areas of skill and knowledge that schools purport to teach. (Philips 1972: 371)

[4] Philips used the term "invisible culture" to refer to Warm Springs language use and ideology.

Questions about how communicative competence is taught, learned and developed can be asked for all societies. Correspondingly, virtually every society provides time and dispensations for children as they learn how to navigate their communicative terrain. When adults enter speech communities for the first time, they must work through their position as inexperienced participants in interaction styles and rules without the dispensations allowed to children. Instead, they must rely on feedback from and negotiate with accomplished and competent participants.

3.3 SPEECH EVENTS

Although the details of the speech communication process may vary, there are some general principles that remain consistent. In all cultures, successful communication includes understanding who can participate in an interaction, when and in what context they can participate, the role of all participants and the many forms that communication can take. Early descriptive models of communication were grossly simplistic and included three basic parts: the speaker, the hearer and the message. These models evolved to focus on the goal of communication, so that the speaker was also designated as the sender and the hearer the receiver of the message. The message was further analyzed to focus on mode and channel of communication. Yet, as Bakhtin complained, this development still ignored fundamental aspects of speech communication:

> Language is regarded from the speaker's standpoint as if there were only *one* speaker who does not have any *necessary* relation to *other* participants in speech communication. If the role of the other is taken into account at all, it is a role of a listener, who understands the speaker only passively. The utterance is adequate to its object (i.e., the content of the uttered thought) and to the person who is pronouncing the utterance. Language essentially needs only a speaker – one speaker – and an object for his speech. (Bakhtin 1986: 67)

As the analysis evolved, it raised questions about how communication actually functions at the linguistic, philosophical and cultural levels.

Roman Jakobson (1960) acknowledged that a linguistic understanding of communication should also provide an understanding of how language functions in context:

> But even though a set [*Einstellung*] toward the referent, an orientation toward the CONTEXT – briefly the so-called REFERENTIAL...
> "denotative," "cognitive" function is the leading task of numerous messages, the accessory participation of the other functions in such

> messages must be taken into account by the observant linguist.
> (Jakobson 1960: 353)

Jakobson proposed a speech event model consisting of six functions that determine different aspects of language. The functions include: the referential, emotive, connotative, metalingual, poetic and phatic. He focused on single utterances and linked a message to the linguistic function it represented. His focus was not to develop a system that could unveil the complexities of the speech community that Bakhtin mentioned. Rather, he focused on the category of language most aligned with the function.

Philosophers John Austin (1961, 1962) and later John Searle (1969, 1983) considered speech communication models of speech acts. They reasoned that the relationship between the utterance and the social world was directly tied to the speech act being used. Austin (1962) attempted to resolve how individuals interpret utterances, referents and meanings while simultaneously recognizing that there are different senses and therefore possible interpretations of referents. Similarly, for Searle (1976), assertions are speech acts in which the words must match the world (words-to-world direction of fit), and directives are speech acts in which the world must match the words (world-to-words direction of fit). The theory focused on the individual perspective and the dualism between mind and the world, speaker and hearer, etc. (see Descartes 1996). Rosaldo complained that Speech Act Theory lacked the connection to different social worlds and their speech communities and "falls victim to folk views that locate social meaning first in private persons and slight the sense of situational constraint" (1982: 212).

In contrast to the approaches presented above, Dell Hymes focused on social units rather than linguistic units and considered the community the center of the analysis:

> The starting point is the ethnographic analysis of the communicative habits of a community in their totality, determining what count as communicative events, and as their components, and conceiving no communicative behavior as independent of the set framed by some setting or implicit question. The communicative event thus is central. (Hymes 1964b: 13)

As Duranti (1997) observes, Hymes built on Jakobson's six-function speech model and re-analyzed it to include sixteen factors, in order to include more of the elements and social and cultural factors involved in the speech event. Hymes argued that speech events are related to all activities governed by norms of rules of speech, and that an event may consist of a single speech act, but will often comprise several (1972: 56).

In order to identify speech events, he identified eight aspects that comprise a speech event that correspond to the acronym SPEAKING (1974a: 55). They include: (1) Setting and scene as the place of speech. It includes physical circumstances, space and place, and cultural definition of gatherings. (2) Participants, speaker(s) and audience, onlookers, etc. (3) Ends or purpose, goal, outcomes. (4) Act Sequence – form and order of event. (5) Key – cues that establish the "tone, manner and spirit of the speech act." (6) Instrumentalities – forms and styles of speech (e.g. register). (7) Norms – social rules governing the event and the participant's actions and reactions. (8) Genre – the kind of speech act or event (55).

Hymes' introduction of speech events exists at many levels of talk, and some specific events function to identify speech communities and are indexical in that they also reflect values, histories, politics, etc.

3.4 VERBAL GENRES

While a speech event focuses on the exchange between speakers governed by rules of speech (Hymes 1972), verbal genres are characterized by communicative routines that are viewed as distinct wholes, separate from other types of discourse, characterized by special rules of speech and non-verbal behavior, and often distinguishable by clearly recognizable opening and closing sequences (Gumperz 1972: 17). Verbal genres can occur within an event as well as be the event themselves. In that sense, they are regularly indexical to other speech events, as well as symbols. Richard Bauman defines verbal genres as:

> one order of speech style, a constellation of systemically related, co-occurrent formal features and structures that serve as a conventionalized orienting framework for the production and reception of discourse. More specifically, a genre is a speech style oriented to the production and reception of a particular kind of text. When an utterance is assimilated to a given genre, the process by which it is produced and interpreted is mediated through its intertextual relationship with prior text. (Bauman 2004: 3–4)

The importance of intertextuality to an understanding of verbal genres was introduced in 1986 in M. M. Bakhtin's "The Problem of Speech Genres." In this essay, Bakhtin considered linguistic style along with content and compositional structure to be speech or verbal genres (1986: 60). As with poetry and other texts, style can be directly related to speech genres.[5] Style cannot be understood by grammar alone. Bakhtin argued

---

[5] Stylistics is the linguistic study of literary texts. See Halliday (1973).

that choice of linguistic means and speech genres is determined referentially through semantic assignments and the expressive aspect. Thus an utterance must have addressivity and is always in dialogue with other utterances, texts, experiences, etc. Speech genres presuppose that other genres have come before and anticipate prospective ones. Furthermore, Bauman writes, "While particular genres may be primarily identified with specific situational contexts of use – for example, curing chants with healing rituals – it is the very nature of genre to be recognizable outside of the primary contexts" (2004: 5). Bauman's concern is "how intertextuality is accomplished in communicative practices, including both production and reception, and to what end" (5). He argues that "genre thus transcends the bounded, locally produced speech event... genre appears as a set of conventional guidelines or schemas" (5).

Briggs and Bauman argue that genre is "quintessentially intertextual" and that when discourse is linked to a particular genre, the process by which it is produced and received is mediated through its relationship with prior discourse so its "contradictory relationship to discourse becomes evident" (2009: 225). Texts are unified and bounded as well as fragmented, heterogeneous and open-ended. "Viewed synchronically, genres provide powerful means of shaping discourse into ordered, unified and bonded texts." Moreover, as Bauman (2004: 5) argues: "It is the very nature of genre to be recognizable outside of such primary contexts." Thus when English speakers hear "Once upon a time," or "On a planet or in a galaxy far, far, away," irrespective of what has been talked about prior, our expectation, in the first case, is that a narrative will begin or is being referenced that may include people, animals, cartoon characters, etc. In the second case we assume there to be another world in space where unexplainable and bad things will certainly happen and where we will all be the aliens and our existence on earth may be in danger!

These genres can be metalinguistic in that they function as a reference to the language situation and awareness of speech communities in some way. In this respect the choice of style and dialect is also a commentary on the language situation (see Chapter 4 reading dialect) (Tarski 1956; Lucy 1993; Morgan 2002). Verbal genres can be culturally specific so that a joke in one culture may be an insult in another. Moreover, in speech communities where there is prejudice against some groups, even a hand gesture of solidarity and victory can be interpreted as an un-American symbol. Finally, as Briggs and Bauman argue: "Choices between intertextual strategies are ideologically motivated, and they are closely related to social, cultural, political-economic, and historical factors" (2009: 238).

3.5 FACE-TO-FACE INTERACTIONS

All face-to-face interactions include an evaluation of the participants from multiple perspectives. Speech communities identify members and understand meaning and intentionality through linguistic use, conversational styles, construction of attitude, subjectivity, etc. Goffman (1967) describes two types of social face: positive, which focuses on the desire for appreciation and approval by others; and negative face, which is the desire not to be imposed on by others. Brown and Levinson (1987) apply these concepts to theories regarding politeness and conversation. In their case, positive politeness establishes a positive relationship between parties. Negative politeness shows deference and makes requests less infringing. Yet politeness, while nice, is also part of the elaborate communication process among individuals. The question is how the individual participates in, works and manipulates in the communication process in order to set the stage for a kind of information game – "a potentially infinite cycle of concealment, discovery, false revelation, and rediscovery" (Goffman 1959: 8).

As in his analysis of social face, Goffman's understanding of indirectness is based on the intersubjective relationship with others and is a discourse practice where "The witness has the advantage over the actor" (1959: 9). The idea that the audience is the witness is very important for the current analysis as well. A witness is more than an empty vessel. A witness is an active participant in that he or she sees, hears, thinks, critiques and infers. The significance of the audience as witness that interprets what someone means suggests that participants do not find indirection surprising, but rather often comment on and argue about the indirection itself. In that sense the indirect act represents an assessment and belief. Maintaining a "cool face" is often difficult, especially in interactions, because indirect discourse requires that all participants (including hearers/witnesses) constantly assess and address potential meanings within and across contexts.

3.6 GREETINGS

Every speech community includes routine exchanges in their repertoire. In fact Goffman (1971) considered greetings to be the marking and validating of the opening and closing of interpersonal access. As a genre, greetings are particularly important because every society seems to employ some form of greeting that represents first contact and recognition of social relations. Yet, although it is possible to learn for-mulaic greetings, it is also important to realize that greetings can also be complex – and they can lead to profound misunderstandings. Greetings can occur in the form of questions, statements and religious expression. Greetings incorporate social context, age, situation, status, etc. and can range from very formal to very informal, and from subtle to elaborate. Greetings can include questions about health, journey and direction, family, community, feelings, etc. One must know when to greet, how to greet and, more importantly, who to greet. Irrespective of where they occur, greetings at least potentially have the same function, although context may make it necessary to alter the greeting, a feature may be indexed so that one pays close attention to signs that might not occur or might be ignored in other contexts. For example, if a handshake is not returned or eye contact is avoided, it could signal that there is a misunderstanding, cultural difference in greeting or an insult.

The necessity of greetings in some societies is shown by Irvine (1974), who writes: "Wolof greetings must occur between any two persons who are visible to each other." Greetings are significant in maintaining social relations and are based on social role and status, and thus incorporate cultural beliefs of inequality. Thus the greeting exchange incorporates the social role of the participant. According to Irvine, how someone greets can vary to a point, because the role created or performed in greeting determines the ongoing social relationship. When greeting, any two persons who engage in an encounter *must* place themselves in an unequal ranking (Irvine 1974: 173). This explains the proverb "When two persons greet each other, one has shame, the other has glory"[6] (175)

Firth looked at greetings in societies in Europe, the US, Africa, Asia and the Pacific, and considered greetings to be "the recognition of an encounter with another person as socially acceptable"; the prime rele-vance is the establishment of perpetuation of a social relationship and the recognition of the other person as a social entity, a personal element in a common social situation (1972: 1).

A classic ethnographic case of greeting is Youssouf, Grimshaw and Bird's analysis of the Tuareg of the Western Sahara entitled "Greetings in the Desert." The authors present a particular case of greetings where they describe the environment as potentially hostile because of the physical properties of the desert, and also because of what they refer to as "psychosociocultural characteristics" (1976: 800). These characteristics

---

[6] High ranking is preferred even though the higher-rank person may end up having financial obligations to the lower-status person.

are in reference to the Tuareg, who are pastoral nomads that live in an area centered in northern Mali where encounters can occur in which territorial rights are ambiguous. The men, who can spend days without meeting another person, experience loneliness and consistently move throughout the desert. As they move throughout the desert, the Tuareg must also be wary of intertribal warfare and intertribal feuds.

Irrespective of the difficult environment, Youssouf, Grimshaw and Bird report that the functions of greetings remain constant, although the context makes changes in tactics necessary and requires special attention to cues, which could be ignored in other contexts. "Encounters in the desert not infrequently occur without either mediators or audiences . . . Our data show that such desert encounters are, because of these characteristics, associated with apprehensiveness and a need for caution on the part of participants" (1976: 800).

Another greeting encounter of some significance that was witnessed by millions occurred in June 2008 when the then presidential candidate Barack Obama completed his acceptance speech after officially receiving his political party's nomination for president. As is the tradition, loud music played, red, white and blue balloons and confetti poured from the ceilings, and he and his wife greeted by making a fist and tapping each other. The greeting, known as "dap," has been widespread in African American culture since the 1970s. Geneva Smitherman offers two definitions (cf. Alim and Smitherman 2012):

> Dap – Respect, one person's fist taps the other person's fist in a vertical position.
> The Dap – A style of handshake executed with elaborate movements; very popular among Blacks during the Vietnam war and today among Vietnam veterans. (Smitherman 1994: 103)

The *Baltimore Sun* referred to it as "a bare-knuckles kiss." In contrast, E. D. Hill introduced a June 2008 segment on FOX News by asking: "A fist bump? A pound? A terrorist fist jab? The gesture everyone seems to interpret differently. We'll show you some interesting body communication and find out what it really says." On July 21, 2008, The *New Yorker* magazine published what they thought to be a satirical magazine cover that depicted Obama in a turban, fist-bumping with his gun-slinging, Afro-wearing wife – as an American flag burned in the fireplace.

On June 6, 2008, Kimberley Best, a blogger at Ezinearticles.com, asked several pointed questions about how the African American speech community might understand the response to the dap:

This isn't something new; it's not like the first astronaut to walk in space, it's what Black people do. It's a sign of respect and support. The question is not what is it; the question is was it appropriate? As we all know when you are in the spotlight, as the Obamas are, any and everything you do will be monitored and analyzed with a microscope – that's just the way it is. But how is this any different from bowing down to address the Pope? Or bow and curtsy for the Queen of England? What's Wrong With Giving a Little Dap?

Both examples highlight what people should know about greetings in their speech communities and the importance of language ideology in their respective cultures. They also suggest that reckoning with the growing complexity of changing notions of space and place and public and private rights to discourse is an ongoing challenge to speech communities.

3.7 CONCLUSION

This chapter shows that while speech communities can be "home" and familiar to members, there are not only numerous linguistic considerations, but also communicative competences that address the social, political and cultural environment. Socialization into speech communities provides members with practice and the insight of others as intuitions about how to be fully competent members develop. It is not enough to recognize speech events, verbal genres, greetings, etc. It is also necessary to know what to say and when to say it, and to understand the potential meanings of interactions. Moreover, in face-to-face encounters, one must negotiate space and recognize its histories, since they include narratives, spaces, etc.

DISCUSSION QUESTIONS

1. Why is socialization important? What aspects of language and interaction can only be learned from competent members during socialization? How does a child become competent in a speech community? How are children socialized into a speech community?
2. What are some examples of speech events?
3. Why are greetings so important in many societies?
4. Please discuss issues that develop when speech communities occupy and claim places and spaces.

FURTHER READING

Heath, S. B. (1983). *Ways with Words: Language, Life and Work in Communities and Classrooms*. Cambridge University Press.

Hymes, D. (1974a). *Foundations in Sociolinguistics: An Ethnographic Approach*. Philadelphia: University of Pennsylvania Press.

Irvine, J. (1974). Strategies of Status Manipulation in the Wolof Greeting. In R. Bauman and J. Sherzer (eds.), *Exploration in the Ethnography of Speaking*. Cambridge University Press.

Lefebvre, H. (1991). *The Production of Space* (D. Nicholson-Smith, trans.; first published as *La production de l'espace* [1974]). Cambridge: Blackwell.

Ochs, E. and Schieffelin, B. (1984). Language Acquisition and Socialization: Three Developmental Stories. In R. Shweder and R. Levine (eds.), *Culture Theory: Essays on Mind, Self and Emotion* (pp. 276–320). Cambridge University Press.

4 The African American speech community

African American English (AAE) is important to African American people. It is about ideas, art, ideology, love and memory. Whether they celebrate or criticize AAE, its continued presence is indisputable evidence of what they have been through and achieved in society today. The speaker who relies on its most vernacular form represents his or her social world and the encroachments of racism, inadequate education systems and class inequities. The successful adult who claims an allegiance to standard, "good" speech uses language as proof that the escape from racism is successful and over. The teenager who confronts and confounds the world with language games and verbal usage that celebrates the dialect is recognizing its power to both simultaneously represent a generation and defy authority. The college student and computer specialist who uses elite speech when working with others and AAE when theorizing and plotting to build an empire is using every creative linguistic resource to build a future. The US president who is constantly attacked in terms of identity and citizenship uses it to demonstrate that he understands what is going on. AAE is part and parcel of social, cultural and political survival.

4.1 CONTACT AND THE AFRICAN AMERICAN SPEECH COMMUNITY

Discussions of language contact in earlier chapters have alluded to the extreme circumstances that can result from the often violent meeting of peoples and their languages. Discussion of the development of the African American speech community and its survival provides an important example of how speech communities often develop, and how dialect difference and language itself may become the context that represents and condemns the contact. The African American speech community refers to the community of speakers whose African ancestors experienced plantation slavery in the US. According to Eltis and Richardson (2007), between 1525 and 1866 an estimated 12.5 million

Africans were shipped to the New World. Some 10.7 million survived the dreaded Middle Passage, disembarking in North America, the Caribbean and South America. Only about 388,000 Africans were shipped directly to North America. According to Henry Louis Gates (2013), some believe that another 60,000 to 70,000 Africans were taken to the US after arriving in the Caribbean, making the total approximately 450,000 Africans who arrived in the US over the course of the slave trade. As Gates (2013) observes: "Incredibly, most of the 42 million members of the African-American community descend from this tiny group of less than half a million Africans. And I, for one, find this amazing."

While there remain numerous unanswered questions regarding specific language backgrounds of Africans brought to the New World, there are several factors about the dynamics of slave communities that are known. First, the development of African-origin communities within the US occurred in two waves (Morgan 2002). The beginning of African slavery was represented by the upper colonies' demand for domestic and manufacturing work and the lower colonies' for agricultural production of rice, indigo and tobacco (Johnson and Campbell 1981).[1] During this first stage, the language contact situation consisted of coastal West Africans, as well as those from countries between Angola and Senegal.[2] Several historians (e.g. Berry and Blassingame 1982) regard this period as one of both linguistic isolation and ongoing contact. For example, those who were sent to the Carolinas were geographically isolated on the Sea Islands and formed very different speech communities from those involved in domestic and manufacturing labor (Berry and Blassingame 1982; Fields 1985).[3]

The second stage emerged around 1793 with the introduction of the cotton gin, which demanded intensive slave labor. The historian Walter Johnson (1999) describes the overall effect of this invention on the African slave population: "In the seven decades between the ratification of the Constitution [in 1787] and the Civil War [1861] approximately one million enslaved people were relocated from the upper South to the lower South . . . two thirds of these through . . . the domestic slave trade."

While the cotton gin's invention was followed by the official cessation of the Atlantic slave trade in 1808,[4] during this same period of

---

[1] According to the 1790 federal census, of the 757,000 Blacks who resided in the US, 700,000 were slaves.

[2] The majority of captives were simply listed as Africans.

[3] This geographic isolation created the social context for the development of the Gullah language.

[4] Although it continued years after (Franklin and Moss 1988).

slavery the plantation systems of the Gulf States and the Mississippi Valley expanded. Slaves in the Upper South had become extremely valuable commodities. By 1815, internal slave trading was a major activity within the US, and between 1830 and 1840 nearly 250,000 slaves were transported over state lines. From 1850 to 1860, over 193,000 were transported, and by 1860 the slave population had reached over 4 million. Slave communities were highly concentrated in specific geographic areas, and, despite intensive labor conditions, opportunities for social and linguistic interaction persisted.[5]

Once the internal slave trade became the dominant character of US slavery, and individuals within extended families were dispersed and clans and national groups forced to move to other states, it became increasingly difficult to determine one's country of origin, and therefore language origin, whether originally from Africa or born into slavery. While the focus here is the development of a speech community, it is important to consider the inhumane nature of life as a slave in the US and the few choices slaves had in their situation. As Gates (2013b) reminds us:

> When we think of the image of slaves being sold "down the river" on auction blocks – mothers separated from children, husbands from wives – it was during this period that these scenes became increasingly common. The enslaved were sometimes marched hundreds of miles to their destinations, on foot and in chains. Indeed, the years between 1830 and 1860 were the worst in the history of African-American enslavement.

The internal slave trade lasted over sixty years and was followed by eighty years of Jim Crow laws.[6] What remains uncertain is how the plantation system and White supremacy's attempt to restrict communication among African Americans affected the linguistic development of AAE.

The harsh Jim Crow laws and the requirement that African Americans display a public social face of subservience among Whites created a life of more misery. The African American population began to flee the South during what is known as the Great Migration. Between 1916 and 1930 over 1 million people headed north. As Carole Marks writes:

---

[5] Between 1790 and 1820 the language contact situation was one where many of the African slaves retained their first languages, a contact variety and some version of English (cf. Dillard 1972).

[6] Jim Crow laws were state and local laws enacted between 1876 and 1965 that could impose legal punishments on people for consorting with members of another race. The most common types of law forbade intermarriage and ordered business owners and public institutions to keep their Black and White clientele separated.

> The great migration represents a "watershed" in the experience of Blacks in the United States because it was the first mass movement out of the South, the beginning of significant industrial employment, and the initial exercising of the rights of citizenship. (1989: 1)[7]

World War II represents the second phase of African American mass movement from the South as many traveled to urban areas to escape Jim Crow and fill the vacancies of the thousands of jobs traditionally held by White men. It also institutionalized the presence of concentrated urban African American communities (Drake and Cayton 1945; Johnson and Campbell 1981; Marks 1989; Adero 1993). The African American population was transformed from mainly agricultural workers and families to individual workers within factories, often with White workers who performed similar labor. As the African American population moved into urban centers, they encountered emigrants from Eastern and Western Europe, Asia and the rest of the Americas. And as a Black American culture and identity continued to evolve, so did a language ideology that reflected the experiences of the slave trade, life as chattels, attitudes toward the verbal controls of Jim Crow laws, and all aspects of Black American social and political history.

4.2 LANGUAGE IDEOLOGY OF THE AFRICAN AMERICAN SPEECH COMMUNITY

The damage done to African American society and American society in general was devastating but not irreparable. Communication styles were in use that allowed ideas, information exchange and most importantly a way to discuss the possibility of freedom. US plantation slavery was a total institution, where all behavior, as well as speech and style of speaking, was greatly regulated. Total institutions (Goffman 1961) are enforced social systems whose primary purpose is to control most aspects of its participants' lives. Total institutions like plantation slavery often lead to antisocieties and underground institutions where people develop language and discourse styles that serve as contextualization cues that show a speaker has agency and that resistance is in play (Goffman 1961; Halliday 1978).

Antisocieties typically emerge when those who dominate individuals require that the subjugated display an attitude that reaffirms the

---

[7] The availability of jobs in the North was partly due to World War I, which effectively halted European migration to the US and led to the loss of menial and factory labor in the North.

dominator/dominated relationship – in the presence of others – by verbal or physical confirmation (e.g. bowing heads or saying, "Yes sir/ma'am"). Communicative styles are highly indexical and intertextual, since they cue and remind one of perspectives and references to events and discourse and language forms. These forms are often not contextualization cues to non-members. For this reason antisocieties should not be viewed solely as underground institutions. They are formed in response to control from those with power and are only underground in the sense that disempowered or marginalized groups rely on and participate in them. Consequently, from the perspective of the non-dominant group, antisocieties are very much above the ground and a significant aspect of everyday speech. These antisocieties are constructed through language use and are submerged in language styles and contextualization cues that are unheard or whose meaning is misunderstood by those in power. Thus they allow people a form of agency in face-to-face encounters.

During US slavery and until the 1960s in the South, Blacks could not exhibit linguistic agency, nor, under the threat of death, could they initiate verbal interactions with Whites (Morgan 2002). This racialized context presumed that race mattered and that Black people did not have the same intelligence and ability as Whites and thus needed to be protected from themselves – by Whites – who also regulated the public attitude and behavior of Blacks. Submission to White supremacy demanded non-verbal communication as well. Control and surveillance were relentless and occurred within all aspects of Black life, especially in terms of day-to-day interactions. Since the discursive practices of all Black people were regulated by White supremacists, all Black communication with Whites in general was performed as powerless, agentless and child-like. Interaction styles included nearly every old-fashioned, overly polite verbal and non-verbal expectation of speech, such as: use formal address when speaking to a White person, do not speak unless spoken to, do not speak assuredly (use hedges), and do not make statements (over-use tag questions) and so on. The discursive requirements also included non-verbal rules, such as stepping aside when a White person approaches, keeping one's head lowered and not looking someone directly in the eye. Thus linguistic and conversational cues of subservience and dependence were necessary as performatives to corroborate the defense for slavery, and later Jim Crow segregation.[8] Goffman refers to the interactional demands of total institutions like

---

[8] The harsh consequences that might result when the communicative dictums described above were ignored have been brilliantly illustrated in many slave narratives and literature about lynching and Black cultural life under segregation

those required for Blacks in the South as "looping," where the act of making a statement is viewed as a symptom of the problem, and a person cannot distance him- or herself from "the mortifying situation" (1961: 36) by any face-saving action.

The late comedian Richard Pryor performed a routine where he portrayed a slave on his 1976 recording, *Bicentennial Nigger*. Richard Pryor provides a two-and-a-half-minute monologue where he acts out the stereotype of an old, chuckling, semi-literate and subservient, but nonetheless contented, *darky*. As he catalogs the degradations of slavery, he continues to chuckle, scratch his head and talk about how happy he was to be a slave in America.

> RICHARD PRYOR: (*In a voice with exaggerated long vowels, and a mimic of stereotypical speech used by actors playing African American servants in 1950s movies*)
>
> I'se so:::oo happy 'cause I been here 200 years.
> I'm just thri::lled to be here. (*laughs under breath*)
> I'm so::oo glad you took me out of Dahome. (*laughs under breath*)
> I used to live to be a hundred and fifty.
> Now I dies of high blood pressure by the time I'm fifty-two.
> That thrills me to death. (*laughs under breath*)

Pryor as the contented Negro describes how difficult his life was during the Middle Passage – even though he was still happy – and then goes on to describe being sold as chattel:

> Took my momma over that way (.) took my wife that way (.) took my kids over yonder (*laughs under breath*)
>
> I don't know what to do. I don't know what I'm gonna do if I don't get 200 more years of this.
>
> Y'all probably done forgot about it. (.)
>
> (*Pryor uses his regular voice*) BUT I AIN'T NEVER GONNA FORGET

Glenda Carpio describes the monologue as not comic and argues, "It is instead darkly satirical, even bitter. His laughter, mechanized and obviously constructed, is piercingly ironic, since, far from expressing gaiety, it is from the start a laughter that kills" (2008: 74). After his linguistic portrayal of the subservient and loyal servant, Pryor reclaims his voice and speaks the truth.

In response to the demand that they have the "attitude" of someone who should be oppressed, the African American speech community challenged the values, attitudes and beliefs that the dominant society

(e.g. Gwaltney 1981; C. Johnson 1982; Walker 1982; Morrison 1987; Simonsen 1986; S. A. Williams 1986; Whitfield 1992; Stevenson 1996; Jacobs 2001).

held toward them (cf. Bryce-Laporte 1971) through the use of existing systems of indirectness found in many African languages (Morgan 1991, 1993). Indirectness occurs when cultural actors recognize talk as symbolic of ideas, values and occurrences that are not directly related to the present context. African American adult indirectness includes an analysis of discourses of power, since these adults know that their cultural practices, beliefs and values are generally not shared by the wider society, who may not be aware that they exist at all. African Americans developed discourse and linguistic strategies to address threats during social encounters and interactions, so that words or phrases could have contradictory or multiple meanings beyond traditional English interpretations. Thus a counterlanguage emerged that was based on indirectness and functioned to signal the antisociety (e.g. ideological Black audience) and provided a means for a speaker to reveal a social face (Goffman 1967) that resisted and contested the practice of racial repression.

Although based on norms of African interaction, the counterlanguage developed in ways that reflected the social, cultural and political experience of African Americans. Thus, in stark contrast to the cross-racial rules of interaction outlined earlier, Black interactions embodied and highlighted an exacting sense of speaker agency (Morgan 1993). This intense focus on speaker agency was co-constructed with a Black audience for whom language forms and styles signal that content or speaker intent is being camouflaged. In other words, within the system of repression, the counterlanguage provided a vehicle to secretively display a positive social face and exercise face-work (Goffman 1967) that protected and confirmed the existence of the antisociety. Its function in instantiating speaker agency was so great that the "act" of talking was potentially political and highly symbolic.

Within the counterlanguage, the basic concept of audience included all Black hearers and potential hearers, as well as the likelihood that there were spies and overhearers/reporters. Thus the audience and hearer, whether immediately present or presumed present through gossip, spies, etc., were socially and culturally constructed entities. As a result, a speaker was also expected to exhibit his or her conversational prowess and manage to direct what was said to a Black audience who, in turn, held him or her responsible for what was said, as well as possible interpretations. Thus, in many profound ways, a speaker's social face, status and standing were always at stake (Smitherman 1977; Morgan 2002).

Sociolinguistic evidence of counterlanguage exists in examples of camouflaged forms. For example, Rickford (1975) and Spears (1982) report that those outside of the African American speech community overwhelmingly misinterpret utterances containing AAE forms such as stressed **been**, the modal semi-auxiliary **come** and the predicate adverb **steady** as in:

1. *Hey, I **BIN** know his name!* (Rickford 1975: 172)
2. He come walking in here like he owned the damn place. (Spears 1982: 852)

In the first example, stressed **been** (BIN) refers to the remote past and can be written as:

1a. *I have known his name for a long time, and still do.*

In the second case, Spears argues that *come* is not a motion verb but functions as a modal semi-auxiliary to signal the indignation of the speaker. In fact, according to Baugh (1988, 1999), *come* functions to convey personal observation and opinion. Thus sentence 2 can be written as:

2a. *I don't like him walking in here like he owned the damn place.*

Spears uses the notion of camouflage to explain why speakers outside the African American speech community and researchers alike misread these forms:

> It is the form itself which provides the camouflage, and the meaning which is being camouflaged ... Word camouflage, then, has to do with meaning and function: they are camouflaged by the form that bears them. In the case of syntactic camouflage, meanings are camouflaged not only by the form that bears them, but also by their syntactic environment. (Spears 1982: 869)

These camouflaged forms may not be detectable without previous socialization in AAE, and speakers of AAE may or may not realize that other speakers don't share this usage. In many respects these camouflaged forms represent the structural adhesive of the counterlanguage.

From the slavery era until the 1960s, the principles described above continued to function in the Southern US within White supremacy dictums of interaction between Blacks and Whites, which were enforced by state-sanctioned policies. These policies considered certain forms of talk by African Americans to constitute and index claims regarding citizenship rights and status. Thus "talk" and "interaction" were constitutive elements of the system of inequity, and participants' social roles were partially constructed through conversation. The counterlanguage included multiple audiences, layers of understanding and concomitant multiple subjectivities. It might not have survived and been adapted had it not been for the dominant Southern Society's relentless monitoring of African Americans' communication and language. Irrespective of the reason for its continued significance in African American interactions, the counterlanguage is the foundation of all African American discourse. Although legal forms of segregation and punishments were removed with the civil rights movement, the importance of indirectness remains a central aspect of African American ideologies of language.

For the African American speech community, language ideology incorporates the knowledge that the construction and assessment of social face and character are simultaneously performed and grounded within the notion of multiple audiences. Since these audiences include those socialized within the African American experience and outside of it, the knowledge of competing ideologies – and how speakers handle them – is also included in the mediation of social face. In fact, the language ideology not only recognizes, but also relies on the knowledge that language varieties exist and represent different positions of power, politics and history. And any member who doesn't know it – should.

4.3 SOCIAL FACE AND FORMS OF SPEECH

The system of social face found in African American communities requires speakers and audiences to have nearly equal responsibility, knowledge and power in interactions irrespective of the power inequalities between speakers. The importance of the tension between subtlety and non-subtlety and indirect and directed speech has been discussed as the contrast between being "cool" and acting "a fool" (Morgan 2002).[9] Maintaining a cool face can be difficult, especially in interactions, because it is often challenged during indirect discourse (see below), which requires all participants, including witnesses, to constantly assess and address potential meanings and intentions within and across contexts. Coolness, while highly valued, is also severely criticized. In *Drylongso*, Gwaltney pays tribute to the cultural value of the cool social stance in his description of Nancy White: "She is the exemplar

---

[9] The cool/fool contrast is at the core of African American language ideology and has counterparts throughout the African Diaspora and Africa (M. C. Alleyne 1980, 1989; Yankah 1995).

par excellence of the highest status that core Black culture can accord – that of the cool, dealing individual" (1981: 143). In contrast, Connor highlights the indeterminacy of African American coolness: "Cool is not just a term, it is a lifestyle . . . It is the most powerful yet intangible force in Black America. It is to be praised and at the same time it is insidious" (1995: 1–2).

A cool social face is the ability to act on symbolic incidents and subtle varieties of cultural practice with verbal eloquence, skill, wit, patience and precise timing. Those who possess coolness are current and trend-setting, calm and detached, yet in control – in any situation (Major 1994; Smitherman 1994). In this sense, social face is not an identity but a per-formative that requires witnesses who corroborate the status of one's social face. Performatives create the state of affairs that they appear to refer to (Lee 1997: 50), and having "no cool" is akin to having a nega-tive social face, and so is to be avoided at all costs. Performatives have felicity conditions and are the doing of an action rather than merely saying something (Austin 1962: 5). Consequently, performatives and per-formativity (Butler 1997) can enact identities, as "they are the product of constitutive constraints that create identities, create performances elicited under duress" (Kondo 1997: 7).

In the discussion that follows, intertextuality of discourse and verbal genres plays a crucial role in displaying the language ideology of the speech community. Discourse genres refer to language and communi-cation styles that commonly occur in socially, culturally and politically defined contexts. In contrast, verbal genres refer to a speaker's use of culturally significant varieties and styles that mediate, constitute and construct contexts. Thus, while both discourse and verbal genres may co-construct various contexts, verbal genres can collide with strongly framed discourse norms eroding or disrupting well-defined social con-texts. The following analysis locates various speech genres within a system of social face that is partially constructed through directed and indirect discourse. This system includes signifying or sounding, adoles-cent instigating, adult conversational signifying, reading a person and reading dialect.

4.4 INDIRECTNESS

An array of hearers, overhearers and passers-by are part of the fabric of African American interaction. Participants and witnesses assess the nature of speech community membership through the use of indirec-tion in order to test, save, show and participate in social face moves and a sense and reference that is shared. Indirectness occurs when there is a mismatch of these indicators. This in turn introduces performativity, in that identity and intention are indirectly made explicit. Intentionality and responsibility are viewed as both socially situated and constituted, so that speakers and audience collaborate in determining what is meant by what is said (Duranti 1993; Irvine 1993). Thus speakers who use indirectness actually mean to target certain individuals, and they mean to do so indirectly.

While African American indirectness can take many forms in discourse, there are essentially two forms that seem to be indicative: (1) pointed indirectness – (a) when a speaker means to say something that is to be heard by a target and others but is directed at someone else; and (b) when a speaker refers to local knowledge to target someone else; and (2) baited indirectness – when a speaker attributes a feature to a general target and audience that may be true for only a segment of the audience.

Pointed and baited indirectness are not mutually exclusive, and one type of indirectness can quickly lead to another. Their main function is to have all participants pay attention to contextualization cues in order to address a target and identify outsiders who are not aware of the norms. That is, for many African Americans it is not logical that a person would respond to something attributed to him or her unless it was true (Kochman 1981).

Pointed indirectness requires local knowledge to understand what a speaker means and is seldom recognized by non-African Americans when it occurs. In contrast, baited indirectness is often noticed, yet misunderstood by most non-speech community members. This is largely because baited indirectness often includes features that symbolize the African American experience. For instance, I heard someone respond to a simple "How are you?" with, "Ain't nothing happening but the rent." They both laughed, although both own rather lavish homes and have sizeable incomes. The expression is the title of an R&B song from 1986 by Gwen Guthrie. It was a widely popular greeting response through the 1990s in the African American speech community.

Speakers who employ pointed indirectness assume a shared local knowledge, and focus on the context and plausibility of a surrogate as the intended target of an interaction. This form of discourse focuses on speaker agency and facility at portraying the local knowledge in play in creative and subtle ways. For example, I once heard a woman tell another woman in front of a group of teenage girls "When I was young I wore too much make-up and looked like a fool." Although she later informed me that she was referring to one girl in particular, her statement sent all the girls into a crisis! So pointed indirectness gives a speaker room to insult someone in an indirect way because it is based on shared cultural knowledge. This type of indirectness is only successful if recognized by hearers as well as targets who share prior knowledge about events or where the context has been established in such a way that the addressed target and those around can determine the identity of the intended target. It is used by all social classes (see Fisher 1976), especially to key signifying (see below), and, in contexts that include non-members, it can function to enact identity, solidarity and/or resistance among speech community members participating in the interaction. Typically, neither the surrogate nor the intended targets respond, since, for this form of indirection, any response corroborates what the speaker says. This is because the statement is constructed within an act that highlights verbal skill, social face and local knowledge. Thus a direct response should not be within a turn of the particular interaction. In the few cases that I have witnessed where the intended target has responded to the speaker, the target has been aggressive and argumentative (Morgan 1994b).

This form of indirectness may become precarious if the surrogate responds to the speaker (e.g. does not perform the role of mock receiver) and does not recognize that it is implausible that he or she is the target. In this case the surrogate runs the risk of embarrassment, especially if the comment is complimentary and the speaker and/or hearers believe that what is said is only true for the intended target. For example, at a middle-class social gathering I heard a woman say to a man who was not smiling and did not have dimples, "I like a man with a warm smile and deep dimples." Unfortunately, the man (surrogate) responded with a flattered and beaming, dimple-less smile, and said "Thank you," which caused everyone, including the intended target, to laugh at the surrogate and his loss of cool.

In contrast to pointed indirectness, baited indirectness occurs when a speaker means to talk about someone in general by targeting possible attributes or features. An example is when someone says directly to you "Nice smile" when you're not smiling, or "Beautiful voice" when you're not singing and they know you can't sing! In its most basic form, it is a cultural secret handshake. It is meant to be "*audienced*," witnessed and heard by those who have the local knowledge and understand who or what the target is. In contrast to pointed indirectness, it is not always assumed that the target has the local knowledge necessary to know that they are being baited and their social face challenged. That is to say, the speaker may not have anyone in particular in mind and in fact lures potential targets into positions that challenge their social face. If a hearer responds at all, whether protesting or affirming the allegation that he or she possesses these attributes, the audience considers the respondent's recognition of the attributes as an indication that what is said may be true for the protestor.

Baited indirectness, which often appears as circumlocution, can employ collective nouns and indefinite personal pronouns, e.g. "something," "someone," that highlight that the attribute being discussed is distant from the specific hearers (Morgan 1994a). Its function is to make unambiguous participant beliefs and attitudes by provoking a response from those who fit the description. The system of indirection outlined above reveals that African American audiences are co-authors (Duranti 1986) who, along with speakers, contribute to and determine the intent of what is said. In this sense, speaker intent is constituted through collaboration and is not considered complete without it. In contrast, direct discourse is marked by the absence of collaboration and the sense that speakers and audiences rely on each other for meaning. It involves the speaker acting as an individual independent of collaborators and with nothing to lose. Either the speaker has no control or refuses to exercise control over what he or she says, or the speaker is in a powerful position so that audience collaboration is not necessary.

There are two types of direct discourse. The first type occurs in institutional settings where the event or context prescribes speaker intent (e.g. school, work). The other case I call directed discourse (Morgan 2002) and is marked by the absence of indirection, audience collaboration and a disregard for social context. Directed discourse is often used to make what is implicit *explicit* and determine truth, etc. African American attitudes toward direct discourse have been discussed in educational, work and legal contexts where formal communication is defined in relation to tasks and individual activities and where power relationships are extreme. Some researchers have called this communication style work or school language (e.g. Kochman 1981; Dandy 1991). This is because how one speaks is often considered part of a job rather than a reflection of the attributes, beliefs or attitudes of the speaker. Consequently, this form of discourse is considered to be functional, rather than truthful or dishonest. Because direct discourse is void of co-constructed intent, it is often viewed suspiciously outside of institutional contexts. This is especially true for direct questions, which many African Americans view as "confrontational, intrusive, and presumptuous" (Kochman 1981: 99) and potentially harmful (Jones 1988).

Within the framework outlined above, direct questions are institutional ways of knowing which are not based on the truth (intentionality) of the questioner or respondent. The Black expression "Talking like a man with a paper in his hand" (Gwaltney 1981: xxiv) refers to those who ask questions without recognizing or understanding that both listening and hearing are culturally constituted and socially situated. Thus, from a Black perspective, questions should appear in social contexts which incorporate or reflect their reasoning, rather than to simply satisfy institutional or intellectual curiosity and need.

While direct discourse is considered formulaic and does not focus on the participants' role or intentions, directed discourse focuses on a clear target and is unpredictable regarding language variety and discourse style. Although they both share an absence of audience collaboration, directed discourse evolves from the notion that speakers are advocates and there is no such thing as an impersonal position (Kochman 1981). Thus, during conversation, directed discourse can occur in response to direct discourse when hearers believe that speakers should possess or demonstrate their own beliefs and intentions. It can also occur within indirect discourse when hearers believe that speakers are misrepresenting themselves in some way.

One cultural enactment of directed discourse is called "reading." This form of interaction occurs whenever a speaker denigrates another to his or her face (Goffman 1967) in an unsubtle and unambiguous manner. Although there may be self-reporting of reading having taken place without witnesses (e.g. in a story, the narrator may simply report "*I READ her!*"), reading is legitimate only when it is accomplished in the presence of other witnesses who corroborate that it, in fact, occurred. It is directed speech to the point that it is often accusatory. When a target gets read, he or she is verbally attacked for inappropriate or offensive statements or what is perceived, by the reader, as the speaker's false representation of his or her beliefs, personal values, etc. It is not unusual to get read for acting out class privileges, failing to greet friends, pretending to have beliefs that are not actually held, etc. (Morgan 1996). The point here is not that a reader is correct or incorrect, but that the reader is willing to jeopardize his or her own face (as well as that of the target) by disclosing what the reader believes is the target's attempt to camouflage his or her beliefs, attitudes, etc. regardless of setting or context.

Another significant aspect of reading involves a prosodic system that prescribes specific responses from speakers, targets and hearers. This prosodic system includes loud-talking, marking, high pitch and timing/rhythm. Loud-talking occurs in the presence of an audience or overhearers when someone talks about someone else at a volume which is either louder than necessary for the addressed target to hear or markedly different in volume (louder or quieter) from utterances which precede or follow. It can occur on a word or an entire segment. According to Mitchell-Kernan:

> Loud-talking often has the effect of unequivocally signaling the intent of the speaker from the perspective of the addressee. That is to say, it assures that intent will be imputed beyond the surface function of the utterance, which might be to seek information, make a request, make an observation, or furnish a reply to any of these. (Mitchell-Kernan 1972b: 329)

The target of loud-talking is always directly addressed, and hearers generally make an effort to pretend that they are not aware of the speech event under way. In contrast to loud-talking, marking is a mode of characterization where mannerisms are mimicked. When marking, a speaker "copies" a language variety out of context. This is done in such a way that the marking is attributable to a "type" of person who is different from the speaker and/or intended hearers. As Mitchell-Kernan explains: "Rather than introducing personality or character traits in some summary form, such information is conveyed by producing or sometimes inserting aspects of speech ranging from phonological features to particular content which carry expressive value" (Mitchell-Kernan 1972b: 333). Thus, marking is a side remark about a person, and the speech style serves as a commentary about the person.

Pitch and timing are also important resources in interaction. High pitch is associated with dishonest, authoritative discourse and low pitch with honest or true discourse and AAE. Pitch contrast can occur across words or expressions and often co-occurs with other linguistic features involved in dialect opposition. Its appearance often reflects the attitude of the speaker toward the interlocutor or topic.

Timing also signals speaker attitude in that rhythm is viewed as an important aspect of what is said. As in other communities (Sacks, Schegloff and Jefferson 1974; Levinson 1983; Pomerantz 1984), skipping a beat (or two) suggests that a speaker has a view or attitude which does not align with the other interlocutors. In contrast, speaking rhythmically (often with regularized intervals between talks and pauses) signals that the interaction is highly marked as African American and likely to lead to conversational signifying.

Finally, laughter (Morgan 2003) and other vocalic expressions like sucking teeth (Rickford and Rickford 1976) often signify disapproval and the opposite meaning of what is being said. Laughter, when used by women, is often the "fool's laugh," and indexes and signals that what is occurring or being talked about is considered foolish. Women also use laughter when they believe someone thinks that they are the fool, and are mistaken in their assumption.

4.5 CONCLUSION

Perhaps the most outstanding quality of African American interaction is the way in which speaker agency and audience instantiation combine to shape and evaluate both the choice of styles across interactions and the choice of varieties within each style. While African American discourse is based on a system of indirectness, the uses of direct and directed discourse styles are viewed as choices. The use of indirect discourse requires knowledge of AAE and, in most cases, American English norms. The pervasiveness of indirectness and the function of direct and directed discourse are learned from adults and as younger children are socialized through play with older children. (See Chapter 9 for discussion of play.)

The African American speech community exists in relation to and in spite of the dominant American speech community. It is an ideology where, to paraphrase Claudia Mitchell-Kernan (1971), if a guest is offered a soul-food dinner and refuses it without a clear explanation, that person may have signified that he or she is rejecting the Black community in general and the hostess and her family in particular.

DISCUSSION QUESTIONS

1. What aspects of the history of African American culture shape the language ideology?
2. How do language ideologies develop?
3. Define indirectness.
4. What type of cultural, linguistic and social information are necessary to identify indirectness in the African American speech community?
5. Describe the importance of social face and coolness in the African American community.

FURTHER READING

Baugh, J. (1999). *Out of the Mouths of Slaves*. Austin: University of Texas Press.
Labov, W. (2012). *Dialect Diversity in America: The Politics of Language Change*. Charlottesville, VA: University of Virginia Press.

Morgan, M. (2002). *Language, Discourse and Power in African American Culture.* Cambridge University Press.

Rickford, J. R. and Rickford, R. J. (2000). *Spoken Soul: The Story of Black English.* New York: John Wiley & Sons.

Smitherman, G. (1999). *Talkin' That Talk: Language, Culture and Education in African America.* London: Routledge.

5 Youth communities: the Hiphop Nation

This chapter investigates the linguistic, discourse and ideological aspects of the Hiphop speech community in the US and globally. The hiphop speech community is largely made up of youth who function both as an imagined cultural community and, just as importantly, as a community of imagination.[1] As Morgan and Bennett argue, hiphop's "artistic and linguistic practices are not merely part of its culture, but the central driving force that defines and sustains it" (2011: 12). Members assume that there are others that communicate and participate in similar activities and practices. The use of the term "Hiphop Nation" to describe the citizens of the global Hiphop cultural community has not been officially declared, but it is increasingly common. Citizenship in the Hiphop Nation is not defined by conventional national, social or racial boundaries, but by a commitment to Hiphop's multimedia *arts* culture that represents the social and political lives of its members (Forman and Neal 2004; Keyes 2004; Morgan 2009c). Moreover, because most Hiphop artists are self-taught or taught by peers in the Hiphop community, it has empowered young people from all socioeconomic backgrounds to participate in their own right.

5.1 THE HIPHOP SPEECH COMMUNITY

Irrespective of where in the world one finds Hiphop, it incorporates local, national and culturally marked symbols to represent space, place and context. The term Hiphop refers to the artistic elements of: (1) deejaying and turntablism; (2) the delivery and lyricism of rapping and MCing; (3) breakdancing and other forms of Hiphop dance; (4) graffiti art

---

[1] In this respect the Hiphop Nation shares the contours of what Benedict Anderson (1983) describes as an "imagined community," discussed in Chapter 2 where people may see themselves as part of a nation even if they do not participate in everyday, face-to-face interaction.

and writing; and (5) a "fifth element" that unites them all – knowledge.[2] Hiphop knowledge refers to the cultural, aesthetic, social, linguistic, intellectual and political identities, beliefs, behaviors and values produced and embraced by its members, who generally think of Hiphop as an identity, a worldview and a way to say the truth. American writer and social activist Kevin Powell (2003) explains the Hiphop lifestyle:

> When I say I am a hiphop head, I mean that I speak hiphop, I dress hiphop, I walk hiphop, I think out of the box, like hiphop, and that, as **KRS-One** famously said, **I am hiphop**. And I understand that hiphop, really, is a reaction to the failures of the United States government to help poor people, since it was poor people who created hiphop in the first place, and that hiphop is also a reaction to racism and oppression. (Powell 2003)

It is not surprising that, all over the world, Hiphop Heads or Headz – as members of Hiphop culture describe themselves – frequently join the chorus and proclaim "I AM Hiphop."[3]

Hiphop language ideology remains central to the construction and continuation of all Hiphop cultures locally and globally (Alim 2006; Alim, Ibrahim and Pennycook 2008; Morgan 2009c; Terkourafi 2010). The inclusion of varieties of dialects and national languages serves as a declaration that Hiphop culture will help reclaim the nation for everyone. In Hiphop speech communities, language and dialect usage is not based on prestige. Rather, usage depends on whether the languages and dialects are spoken and heard in the local and larger speech communities. Because Hiphop doesn't privilege one dialect over another, Hiphop culture enables all citizens of the Hiphop Nation to reclaim a range of contested languages, identities and powers. Bennett further describes the philosophy behind Hiphop's language ideology:

> We may, also, look at the sharing of language as a collaborative creative performance, whose qualities of being mundane or so common as to seem "natural," do not in any way diminish the artistry and creativity that inform the skills that every human being must bring to the everyday practice of communicating with each other. We offer attention to those who are more skilled then others such as when we describe somebody as having "a way with words" or, admire what in the 18th century would have been called a "turn of phrase." In this sense, a speech community is not only an "imagined community," a speech community is, also, an "imagination community" as members

---

[2] Afrika Bambaataa of the Zulu Nation introduced "knowledge" as the fifth element of Hiphop although some argue that it is beat boxing (vocal percussion). See Price (2006), Chang (2005) for further discussion.

[3] See Alim, Ibrahim and Pennycook (2008), KRS One (2009) and Morgan (2009c).

of a speech community draw from a shared set of creative linguistic skills and values in order to communicate with each other in ways that those outside of that community may fail to appreciate or understand. (Bennett 2012: 1–15)

Youth in the US and globally are socialized into hiphop through ritualized practices and activities that include extensive practice and evaluation among friends and rivals. It is only when they have gone through some aspect of this socialization that they can "represent" hiphop. Membership in the community is instantiated and mediated through audience corroboration and collaboration (Duranti and Brenneis 1986). In the US, the right to represent the Hiphop Nation is substantiated by members' (1) purchase and copying of recordings, (2) memorization of rap lyrics, (3) practice and free-style performance, (4) loyalty to crews and/or individuals, (5) participation in some aspects of hiphop's elements and in evaluation of artists' skills (Morgan 2009c). Internationally, members are involved in some aspect of the first three activities. These recurring activities often result in the emergence of two groups who represent and protect hiphop, and express a commitment to hiphop culture: the *core* and *long-term (LT)* members (Morgan 2009c).

Hiphop speech community members have extensive knowledge of many aspects of verbal and artistic and performance skills, including shifts in aesthetics. They begin as adolescents who have an uncompromising expectation that an MC be exceptional and able to accept severe criticism. They develop their methods and values of critique – including how to handle critiques directed at them – through an elaborate process. In the US the core audience of the Hiphop Nation includes adolescent males and females between 12 and 17 years old. They experience hiphop as a generational and popular activity, and may listen to, memorize and write raps and rhymes, dress in the current hiphop style, keep up with the current dances, and tag or at least practice graffiti writing (Wheeler 1992).

Whether made up of artists or enthusiasts, the core audience develops through at least three overlapping stages that apprentice and socialize them into hiphop culture and the evaluation of skills in the four elements of hiphop.[4]

> Stage 1: Boys in this stage almost exclusively draw action figures and write their names in various graffiti styles, while some girls

---

[4] The following stages include generalizations regarding gender roles. While girls, in particular, may participate in some of the activities described as relating to boys, it only happens occasionally in pre-adolescence, and usually involves siblings and other same-age family members.

may draw action figures along with a variety of cartoon characters and begin writing names (graffiti and multiple styles). It
is at this point that they both begin to think of their names as
potentially tags and a graffiti personal identity. They also begin
to practice hiphop dance moves.

Stage 2: Both boys and girls repeat and copy their favorite artists
and memorize their favorite songs. They listen to hiphop online,
on the radio, and in cars and bedrooms across the country. These
core members may not know the meaning of the lyrics, and
when they suspect a reference may be regional or purposefully
indirect, they consider it their mandate to determine what the
word means and then to strategically employ it. They discover
meanings by scanning websites, listening to interviews, and
talking to their friends and cousins from other parts of the
country, etc.

Stage 3: It is common for the core to participate in all elements of
hiphop and to begin to practice and focus on what they enjoy
the most. The revelation that they are more than consumers of
hiphop is often accompanied by evidence of emerging critiques
as the young recite, at length, the lyrics of their favorite childhood raps and describe their dance and graffiti styles. (Morgan
2009: 57–58)

While these stages do not occur in the same way internationally,
socialization does occur. In her introduction to *Languages of Global Hiphop*
(2010), Marina Terkourafi recalls her youth in the mid 1980s in Herak-
lion, Greece, when she was introduced to hiphop culture. A new student, whose family had emigrated, returned from Germany with a new
dress code – "consisting mainly of hooded sweatshirts – a new style of
'calligraphy' (graffiti) – which we quickly adopted for the headlines of
the class newspaper – and, last but not least, a new style of dance:
breakdancing" (Terkourafi 2010: 1). She reports that same summer she
and some high-school friends watched *Beat Street* (Lathan 1984), the classic Hiphop movie that featured the five elements of Hiphop, at the
local open-air cinema. Versions of the above story are often repeated
throughout the world as a generation in the 1980s was introduced to
Hiphop culture through the movies *Beat Street* (Lathan 1984) and *Wildstyle*
(C. Ahearn 1983).

Eddie Huang, a chef, writer and lawyer in the US, recently described
his realization that hiphop was not just a passing fad.

I think hiphop is real for a lot of White and Asian kids, but there's a
point of diminishing returns. That's when they make an upward

assimilation. I didn't listen to hiphop for strategic reasons. I loved it, I needed it. Watching my White and Asian friends move away from hiphop opened my eyes to this rite of passage that I was never going to join – the ascendance into Whiteness.... I was down with the rotten bananas who want nothing to do with that. (Huang 2013: 110)

5.2 YOUTH LINGUA FRANCA

During the late 1990s, there were sporadic reports of Hiphop cultural sightings throughout the world. While world travelers were accustomed to seeing Hiphop performers in Western Europe, they were stunned to see it celebrated and practiced throughout Africa and in places like Lithuania, China and Mongolia. Today, Hiphop is the lingua franca for youth around the world. It is not simply a language of wider communication, but rather a model of how to simultaneously represent culture and society while challenging traditions, the nation-state, identities, etc. Hiphop artists throughout the world perform their raps/messages in local and national languages, with hands raised as they "shout out" to their crews, neighbors, governments and ancestors – "*Holler If Ya Hear Me!*"[5] As a lingua franca, Hiphop is a global imprint that is familiar, yet unique and customized to "*get in where you fit in*" for each locale.

The notion that everyone has the right to be represented affects every aspect of Hiphop culture, and, while inclusive, it does not necessarily guarantee a harmonious result. The movement of Hiphop culture throughout the globe has been conceived of as a Hiphop Diaspora (Motley and Henderson 2008, Omoniyi 2009) that shares some of the characteristics of ethnic constructions of diaspora. Global Hiphop scenes are sometimes quite accurately described as translocal (Bennett and Peterson 2004) because they so often represent complex cultural, artistic and political dialogues between local innovations of diverse Hiphop art forms, and transcultural interactions between local Hiphop scenes in cities and nations outside of the US, as well as interactions between local scenes and US-based Hiphop media (Mitchell 2001, Alim, Ibrahim and Pennycook 2008). The globalization of Hiphop is, also, sometimes explained in terms of the concept of "glocalization" (Robertson 1995; Androutsopoulos and Scholz 2002; Alim, Ibrahim and Pennycook 2008) because it simultaneously engages the intersections of global and local dynamics. In their analysis of European Hiphop, Androutsopoulos and

---

[5] Tupac Shakur. 1993. *Holler If Ya Hear Me*. Strictly 4 My N.I.G.G.A.Z. Interscope Records.

Scholz suggest that glocalization amounts to a "recontextualization process, wherein a globally available cultural model is being appropriated in various reception communities" (2002: 1). As Hassa explains, these models are "then integrated into a new social context" (2010: 48).

Transculturation in global Hiphop represents a process of continuous cultural exchange within and across national, local and online Hiphop cultures, and rejects the unidirectional model of cultural transmission implied by the concepts of acculturation, appropriation or cultural imperialism. Consequently, global Hiphop cultures retain many qualitative features of African Diasporic cultures (Osumare 2008), and US-based Hiphop cultures, while simultaneously engaging in dynamic and prolific processes of aesthetic innovation, production and diversification. While the translocal dynamics of the Hiphop Diaspora mean that there are countless routes of cultural interaction and exchange, there are at least two major routes of cultural globalization in the brief history of Hiphop culture that the numerous other pathways cross over and over again.

The first Hiphop Diaspora route relates to constructions of the origins of Hiphop culture. While Hiphop may have emerged in New York in the 1970s, many of Hiphop's diverse global and multicultural origins can be tied to African Diasporic cultural forms and communities (Osumare 2008). Especially in the case of rapping/rhyming, it is almost impossible to isolate a single cultural trajectory, because the aesthetic and linguistic features of lyrical rhyming can be found throughout Africa and the Caribbean, as well as the US. David Toop traced these many trajectories in his discussion of the origins of Hiphop culture when he wrote:

> "Rap is nothing new," says Paul Winley. Rap's forebears stretch back through disco, street funk, radio DJs, Bo Diddley, the bebop singers, Cab Calloway, Pigmeat Markham, the tap dancers and comics, the Last Poets, Gil Scott-Heron, Muhammad Ali, acappella and doo-wop groups, ring games, skip-rope rhymes, prison and army songs, toasts, signifying and the dozens, all the way to the griots of Nigeria and the Gambia. No matter how far it penetrates into the twilight maze of Japanese video games and cool European electronics, its roots are still the deepest in all contemporary Afro-American Music. (Toop 1992: 19)

The second major route of global Hiphop culture represents the movement of Hiphop culture into local youth cultures all over the planet. While multi-ethnic collaboration produced early Hiphop cultures, African Americans played a vital cultural and political role. As Perry argues: "promiscuous composition does not destroy cultural identity...The African aesthetic origins of Hiphop, as with all Black American music, allows for it to have a shared resonance among a wide range of diasporic and continental Africans" (2004: 12–13). Moreover, these African aesthetics, in addition to representing a shared cultural terrain for members of international African Diaspora cultures, have also been shaping the aesthetic consciousness and tastes of non-African Americans for centuries. The world's youth have responded with a stunning proliferation of Hiphop-based artistic and cultural production. Along with Hiphop's cultural norm of inclusion, global Hiphop remains symbolically associated with African Americans and has incorporated many aspects of African American language ideology.

As Morgan reveals:

> it is not mere words and expressions that create a bond among Hiphop followers throughout the world. Rather, it is based on African American language ideology where the words signify multiple meanings and critiques of power. Hiphop represents African American English as a symbolic and politicized dialect where speakers are aware of complex and contradictory processes of stigmatization, valorization and social control. The Hiphop speech community is not necessarily linguistically and physically located but rather bound by this shared language ideology as part of politics, culture, social conditions and norms, values and attitude. (Morgan 2009c: 62).

Hiphop language ideology remains central to the construction and continuation of all Hiphop cultures, local and global (Alim, Ibrahim and Pennycook 2008, Morgan 2009c, Terkourafi 2010) in that the usage of varieties of dialects and national languages serves multiple functions. It acknowledges participation in and knowledge of the culture and range of languages and local varieties and their social significance. Through usage that acknowledges, ignores and recontextualizes multiple varieties, hiphop culture reclaims the nation as responsible to and representing everyone.

5.3 THE WORD: HIPHOP PHILOSOPHY AND IDEOLOGY

The WORD brings hiphop into being as an art, a culture, a space and place, and people with a history, social consciousness, ideology and much more. However, it is not mere words and expressions that create a bond among hiphop followers throughout the world. Rather, it is based on African American language ideology (see Chapter 4) where the words signify multiple meanings and critique power. Hiphop presents AAE as a symbolic and politicized dialect where speakers are aware of complex and contradictory processes of stigmatization, valorization and social control. The hiphop speech community is not necessarily linguistically and physically located, but is instead bound by this shared language ideology as part of politics, culture, social condition and norms, values and attitude.

For hiphop, everyday language creativity requires knowledge of a linguistic system as well as how language is used to represent power. It uses language rules to mediate and construct a present which considers the social and historicized moment as both a transitory and a stable place. In this respect, hiphop represents the height of fruition of discursive and symbolic theories of identity and representation. It incorporates symbols and references based on shared local knowledge and produces a frenetic dialectic by interspersing and juxtaposing conventions and norms in the form of language and dialect varieties (Morgan 1998, 2001, 2002). Hiphop then introduces contention and contrast by creating ambiguity and a constant shift between knowledge of practices and symbols. Thus, while the Hiphop Nation is constructed around an ideology that representations and references (signs and symbols) are indexical and create institutional practices, what the signs and symbols index in relation to power remain fluid and prismatic rather than fixed. The use of a famous phrase or line is not enough to claim WORD as an ideology. Rather than be imitative, the objective is to be creative within an existing ideological system. For example, Urla's (2001) discussion of the construction of Basque nationalism in Spain includes an analysis of the use of African American expressions and cultural references among the music group Negu Gorriak. Their mere use of these references helped represent and symbolize a Basque identity and nationalism that could be understood by anyone in the world. The expressions linked their struggle to the civil rights and Black Power movements in the US, a struggle known world-wide as one for basic civil and human rights. Consequently, Negu Gorriak's usage of African American linguistic and cultural references and expressions found in Black films and music served not to simply imitate US and African American culture, but also to represent the Basque nationalist struggle as a righteous struggle.

Those involved in Japanese hiphop also faced the challenge of how to reference and use African American language and symbols in ways that are not imitative, but representative of Japanese hiphop. In fact, early Japanese participation in hiphop was initially viewed as mimicry. According to Fischer, "Verses were constructed in ways that either actually used AAE and/or Hiphop language phrases or AAE sentences were translated into Japanese and then performed over beats" (2007: 25). Japanese fans of hiphop who lived abroad registered their embarrassment, as did African American visitors to Japan. In response, MCs began to manipulate the Japanese language to achieve rhyme and rhythmic flow. In fact, Condry reports that "the skepticism was transposed from the formally dominant discourse of hiphop's association with African-Americans and the English language (in contrast to Japan's ethnic and linguistic setting) to a new discourse challenging Japanese hiphop's authenticity on the grounds that it was simply commercialized (*komasharu*) pop music fact" (Condry 2006: 13). Fischer writes, "In the 1990s, emcees like K Dub Shine and producers like DJ Yutaka brought cultural and linguistic knowledge of Hiphop style to crews in metropolitan areas like Tokyo . . . In addition, emcees, in line with the Hiphop mantra of 'keeping it real' began to incorporate dialects and narrative traditions (such as Osaka-ben and Osaka comedy)" (2007: 3). Artists' messages began to take on subjects important to Japan's youth, including the education system, the sex industry, teenage bullying victims turned schoolyard murderers, and even America's handling of the war on terror (Condry 2006; Fischer 2007). Similarly, in Germany, AAE language ideology also prevails (Brown 2006; Richardson 2006). As Richardson notes, "Hiphop carries with it a paradigm, an aesthetic, and ideologies brought about through culture-specific sociopolitical and economic realities" (2006: 95).

Those in hiphop consider this language to be visible, yet unattainable, unless one respects hiphop's language ideology. It is the barely perceptible antilanguage (Halliday 1978) and counterlanguage (Morgan 2002) that produce potentially dangerous discourses with power. That is, African American youth respond to society's attempt to stigmatize and marginalize AAE usage by their continued innovations within the norms of both dialects (Morgan 2002). Consequently, discourse styles, verbal genres, and dialect and language contrasts become tools to represent not only African American culture, but also youth alienation, defiance and injustice in general.

Central to the Hiphop speech community is the linguistic and ideology border that regulates membership. As discussed above, one aspect of hiphop culture's complexity, and an aspect of its language ideology, is that it insists that members be informed and knowledgeable about potential meaning and contextualization cues. Yet it is impossible to know all potential meanings, since some are popular, local, regional, historical and context-dependent, and may require prior knowledge. Nonetheless, an incorrect interpretation of what someone says guarantees a loss of social standing. It is this interplay of certainty and uncertainty about meaning and intention that brings play and seriousness into hiphop. The interplay that comes from indirectness is an integral part of this system. This is particularly true when it comes to making meaning in conversations about topics that may be avoided and considered taboo in some speech communities, while common and embraced by other speech communities. In many respects, the business of hiphop culture is to continuously challenge and change the "information game" (Goffman 1959: 8) in order to get to the truth and what is real. For many, especially those who express their "true" and "real" attitudes and beliefs in social contexts that are hostile to their beliefs, indirectness becomes an indispensable discourse strategy.[6]

As mentioned above, by the 1990s AAE language and discourse had become a symbol of both truth/realism and disaffection among youth throughout the US. Urban youth recognized, co-opted and capitalized on directness and indirectness, dialect contrast and signifying, and incorporated them in dress, body and art. It is in this respect that hiphop represents the integration of the African American experience within American culture. Black urban youth and youth of all backgrounds have taken counterlanguage and in turn exploited it by focusing on the following tenets:

(1) Sounds, objects and concepts embody and index memory, community and social world.
(2) Choices of language and dialect can signify status, beliefs, values and specific speakers.
(3) All meaning is co-constructed (co-authored).

The first tenet refers to the importance of signifiers or indices and emblems of social life. These may include the use of and references to AAE, general English, proverbs, popular and children's television, kung fu movies, neighborhoods, streets, public transportation systems, prisons, police stations and the things youth must deal with. However, these items' value may change quickly. Thus it is not only that the popular items have exchange value for youth culture: it is also a question of how they function within a system of markedness where the notion of normal, expected and stable are disrupted by forms, references, expressions and so on that question what is considered normal and accepted. Moreover, a system of markedness functions within popular and local trademarks and brands (cf. Coombe 1998; Bucholtz and Hall 2004), and youth may use the system to mark the same symbol as both positive and negative in any given moment.

---

[6] This is in reference to Goffman's contention that crucial facts exist beyond interactions and are concealed within them: "For example, the 'true' or 'real' attitudes, beliefs, and emotions of the individual can be ascertained only indirectly, through his avowals or through what appears to be involuntary expressive behavior" (1959: 2).

The second tenet is concerned with identity, ideology, power and attitudes toward language use. It directly refers to the possibility of altering symbols and trademarks as a means to exploit and subvert them. It seems that Hall may have had youth in mind when he described identity as the changing same (see Gilroy 1994), and "not the return to roots, but the coming-to-terms-with our 'routes'" (1996a: 4). Youth expose and "flash" their routes all the time, on their way to asserting their difference as well as their sameness, and recognizing the power in the expression of their identity. Adolescent social identity is one that experiments, and thus fuses crucial identity issues into play and back again. What's more, identity is viewed through referential and indexical language use where the discourse evokes times, places, experiences and ideologies that accentuate not only the terminology itself, but also the power of the discourse ideology.

The third and final tenet makes obvious that neither youth nor the artist stands alone as an independent, disconnected and de-contextualized individual. Rather, the ties to the audience/generation, speech community and urban youth bring him and her into existence. In this sense, an artist is a composite of the audience – representing experiences that are shared – and the audience determines whether the artist can assume that role. The artist must represent where he and she is from, irrespective of how distant it may seem to others.

As discussed earlier, hiphop's language ideology, while mediated through the tenets discussed above, is also concerned with the play, plea-sure and politics inherent in contrasting and perfecting one's knowl-edge of many aspects of linguistics. When MCs believe that they have extraordinary linguistic ability and are connoisseurs of word formation, they may refer to their word choice as slang. This is especially true for the manipulation of lexical and morphological norms. Hiphop artists constantly change word classes and meanings, resulting in a sense of chaos, movement and urgency.

5.4 NEGOTIATING NORMS AND VALUES: THE REAL HIPHOP SPEECH COMMUNITY?

The conflict over the content of hiphop lyrics occurs regularly in France, the world's second-largest Hiphop market, and one of the largest pro-ducers and consumers (Béthune 1999; Krims 2000) of Hiphop culture. Its immigrant population is largely from North and Sub-Saharan Africa. They mainly reside in subsidized housing in the suburbs of Paris known as *les banlieus* or *le Ghetto* – troubled suburban areas that are the rough equivalent of inner cities in America. France's MC Solaar, who was born in Senegal and whose parents are from Chad, has topped French charts with his singles and albums for nearly two decades, and has had best-selling albums in dozens of other countries. He also collaborated with Guru of Jazzmatazz on their popular recording *Le Bien, Le Mal: The Good, the Bad* and worked with Missy Elliott. In 1995, Solaar was named Best Male Singer in the Victoires de la Musique Awards (the French version of the Grammy Awards). During the 2005 youth riots outside of Paris, France, youth blared Hiphop to fuel their battle cries. In 2003, four Hiphop singles were nominated for the Victoires de la Musique.

One moment in hiphop that was commercial, local and global was the response to the popular song "*Ni**as in Paris*" from the 2011 *Watch the Throne* album of Jay-Z and Kanye West. This hiphop album was highly anticipated, and Jay-Z boasted that not a single sound of the album would be leaked. Billboard.com described the album's first-day # 1 global release as having an old-school feel because fans all had to wait and download at the same time from "NYC to Australia." "*Ni**as in Paris*" quickly achieved platinum status but it initially received mixed criticism. Its beats and production were praised, but its tribute to luxury consumption, sexism, and success and partying was widely criticized.[7] The song actually incorporates multiple types of indirection and signification. It is also interspersed with dialogue from the 2007 film comedy *Blades of Glory* starring Will Ferrell. A sample of the lyrics include:

Jay-Z:

Ball so hard, I'm shocked too, I'm supposed to be locked up too
[If] you escaped what I've escaped
You'd be in Paris getting *f**cked* up too

Ball so hard muther *f**ckas* want to fine me
(That shit cray, that shit cray, that shit cray)

Kanye:

Doctors say I'm the illest
Cause I'm suffering from realness
Got my n**as in Paris
And they going gorillas, huh!

It should be noted that the title song is a Hiphop version of indirection and counterlanguage (Morgan 2002) and a shout-out to the African American artists who have found refuge from American racism

---

[7] See http://rapgenius.com/ for more discussion of meaning and references.

in Paris. Some of these artists include James Baldwin, Josephine Baker and Richard Wright. In James Baldwin's speech to the Washington DC National Press Club on December 10, 1986 he discussed his views of "Ni**as in Paris." Baldwin arrived in Paris in 1948 when he was young, did not speak French and had only a one-way ticket. He said: "I was getting out of here." He knew "In New York somebody was going to call me ni**er just one time too often and someone would have to die. I didn't care who died . . . I didn't know what would happen in Paris, but I knew what would happen here."

While living in Paris people often said, "You must be very happy to be here because we don't treat Negroes the same way they are treated in the States." Baldwin reported that "I looked around here and I could see that they could be so tolerant because the Black people were in the colonies. They weren't in Paris. My mama didn't raise no fool. I realized at once that Algerians were Ni**ers in Paris."

The lyrics are replete with embedded references. Some examples include *Ball so hard*, which refers mainly to the game of basketball, where hard play may mean a monetary fine. It also refers to aggressive and decisive action, and the role of *baller* is someone who is powerful, rich and successful. The lyric *I'm supposed to be locked up too* refers to Jay-Z being fined in basketball, but it also implies that as an artist and businessman his prowess and swagger had to be "hard" in order for him to achieve and believe he could be a ghetto success story. The typical story would be that he is locked up and in jail like so many young people from his neighborhood. Thus what he escaped is American racism, poverty and injustice. The word *cray* is a reduced form of "crazy," meaning in this sense unbelievable. In Kanye's verse he describes himself as *illest* – a term used in hiphop since the late 1970s. *Ill* refers to the opposite of sick. He is so well that he is at the top of the hiphop game and above anyone else (Morgan 2009c: 75–84).

The *going gorillas* reference is particularly complex because, in African American culture, any reference to primates is a potential trope for a racist remark. It has multiple references in this lyric. One meaning has to do with the Rodney King beating. The LA bureau chief for ABC News at the time the Rodney King tapes were broadcast was Kathy O'Hearn. She describes how, when her staff realized the police officers had reported the scene as similar to the movie *Gorillas in the Mist*, there was disagreement in the newsroom as to whether the reference was insulting to Black people.[8] She describes the newsroom scene as all White males and one female, and that none of them had a clue.

---

[8] Laurence Michael Powell, one of King's arresting officers, had described through radio message a domestic disturbance involving two Blacks as something straight

The LA-based hiphop group Da Lench Mob were clearly insulted, and expanded on the attributes of the term gorilla when they released *Guerillas in tha Mist*. The lyrics begin with the lines: "Come down and beware of the Black fist / The guerillas straight mother f**cking killers is the mist." It ends with: "So you better run yo / Run your ass out the jungle / Cause hear the guns go – and we don't miss / Da Lench Mob, the guerillas in the mist!" Currently, there are also T-shirts, posters and competitions to represent King Kong on the Eiffel Tower, as well as consistent references online to guerillas, White women, King Kong and the Eiffel Tower. These references are sexist, racist and at times satirical. The point is that it is the knowledge of all the references that makes the line meaningful.

In recognition of and response to the themes of "Ni**as in Paris" in the US, Yasiin Bey, previously known as Mos Def, recorded "Ni**as in Poorest" as a remake/parody and critique of the consumerism and lack of political and social outrage in the song.[9] It is part of his *Top 40 Underdogs* where he remashes popular songs. He signifies on the Jay-Z and Kanye through references to Malcolm X rather than Will Ferrel in *Blades of Glory* and highlights the social conditions of many young followers of hiphop in the US. The following is a sample of the lyrics:

> Poor so hard, who getting faded? Little Maurice in the sixth grade
> No mama, no father, role model, the dope game
> Poor so hard, that shit crazy!

In this case, one is not balling and bragging but describing life in poverty in urban America. *Faded* refers to using drugs, and Maurice symbolizes those who idolize hiphop artists but live a life of poverty rather than privilege. This back and forth of signifying on life and each other is classic hiphop. However, the global realities of "get in where you fit in" occurred when France actually stepped in as itself. It illustrated the challenges of the rules of battle for fairness and hiphop.

In the campaign between then President Nicolas Sarkozy and challenger François Hollande, "Ni**as in Paris" became a theme song for Hollande. Its use was not in the tradition of Yasiin Bey above, where an MC displays his or her lyrical and analytical skills. Instead, it was used as a symbol of representation of the discrimination against the poor and immigrants in France. Ashley Fantz (2012) of CNN reports that at the height of the campaign there appeared a video clip set to the

---

from *Gorillas in the Mist*. Powell's comment was seen as racist, comparing Blacks to gorillas, and was used against the officer during the Rodney King trial.

9 Please see www.okayplayer.com/news/video-yasiin-bey-ngas-in-poorest.html. This also exists at other online locations.

soundtrack of "*Ni**as in Paris*." She writes that when Kanye West raps "Got my ni**as in Paris, and they going gorillas," the video and contact suddenly take on a different characteristic:

> Hollande is shown leading discussions between men in suits and then talking to voters of multiple races and ages. Crowds in the street and the subway smile excitedly as Hollande approaches them. Supporters raise their voter cards to the camera. A man shouts, "To hell with Sarko!" – a common shorthand reference to Sarkozy. A Black woman holds the French flag and exclaims, "François, président! Inshallah, Inshallah!" – Arabic for "God willing." "We support François because he supports us," says a young Black man wearing a hoodie. "All of Creil, all of us." (Fantz 2012)

Hollande had been criticized as boring, but suddenly he has swagger as he walks among Black, Arab and multi-ethnic supporters in the working-class suburb of Creil. The ethnic community of mainly Black and Arab voters surrounds him. The message is clear. As president he would have a genuine interest in integration and would include different generations and cultures in his government. The video shows Hollande campaigning in the *banlieus*. Moreover, "One thing French viewers found incredibly clever is that we see and hear several references to the town of Creil, often synchronised with the song's line 'That shit cray' – 'Cray' being how the town's name is pronounced."

The video was actually put together by an independent organization and was shown to the campaign after it had reached over 100,000 views on YouTube. It was essentially a prank that went viral there. It was a surprise to many that Hollande did not disassociate his campaign from the video. When ABC Radio National's Philip Adams hosted the program "Hiphop and the French Elections" on May 7, 2012, his guests were Toni Mitchell of the University of Technology, Sidney and Lester Spence from Johns Hopkins University. Mitchell is the author of *Popular Music and Local Identity*. Spence is the author of *Stare in the Darkness: The Limits of HipHop and Black Politics*. When asked what the song "*Ni**as in Paris*" is about, Mitchell responded that it was racist and about getting high in Paris and degrading women. During the interview he added that it was an inappropriate, classic kind of retrograde and that "French hiphop is infinitely more sophisticated and much more poetic." Mitchell then stated: "Why they would use a stupid, asinine and moronic American clip is beyond me." One immigrant to France described the video in another way:

> But put those images to hiphop music, throw in some dynamic editing, and suddenly, damn, François Hollande seems hardcore.

Voting looks cool and purposeful, the carte électorale (voter
registration card) as hip to brandish as the middle finger. Even without
the song, the video has its rebellious moments, like when a Muslim
woman says "François Président, inch' Allah, inch' Allah" ("François
for President, God willing, God willing") – the Muslim population
being a huge source of controversy here in France. (Salzberg 2012)

Thus they are indirectly signifying on the racist past (and present?)
of America and are recognizing France's support of African American
artists and intellectuals. Their use of indirection in this case is especially
interesting because it may be the case that the people of France are
much more aware of this history than African Americans or many other
Americans.

5.5 CONCLUSION

Hiphop is the lingua franca of global youth; it is unifying young people
across racial and national boundaries while honoring their diversity,
complexity, intellect and artistry. It is also challenging those involved
in artistic, political and social analysis. It continues to raise questions
about how speech communities based on different languages and on
different and often conflicting communication norms adapt and incorporate practices developed in other speech communities. The Hiphop
Nation has done more than heed Public Enemy's famous call to "Fight
the Power." The Hiphop Nation has *created and become* the power. US
and global Hiphop heads have put into practice and expanded upon
Franz Fanon's theory that an individual or group that "has a language
consequently possesses the world expressed and implied by that language ... Mastery of language affords remarkable power" (1967: 18).
Citizens of the global Hiphop Nation have not merely mastered a language, they have formed a new one and used that new language to
redefine, name and create their many worlds and worldviews. The
future remains as complex as ever. Through their unprecedented global
movement of art and culture the citizens of the Hiphop Nation have
used their unique and collective aesthetic voices to both "possess"
and transform the world, a process that has not, merely, "afforded"
them power but has also enabled them to produce new forms of power
and of knowledge. Global Hiphop will not necessarily follow a consistent path, but it will be critical. It will be based on the power of the
Word.

DISCUSSION QUESTION

1. Describe the elements of the Hiphop speech community.
2. What is the Hiphop Nation?
3. How does the Hiphop community represent both local and global speech community knowledge?
4. Explain what is meant by lingua franca.
5. Describe socialization into the Hiphop speech community.

FURTHER READING

Alim, H. S. (ed.). (2006). *Roc the Mic Right: The Language of Hiphop Culture*. New York: Routledge.

Androutsopoulos, J. and Scholz, A. (2002). On the Recontextualization of Hiphop in European Speech Communities: A Contrastive Analysis of Rap Lyrics. *Philologie im Netz* 19: 1–42.

Durand, A.-P. (ed.). (2002). *Black, Blanc, Beur: Rap Music and Hiphop Culture in the Francophone World*. Lanham, MD: Scarecrow Press Inc.

Morgan, M. (2009c). *The Real Hiphop: Battling for Knowledge, Power, and Respect in the LA Underground*. Durham, NC: Duke University Press.

Rose, T. (1994). *Black Noise: Rap Music and Black Culture in Contemporary America*. Hanover, NH: Wesleyan University Press.

6 Voice and empowerment in gender and sexuality

This chapter is concerned with the language, discourse and social aspects of women's speech communities and the effects of linguistic and discourse features that are indexed as gendered. It is also concerned with changes and emerging issues in speech community norms regarding gender and sexuality. Across cultures, different communication styles flourish at various levels of complexity in terms of language use and semiotic resources. The language and interaction practices of gendered speech communities are not special and unique to women. Rather, they are practices that are indexed in societies and culture as women's speech. These range from the poetry of Bedouin society (Abu-Lughod 2000), the wedding songs of British Gujarati women (Edwards and Kaatbamna 1989) and the signifying laughter of African American women (Morgan 2002, 2003) to online communities that mirror gender stereotypes in face-to-face-interactions (Herring 2005). This chapter reveals how language mediates and constructs identity, how we associate language with gender and sexuality, and how values and attitudes regarding gender are represented, enforced, resisted and manipulated. To answer these questions, this chapter focuses on both public and popular culture and African American women's speech.

6.1 WOMEN AND PLACE

Speech communities that are formed around women's lives, groups and activities abound throughout the world. This is true even though many women live in societies where, because of their gender, their voices are treated as different from those of men. As social dominance theory argues (Sidanius and Pratto 2001), group hierarchies ranging from dominant to subordinate are common in all cultures and societies. Ideologies and myths that legitimize inequitable status also circulate within most societies. These ideologies include beliefs, attitudes, values, stereotypes, and rituals that justify practices and policies that benefit dominant and powerful collectives. Therefore it is not surprising that Sidanius and Pratto (2001) have also found that, in relation to gender, social dominance orientation tends to be elevated in men, who tend to be involved in authoritarian roles such as the police, military and business that exacerbate the hierarchy. At the same time, women tend to be involved in roles such as caregiver, social worker, etc. that attenuate this hierarchy (Pratto 2005). As Michelle Rosaldo observed:

> Every known society recognizes and elaborates some differences between sexes, and although there are groups in which men wear skirts and women wear pants or trousers, it is everywhere the case that there are characteristic tasks, manners, and responsibilities primarily associated with women or with men ... But what is perhaps most striking and surprising is the fact that male, as opposed to female, activities are always recognized as predominantly important, and cultural systems give authority and value to the roles and activities of men. (Rosaldo 1974: 18–19)

While social dominance research supports Rosaldo's observation, her analysis also suggests several significant factors often missed when studying male dominance. Although dominant hierarchies may exist in societies, they are not always in play. Being a member of a speech community requires knowledge of the range of possibilities and what may set the recognition and enforcement of hierarchies into motion. Since language use, discourse styles and speech genres play an important role in sustaining social positions and relations in society, a closer examination of what women do with language will reveal more about women and their roles and behavior in their speech communities. As Elinor Ochs has argued:

> the relation between language and gender is mediated and constituted through a web of socially organized pragmatic meanings ... Knowledge of how language relates to gender ... entails tacit understanding of (1) how particular forms can be used to perform particular pragmatic work (such as conveying social stance and social action) and (2) norms, preferences, and expectations regarding the distribution of this work *vis-à-vis* particular social identities of speakers, referents, and addressees. (Ochs 1992: 341–342)

Actual studies of language and gender in speech communities began in the late 1970s. Earlier assumptions of general linguistics were that women's language is more conservative than men's, and that women adopt innovative features more quickly than men (Jespersen 1992). Quantitative studies of language behavior that emerged beginning in the late 1960s focused on mainly social categories of class. The data collected were mainly from males, although some females were included.

Sociolinguists of the 1970s were concerned with discovering the relationship between language usage and social stratification. Research conducted by Labov (1972a) in New York City and Trudgill (1972) in Norwich, England identified linguistic features that characterized a speech community and found that a sociolinguistic pattern appeared that connected these features to non-linguistic variables. The presence or absence of spoken (r) in New York City and variations of the pronunciation of (ing) in Norwich reflected social stratification patterns. This research also revealed style shifts where there was a correlation between use of prestige variants and the formality of the speech situation. A final pattern was associated with the sex of the speaker. When data were divided by sex, women's usage was closer to the standard than that of men of the same social class. This description cast middle-class women's language as conservative when compared with men's. While many critiques of these findings are discussed below, the question for speech communities is this: if the data are true, what do these findings mean in terms of how one understands membership and full participation?

The issue of voice and empowerment in gender and sexuality concerns the language ideology of a culture and society, and especially concerns which social contexts may be considered to be masculine, feminine, strong, weak, etc. What is considered powerful speech, as well as how speech is used to represent and negotiate power in interactions, are two significant aspects of interaction and representation that women throughout the world navigate. These are treated as distinct because speech from those in powerful positions is marked as powerful speech, while speech within groups of women may be indexed as having power, even in situations where women's speech is marginalized.

At the same time, members of speech communities may also recognize that the cultural hegemony that is sustained, enforced and reproduced can also be incorporated and acted on discursively and literally to highlight the representation of others who reside outside its boundaries (cf. Gramsci 1971; Bourdieu 1991). That is to say, membership in a speech community includes local knowledge of the way language choice, variation and discourse represent generation, occupation, politics, social relationships, identity and more. The re-examination of language and gender research and theories that relied on traditional Western languages and boundaries was hastened through research on women in non-Western societies who clearly did not fit the Western woman stereotype. It became increasingly clear that a more complex notion of culture and society and social and cultural roles was required. The power of discourse and language is that these systems exist together with and incorporated within other social and cultural practices and relationships. This seems to be a central factor in all speech communities, irrespective of the degree of male social dominance and female oppression. When considering whether there are common mechanisms used by women to represent their voices, one must consider the question of what speech acts, genres, expressions and linguistic forms etc. are marked and indexed as gendered. Examining women speech communities from this perspective reveals striking similarities concerning how societies frame women's speech and how women access powerful speech.

6.2 LANGUAGE AND GENDER IN THE US

In the US the untangling of perspectives on women's role in language and discourse began in earnest in the 1970s, amidst the political struggles of the growing women's movement. In response to questions raised about society's implicit and explicit views of women's rights, Robin Lakoff (1975) published *Language and Woman's Place* (*LWP*). The publication began as a journal article in 1973, and quickly became the most influential and provocative treatise on language and gender. In the 2004 reprint of her book, Lakoff explains the political times and the influence of the feminist movement on her thinking:

> The original essay was situated at a revolutionary moment, in both linguistics and women's history... There was the youth revolution against the Vietnam War... There was women's liberation, born out of the civil rights and anti-war movements, but by about 1968 taking off on its own. The third (and more obscure) revolution occurred within transformational linguistics, the creation of generative semantics. Each of these contributed to *LWP*. (Lakoff 2004: 15)

In *LWP* Lakoff argued that women and men talk differently, and that women's speech both supported and represented the presence of male dominance in society. Her argument was based on observations and intuitions of middle-class White women and focused on what she considered to be the two main forms of discrimination in women's language: that women are taught a weaker form of language than men (e.g. tag questions), and the existence of an inherent sexism in the structure and usage of language itself (e.g. euphemisms for women). This description is described as the *difference* and *dominance* perspective (see

Wolfram and Schilling-Estes 1998; Eckert and McConnell-Ginet 2003; Talbot 2010), and research and theories about this dichotomy represent the first period of systemic investigation into the relationship of gender and language. This research focus, however, was regularly criticized, as Jennifer Coates explains:

> In the early years... research into the interaction of language and gender relied on a predominantly essentialist paradigm which categorized speakers primarily according to biological sex, and used mainly quantitative methods. Next, in the 1970s and 1980s, came a period which recognized the cultural construction of categories such as gender; during this period, more qualitative, ethnographic approaches predominated. In recent research, a more dynamic social constructionist approach has emerged which makes possible the combination of quantitative and qualitative research. (Coates 1998: 3)

In spite of advances in both focus and methodology, as the field of language and gender research methodology and analysis grew, its subject of study implied that American women are middle-class White women. The analysis of women's language was also submerged in linguistic arguments that mirrored the social dominance theory described above. Much of the research considered men's language to be the norm, and women's speech was analyzed in relation to it. Nancy Henley's (1995) comprehensive review of ethnicity and gender research in linguistics critiqued this problem and argued that the language of working-class women and women of color had been on the periphery as unique, marginal or special case, rather than as one among many examples of language use.

Generally, when US women's language is discussed, it is a question of whether middle-class White women deviate more or less from the male prestige standard. Though prestige usage is considered conservative for middle-class women, it is a social class standard and may not be conservative for working-class women, for whom it can be innovative. In contrast, the African American standard is based on vernacular rather than middle-class male usage. It is not associated with power in society – but it *is* associated with masculinity.[1] Because Black women's language has been viewed as the same as Black men's vernacular speech, it has been considered harsh, direct language rather than prestigious. AAE usage among women also implies membership in the Black speech community, and can be considered conservative or innovative

---

[1] Morgan (2002) also argues that early speech style restrictions on Black men in particular feminized and infantilized them.

depending on the linguistic analysis and whether the social factor is race, class or gender (see Nichols 1998).

Because of these inconsistencies, descriptions of women's language as conflicting when compared with men's are what Cameron and Coates (1989) consider part of the folklore about women. They argue that it is based on the notion that "male behavior and male norms are prototypical" (1989: 24).

6.3 THE LANGUAGE OF RESPECTABILITY: CONSERVATIVE AND INNOVATIVE

As Cameron and Coates (1989) argue, what is designated to be conservative and innovative use of language can at times refer to the same occurrence. This is because in most societies the standard language is based on male usage and is directly associated with power in society. Questions of innovative and conservative forms can also be considered within the social contexts of many women's lives. The combination of respectability, citizenship and womanhood is a consistent theme in works directly pertaining to African American women's language as well. Evelyn Higginbotham argues that the claim to respectability was the only recourse that women had to oppose the social structures and symbolic representations of White supremacy when "crude stereotypes of Blacks permeated popular culture and when 'scientific' racism in the form of Social Darwinism prevailed among professional scholars and other thinking people" (1993: 188). She describes this "politics of respectability" as essentially "the discourse of respectability" at a time when "African Americans' claims invariably held subversive implications" (187–188).[2]

The notion of respectability is also present in Japanese women's language use. Inoue (2006) argues that scholars have described women's language as important to the continuation of the national language and part of the cultural heritage. Sueo Kikuzawa, one of the first modern linguists to bring attention to women's language, observed: "Women's speech is characterized by elegance, that is, gentleness and beauty. Moreover, such characteristics correspond with our unique national language" (Kikuzawa 1929: 75). Inoue (2002, 2006) describes a national

---

[2] Thus while Butler (1990) interrogates the meaning of women within historical and political contexts regarding sexuality, Harris (1996) is concerned with the transition of Black women from being viewed as legal property to being viewed as human beings.

angst where scholars have "systematically located male–female differentiation at all levels of language – phonology, semantics, morphology,
syntax, speech acts, and discourse (in the technical linguistic sense),
as well as extralinguistic features such as pitch; they have explained
how female-specific values, attributes, and social roles are registered
in speech forms and in the management of conversation" (2002: 393).
Yet, she reveals, "most women in Japan do not have access to – did
not systematically learn and cannot skillfully produce – the speech
forms identified as women's language ... people in the cultural, class,
and regional peripheries would tell us that statements such as 'men
and women speak differently' do not apply to *their* everyday linguistic
experience" (Inoue 2006: 3).

6.4 DISCOURSE, NARRATIVE AND VERBAL GENRES

As discussed in Chapter 4, African American women's verbal genres
and narratives, and their conversation styles, are characterized by an
elaborate system of indirectness and contrast with Standard English
verbal styles (Morgan 2002; Spears 2009). Much of the research on verbal
genres of African American women has focused on indirectness like he-
said-she-said routines, signifying and reading. There have been several
developments in these areas.

Although signifying or playing the dozens is a form of play, it is often
considered the province of males. However, research on women and girls
reveal that it is part of an elaborate system of indirection (Smitherman
1977; Morgan 1996, 2002, 2003). Mitchell-Kernan describes signifying as
"the recognition and attribution of some implicit content or function
which is obscured by the surface content or function" (1972b: 317–318).
In 1971, Claudia Mitchell-Kernan's study of African American language
and culture in Oakland demonstrated that women participate in conversational signifying (1971: 65–106) and employ linguistic practices
similar to those of men.

Unlike their male peers who mainly "play" signifying games, girls are
much more invested in what was actually said, who said it and heard
it, and whether the person who said it actually meant it. Girls learn
that *who* talks about another girl behind her back risks being labeled
an instigator. The entire ritual involves investigation, evidence, con-
fession and resolution in the form of apology or confrontation. Goodwin's (1990) analysis of he-said-she-said disputes among African American girls details the elaborate lengths to which participants are willing
to go in order to determine who said what behind someone's back.

Goodwin (2003, 2006) has also found Carol Gilligan's (1982) claim that middle-class White girls are conflict-adverse to be an exaggeration when numerous activities are analyzed. At the same time, when working-class African American and Latina girls introduce conflict and uncooperative interactions that challenge one's position, they may consider it a form of play. Thus rather than learning to "play nice," girls are socialized to be assertive, take and give criticism, and resolve conflict as part of play.

As African American girls grow into women, their expression and defense of social face appears in everyday conversations rather than rit-ualized routines. Morgan (2002) found that signifying and instigating also occur in adult conversations, although through the use of more indirect reference and indexicality. She also reports that for teenagers, he-said-she-said events include discourse strategies that not only intro-duce potential conflict, but also use strategies that re-establish the social order as well. These include investigating and clearing the messenger (instigator), investigating, interrogating and clearing "so-called" friends and the offending parties' voice and, finally, resolution.

Another discourse feature found in African American women's lan-guage research is reading dialect (Morgan 2002). Reading dialect occurs when features of AAE and General English (GE) are contrasted. Mem-bers incorporate distinct dialect forms and functions, contrast them with their possible linguistic counterparts in the other dialect, and con-stantly make use of the possible meanings implied by the particular forms and functions chosen. Another verbal feature found in discourse is what Morgan calls "the Black woman's laugh" (2002, 2003). It is similar to Erving Goffman's (1981) response cries in that it indexes the thoughts of the speaker. In the case of AAWL, Morgan argues that it is often called the "fool's laugh," and indexes and signals that what is occurring or being talked about is considered foolish and not in any way funny.

In her analysis of a radio panel discussion convened in 1992 follow-ing civil unrest in response to the Rodney King verdict, Mary Bucholtz (1996) found that the women used reading dialect and other discourse strategies to frame the discussion. Of the six panelists, five were African American (two women and three men), and one was a White male. Bucholtz found that the women used several discursive strategies that constructed social identities. At times, the women interjected distinc-tive phonological features and vernacular lexical items that serve to establish solidarity. At other times grammatical and discourse strate-gies were used to index solidarity. In other instances, the women pan-elists used questions and deixis in a way that weakened the role of the moderator to control the interview. She argues, "The panelists' use of the vernacular as an emblem, rather than as the primary linguistic code, demonstrates that the social meaning of the language is retained, or even enhanced, within an institutional context" (Bucholtz 1996: 279).

Michele Foster (1995) further examines women's speech in institutional contexts and contests the notion that middle-class African American speech patterns align more closely with Standard English than those of working-class African Americans (Labov 1969). Her data come from observations of and interviews with African American female teachers. By using the framework of performance theory and discourse analysis, Foster concludes that the African American women in her study intentionally and systematically used features of African American discourse style, such as code-switching, in order to express their identity and solidarity with students. Thus not only did the middle-class women retain their ability to communicate in the African American vernacular, but they also used African American discourse to index a social identity and communicate a particular stance or point of view (see Stanback 1986). She concludes: "African American English enables these women to communicate cognitive, affective content not available in the standard form of the language, to create and maintain social relationships and express solidarity with listeners" (Foster 1995: 347).

The significance of indirectness and signifying and reading in interaction is magnified in African American women's narrative practices. There are several narrative styles identified in African American folklore, writing and art. For example, Gwendolyn Etter-Lewis finds that African American women routinely use three narrative styles – unified, segmented and conversational – within interactions and narratives (1996: 178). These styles appear in a non-contiguous yet complementary fashion as they shift according to topic, imagined audience, local knowledge and so on. These narratives are co-authored (Duranti 1993) by the speaker and the audience, and include issues of changing values and culture, especially regarding what it means to be a woman, and of morality, personal responsibility and sophistication. Sonja Lanehart (2002) interviewed intergenerational female family members to determine attitudes toward language, literacy, identity, ideologies, education and sociolinguistic contexts. She found that both societal standards and notions of identity influence the women's attitudes toward standardization and the vernacular. Lanita Jacobs-Huey (2006) examined women's discourse practices in the cultural setting of a beauty salon. She found that interactions between Black women relied on knowledge of indirection as well as discourse markers representing the attitude of the speaker. She also found that in the African American speech community symbols of beauty, race and gender regarding hair types, styles and maintenance, as well as discourses of authority and respect, were common themes in any interaction about hair. Jacobs-Huey (2006) discovered that embedded in these interactions were complex contextualization cues (see Chapter 7) and representations of racial and gender politics.

In my research on laughter, I focus on the body of linguistic and symbolic resources women employ to express their ideas, identities, roles and relations to each other.[3] Through narratives, conversations and interviews I analyze two generations of women's language and cultural practice, especially as they negotiate their race, gender, class and sexuality. In particular, I focus on what Erving Goffman (1981) calls response cries. Response cries are instances of what appear to be self-talk in conventional conversations that also functions as reference to beliefs outside of the talk. In studying African American women's discursive practices, I pay close attention to direct and indirect discourse, and verbal genres such as instigating, conversational signifying and signifying laughter.[4]

Laughter is a special category in indirect reference and serves an indexical function in interactions by highlighting the speakers' critical attitude toward a situation or topic. Indexicality incorporates all aspects of context in order to construct referential systems of signs and symbolism – the core ingredients for ambiguity and indirection.[5] Thus indexicality may not only reveal and display cultural knowledge, beliefs and practices; it may also serve as an endorsement to cultural insiders that a particular set of interpretive beliefs and practices are in play. Similarly, what I call "the Black woman's laugh" (Morgan 2002) can seem out of context if one does not possess the interpretive framework to recognize and respond to that which is implicit and indexed and that which is explicit. This is because the Black woman's laugh often occurs within narratives and discussions of bigotry, patriarchy, paternalism, social-class privilege, sexism and other situations that may also be responded to with outrage and indignation. Consequently, in conversations and narratives, African American women's laughter often signals an indirect critique on situations where injustice and the exercise of power highlight the event under discussion.[6]

---

[3] This discussion is based on ethnographic fieldwork conducted from 1989 to 1999. It includes interviews and conversations that were audiotaped and videotaped.

[4] I will not discuss the use of AAE and GE contrast (Morgan 1996, 2002) to index the language ideology of the speech community, although I am aware that the women incorporate them in their discourse.

[5] See Peirce (1955), Silverstein (1976) and Hanks (2001) for further discussion of indexicality.

[6] Men also use this laugh, but within the culture it seems to occur more frequently among women without additional comment.

This laugh is easily misinterpreted because it occurs as a reflex within discourse that is tragic or may have dire consequences for the speaker – who never provides an explanation for why she's laughing. As a response cry, it is meant to be overheard and aligns speakers with events. Yet this form of self-talk also aligns the speaker with a competing or contradictory assessment of the discourse. For instance, Irma Washington and Judy Murray's discussion of jazz in Chicago reflects the values and attitudes of families and women. They have been friends for over forty years, although they never socialized together until they were adults. Their description of the importance of jazz clubs includes various styles of speaking, as well as an insight into how they were viewed by the community at large.

Irma Washington (IW); Judy Murray (JM); Marcyliena Morgan (MM);

1   IW: Ok ((laughs)) I went to the average teenage dance ((laughs)) OK but
2   they – we, we did have a center on 19th and Archer. And every
3   weekend we would have dances there. (.3) Then a few **OTHER**
4   times ? we would sneak out?
5   MM: What were the names of some of the places you went to?
6   IW: Crown Propeller, was one. And, ((laughs)) and let's see it was one,
7   one called – I think it was the Peps – 48th Street.
8   MM: That's for dancing right? They danced a lot there?
9   IW: Yeah. That was it!
10 JM: What did you think of the Peps?
11 IW: Wi::::ld. That's where – that was my style. Wi:::ld. It was always
12   crowded. You know, it was nice, it was nice. That's where all the
13   high school kids went.
14 MM: So you never went to the Peps? ((to JM, who shakes her head))
15 IW: Na::w? ((looking at JM)) How you miss that? ((looking at MM)) And she
16   living right in the HEART of the city.
17 JM: My mother wouldn't LET me go!
18 IW: **DIDN'T YOU HEAR ME SAY** we was **SNEAKING** out?

Irma Washington responds to the question about going to jazz clubs by framing her statement in line 1 *"I went to the average teenage dance"* with laughter that provides an explanation for why she's laughing. Although she does not come forward with the full details about her excursions into the jazz scene, Irma Washington does acknowledge that – at times – she would sneak out to attend dances (line 4). And after naming a few more of her favorite dance clubs, she laughs again and names another club (lines 6–7). Her friend Judy Murray is present during the interview, yet she is surprisingly silent and does not confirm anything her friend is saying. Instead, in line 10 Judy Murray asks Irma Washington what she thought of Peps, and she responds:

Wi::::ld. That's where – that was my style. Wi:::ld. It was always
crowded. You know, it was nice, it was nice. That's where all the high
school kids went.

Irma Washington's description of Peps ranges from wi::ld to nice and
ends with the unassuming explanation that "all the high school kids
went" there. Yet, her use of vowel lengthening on wild, contrasted with
repeatedly saying how nice it was, suggests that some part of the story
remains untold. What's more, when I indicated to Judy Murray in line
14 my understanding that she never went to Peps, she confirmed it –
much to her friend's surprise. The way Irma Washington handles Judy
Murray's statement addresses the conflict during the period between
the secular and sacred life. First, Irma Washington asks Judy Murray
how she missed the clubs and then signifies in line 15 when she begins
to talk about Judy – to me. Judy responds with a statement that indexes
the piety of the period: "My mother wouldn't LET me go!" Finally, Irma
Washington uses directed discourse and employs loud-talking in line 26
in response to Judy Murray's insistence that her mother wouldn't let her
attend the jazz club. According to Mitchell-Kernan (1972b), loud-talking
always signals that what is meant is not being directly stated: "That is to
say, it assures that intent will be imputed beyond the surface function
of the utterance, which might be to seek information, make a request,
make an observation, or furnish a reply to any of these" (1972b: 329).

In this way, the laugh becomes representational self-talk, where the
speaker indexes historical and social events and situations of power
inequity that contrast and expose the speaker's – and culture's – attitude
towards talk. Similarly, Goffman describes how self-talk helps index that
an alternative view, community, etc. may be represented:

> Its occurrence strikes directly at our sense of the orientation of the
> speaker to the situation as a whole. Self-talk is taken to involve the
> talker in a situationally inappropriate way. It is a threat to
> intersubjectivity; it warns others that they might be wrong in
> assuming a jointly maintained base of ready mutual intelligibility
> among all persons present. (Goffman 1981: 85)

Thus the contextually inappropriate response in the form of self-talk
marks the laugh as indicative of a strong and positive social face of the
speaker (Morgan 1996). It represents a negative, sarcastic or ironic attitude of the speaker toward her own remarks, the person who asked
a question or the situation as a whole. In this way, the laugh not
only signals that the statement is misleading: it also makes ambiguous
whether the speaker thinks the questioner or listeners might be fools!

The response cries of Irma Washington function to signal that something significant is not being said in the interaction that is important to know in order to understand what the women are actually saying. These cries suggest that the hearer listen closely and use her knowledge of the situation and culture.

6.5 CONCLUSION

Women's language and discourse are part of the chorus that sings the culture. Many of the women described in this chapter would argue that their use of indirectness and laughter is the result of growing up in a city where people love the power of their language and their laugh. They are right; but there is more to the story. African American women are well aware that they have paid and continue to "pay their dues," and their discourse joins in with their non-vocal cues like the hand on the hips – or in your face – and the slow rolling of the eyes. The system of indirectness described in this chapter produces powerful speech in that it comments on and references all aspects of social life. It provides attitude and constant assessment. Yet these women's discourses are not the secret handshake of a group wrapped in hidden ritual. Instead, they are discursively layered critiques by women who want to tell what they think, know and feel – if you are willing to acknowledge their symbols, histories, social realities, and joys and pains first.

While I have focused on women's interactions, both men and women who are socialized within the African American experience share their ideology of language use. These women's discourse styles provide insight into how language embodies who a person is as well as how people consider language to be a tool to represent and index their ideas and culture. It is a window onto the complexity of representation and meaning, and the elaborate constructions on which speakers rely to express lives deeply layered in memory, rights, family, politics, art, culture and music.

DISCUSSION QUESTIONS

1. Why have women's speech communities been under-represented in language research?
2. What are some language stereotypes of women?

3. Why are women seen as both linguistically conservative and innovative?

FURTHER READING

Coates, J. and Cameron, D. (eds.). (1989). *Women in Their Speech Communities.* London: Longman.

Eckert, P. and McConnell-Ginet, S. (2003). *Language and Gender.* Cambridge University Press.

Gal, S. (1991). Between Speech and Silence: The Problematics of Research on Language and Gender. In M. D. Leonardo (ed.), *Gender at the Crossroads of Knowledge: Feminist Anthropology in the Post Modern Era* (pp. 175–203). University of Chicago Press.

Inoue, M. (2006). *Vicarious Language: Gender and Linguistic Modernity in Japan.* Berkeley: University of California Press.

7   Online speech communities

This chapter explores the concept of speech community within online technology, virtual communication, media systems and institutions, social networks, communication frames, and symbolic representations and social constructions. It examines the various ways that the Internet affects and builds communities around youth culture, language, discourse, gender and sexuality, and racial and ethnic identity. As the legal scholar Lawrence Lessig argues in his book *Free Culture*, the Internet was built based on the tradition of free will, speech, markets, trade, enterprise and elections (2005: xiv). It developed as a culture that would be available to anyone to use, irrespective of where they are, or who they are, or what they have or don't have. The freedom of the Internet has allowed people to connect with existing communities and create new communities of interlocutors who have redefined our notion of friendship, boundaries, protest, advocacy, education, sharing and communication itself. These online speech communities have developed through an emphasis on language and discourse style, indexicality and multiple levels of intertextuality. Thus online users are, as Danet and Herring state, "members of one or more *speech communities* who bring to their online encounters shared knowledge, values, and expectations for linguistic interaction" (2007: 7).

7.1 IDENTIFYING SPEECH COMMUNITIES

On September 2, 2005, I was on the faculty of Stanford University in Palo Alto, California and directing the Hiphop Archive. On August 29, 2005, Hurricane Katrina made landfall as a category-three hurricane in southeastern Louisiana.[1] Katrina became one of the most destructive and deadly hurricanes in US history. The majority of deaths occurred

---

[1] This was its second landfall.

due to the storm surge, and in New Orleans, Louisiana the levees did not hold. At least 1800 people died.

As the devastation and apparent abandonment of those affected by Katrina slowly unfolded, it became clear that a disproportionate number of those harmed the most were poor and Black. The confusion and slow response of the government outraged many people in the US and the world. I worked with about ten students who conducted research on various aspects of hiphop culture and language. The final outrage for the students was the publication of photos of people wading through the flood water carrying food from abandoned grocery stores. The caption of an Associated Press photo – of Black people wading through the water with food – described them as *looting* food. A Getty Images photo – of White people wading through the water with food – described them as *finding* food.[2] The students argued that the photos were indexing race and noted that the images were only available online – and therefore not visible to the poor and Black people affected by the hurricane.

One asked if they could use the Archive's technology to "put it on blast." They intended to broadcast to the Black community that a terrible situation was being made worse because of what they considered to be racist reporting. Someone mentioned that posting of the captioned photographs hadn't been reported on the televised news and "the 'hood needs to know." This event took place amidst the warnings that a digital divide was preventing minorities from participating in the technology revolution. I suggested they use phones, since, at the time, mainly the middle class could afford cell-phone rates, Facebook had just gone public (in 2004) and was not well known, and MySpace was not regularly used as a social medium. The response was: "It will go faster if we get them on their two-way too. We're putting this on blast." I watched as they sent e-mails and photos to colleges and universities throughout the country.

Blogging was just becoming a popular form of communication, and they blogged on Black Planet, the social networking site, and also entered forums. In order to contact friends from their neighborhoods they would "hit up my friends on the two-way," a pager that used text messaging. Someone explained to me that "people in the 'hood with two-ways are usually with their friends so if they know, all their friends will know too. And then everybody will know." They contacted every social group related to school, church, family and their community that they knew. They kept saying, "No one is talking about this. Let's put it on blast!" Within five hours the news outlets began covering the

---

[2] See Tania Ralli (2005). "Who's a Looter? In Storm's Aftermath, Pictures Kick up a Different Kind of Tempest." *New York Times*, September 5.

outrage over the descriptions of the photos. One of the students received an e-mail from a friend who was studying abroad in Paris. "Have you heard about the two photos from Katrina?"

During a September 2, 2005 live broadcast for Katrina on NBC to raise money for the American Red Cross Disaster Relief Fund, a controversy developed regarding comments made by hiphop star Kanye West. He was presenting with actor Mike Myers when he began an unscripted appeal for help for victims suffering from flooding and loss of home and life after the levees broke. West said:

> I hate the way they portray us in the media. You see a Black family, it says, "They're looting." You see a White family, it says, "They're looking for food." And, you know, it's been five days [waiting for federal help] because most of the people are Black ... So anybody out there that wants to do anything that we can help – with the way America is set up to help the poor, the Black people, the less well-off – as slow as possible. I mean, the Red Cross is doing everything they can. We already realize a lot of people that could help are at war right now, fighting another way – and they've given them permission to go down and shoot us!

> (Mike Myers speaks his scripted lines asking for donations to the Red Cross.)

> West: George Bush doesn't care about Black people![3]

While I will never know the influence those students had on getting the word out, I do know that they understood their strategies of how to communicate across multiple environments and speech communities, as well as the limits and potential of technology. Their posts relied on knowledge of both direct and indirect representations of American cultural and societal beliefs and policies about race and social class. And I also know, because they told me and couldn't stop smiling, that they thought they had reached out to their speech community and put information they wanted them to know "on blast!"

7.2 HAND-HELD SPEECH COMMUNITIES

The Internet, with its profusion of social networking sites and ever increasing formats for communication, both challenges the notion of speech communities and enthusiastically confirms its existence. The rise of online communities and networks for communication occurs

---

[3] Later, President Bush said that this accusation was one of the most difficult moments of his presidency.

through language and discourse that are often indexical and important in establishing values of communication, rules of interaction, representing identities, etc. The Internet consists of numerous platforms for communication. These include virtual worlds, e-mail communication and chat groups. It also includes the World Wide Web, which links all computers on the Internet with mutually accessible documents, instant-messaging sites that allow conversations to take place in real time and blogging, where messages are posted at intervals and comments are possible, and microblogging, where users exchange content with short sentences, individual images or video links. Deborah Tannen (2012) has observed that the Internet incorporates Gumperz's (1982) notion of contextualization cues in that linguistic forms may signal contextual presuppositions and metamessages. In this sense participants endlessly assess the process of reframing and negotiating context and intentionality, both to construct and determine the significance of a message (see also Bauman and Briggs 1990). Tannen believes that these written contextualization cues and the metamessages they signal are particularly significant for Internet communication. Their importance in online use may be directly related to their offline significance.

While many communicative and discourse rules are identical to or are based on face-to-face interaction in the culture of the site's physical location or to whom the site is directed, they are constantly manipulated by users who consider language creativity and freedom to be part of Internet culture and language ideology. Thus while Internet communication often includes the shortening of regularly occurring words and expressions online into acronyms or other forms, online terminology can also appear in conversation with the complete meaning intact (Crystal 2006). Moreover, membership is often constituted and challenged through language ideology as interaction has evolved from e-mails and forums to social networking and various forms of interaction through blogging, where the blogger can choose to include conversations through comments and posts. There are now various ways to expand interactions and allow multiple levels of participation and interactions and comments over time. In all cases, information and meaning are being negotiated and assessed. At the same time, unlike face-to-face speech community contexts where participants may suffer severe consequences and loss of social face if they break the rules, online communication may offer many linguistic face-saving possibilities and strategies. As Gershon observes, "Just as people's ideas about language and how language functions shape the ways they speak, people's ideas about different communicative media and how different media function shape the ways they use these media" (Gershon 2010: 8).

For example, according to the World Bank in 2013, sub-Saharan Africa had 650 million cell-phone subscribers. For most of these subscribers, this was their first phone. The explosion of cell phones was possible because of the introduction of fiber-optic cables and national network lines allowing for such services as mobile banking. Lazuta (2013) quotes the World Bank: "More people have access to [the] internet today in Africa than they do to clean water, or even sanitation... So we can say this has been the most significant revolution in terms of changing the African landscape and how people live their daily life." Yet as Archambault (2013) has found in Mozambique and McIntosh (2010) in Kenya, this "revolution" in the African landscape has changed many aspects of social life and the speech community in general.

Both authors consider the overall effect that cell-phone usage has on communicative and other cultural norms. Archambault conducted her fieldwork between 2006 and 2009 in Liberdade, Mozambique, and describes the situation as one where residents experienced abrupt changes in their social environment from surviving within a wartime economy of extreme scarcity to one characterized by a sudden influx of modern consumer goods. She reports that phone usage allowed for more secrecy in terms of how someone lived, whom he or she saw and who saw him or her. In particular it undermined patriarchal authority, and women could text without men and others knowing. The phone was also seen as distinguishing "those who live" (*os que vivem*) from "those who merely survive" (*os que so sobrevivem*) (Archambault 2013: 89)

McIntosh found that in Kenya, cell phones are associated with a change toward modernity, but not without a cultural price. In fact, she argues that in Kenya cell phones can represent disappointment and danger, but also revitalize kinship and reinforce daily life in general. She also reminds us that in Kenya's 2007 elections "text messages were used to coordinate mass political terror along ethnotribal lines, reifying divisions considered antithetical to liberal nationalism" (McIntosh 2010: 337).

McIntosh is concerned with text messages among the Giriama, who live on the outskirts of the coastal Kenyan town of Malindi. She describes the Giriama as among the most impoverished peoples of Kenya, "but their text messages sometimes take a form that would be familiar to Western youth accustomed to digitally mediated communication" (2010: 337). They use what she refers to as condensed English, much like Westerners. McIntosh suggests that this usage alters long-held beliefs about communication and ideologies about surrounding languages.

Condensed English may appear to represent the diffusion of a global style, but the meanings Giriama attach to it speak to distinctly local fantasies of and anxieties about what it might mean to be a global participant. Furthermore, English derives its very significance by serving as a foil for the other codes used in texting; the possibility of using English incites the performance of alternative, local personae in African languages, and English is marked in contradistinction to such personae. Meanwhile, by contrast with English (and to some extent, Kiswahili), the Giriama natal tongue may be being asked to carry a particularly heavy signaling burden in text messages. (McIntosh 2010: 350)

Yet it is clear that online communicative events are evaluated in terms of linguistic formality and style as well as pragmatics. Much like the knowledge necessary to process greetings discussed in Chapter 3, online communication relies on the consideration of multiple contextualization cues to determine identity. As D. F. Harrell (2010) explains, "Creating identities in the real world is an active creative act of imagination. Everyday people construct and maintain real world identities through how we talk, what we like, what we wear, how we move, what we use, and more." The question, he asks, is "how can we design better technologies based on the wisdom of everyday people who must navigate membership in multiple or marginalized categories?" Harrell's answer to the question is to develop a deeper understanding of intentionality and social identity representation.

7.3 INTENTIONALITY AND SOCIAL IDENTITY IN CYBERSPACE

According to Alessandro Duranti:

intentionality [is] the "aboutness" of our mental and physical activity, that is, the property that our thoughts and embodied actions have to be directed toward something, which may be imagined, seen, heard, touched, smelled, remembered, or maybe a state of mind to be reflected upon (in this case, a second-order intentional act). This property of being directed does not presuppose that a well-formed thought precedes action. (Duranti 2006: 36)

The interest in intentionality in computer science is two-fold. It is directly related to a commitment to capture the process of constructing social identity through both physical representation (e.g. an avatar) as well as some aspect of linguistic symbols (e.g. the word *loot* for Blacks and *find* for Whites). The second interest is in determining how participants in online communities use language symbols to construct and maintain their identity and to challenge and evaluate identities. Thus in terms of Internet theorizing, intentionality is a significant philosophy and process that identifies speech communities and is a major source for revealing the nuances and culturally indexed aspects of identity. As artificial intelligence (AI) has advanced, those involved in computational media have become more critical of the lack of ability to capture "complex phenomena and subjective experience of social identity" (Harrell 2010: 15). The arguments of Agre (1997) and others are concerned with AI's minor success in representing the emotion and unpredictable nature of the social world. The concern is that the world be captured within the ideology surrounding the Internet described by Lessig (2005) above, rather than represent the beliefs and values of a particular speech community. Many of these issues center around learning, planning and stereotypes in gaming.

Everett and Watkins (2008) in their description of race and gaming, report that the first human-like figure was Mario, developed by Nintendo™ in the early 1980s. Mario began as a carpenter but was soon given the occupation of plumber. His identity as Italian was ethnically marked through the use of expressions and stereotypical speech like "It's-a-me, Mario." While Mario may have been a stereotype, as technology became more sophisticated, gamers were able to create realistic environments and worlds similar to the real world. In 1997, when the game Grand Theft Auto (GTA) was first introduced, questions were raised concerning how culture and social life were represented with GTA's attempt to introduce realism and construct an urban neighborhood. This neighborhood is roughly a play on stereotypes and is restricted to violence, aggressive language and profanity, and images of criminals, prostitutes, police, gangsters, pimps, etc. Everett and Watkins refer to these as racialized pedagogical zones that "*teach* not only entrenched ideologies of race and racism, but also how game-play's pleasure principles of mastery, winning, and skills development are often inextricably tied to and defined by familiar racial and ethnic stereotypes" (2008: 150).

While debates surrounding stereotyping communities in gaming continue to rage, for computer scientists the question became whether it is possible to write algorithms that addressed when and how one is suggesting an attribute of identity. As part of a movement launched at MIT called critical computing, there is a concerted effort to address many of the social, cultural and political issues in the world. "Critical computing refers to the potential for using algorithmic processing and data structuring as a basis for expressing commentary about, and making impactful change upon, the real world" (Zhu and Harrell

2008: 2).[4] In particular, computer scientists argue that paying attention to intentionality is one way to challenge the nature of stereotyping in gaming.

To test the applicability of intentionality models, Zhu and Harrell (2008) introduced the concept of a scale of intentionality, inspired by Searle (1983). They consider this approach a critique of AI, as an expressive way to narrate user and system agency and to explore characters that can vary between operating as avatars and narrated agents. Although Searle's theory of intentionality is focused on the subject and speaker rather than the audience, Zhu and Harrell (2008) are concerned with both how the audience believes that intentionality is in play and how they respond to it. They explored the effectiveness of an intentionality scale to address the cognitive process known as conceptual blending – "the human ability to dynamically integrate and generate new concepts" (Zhu and Harrell 2008: 2). They developed an algebraic formalization of this process to serve as the basis for generating narrative-content, blending-based, creative imagining through the narration of daydreaming. They explain:

> Our system invokes a scale between narrating highly user-controlled character behaviors directed by the user's actions and desires within the story world and highly autonomous ones that exhibit situated 'aboutness' regarding the system's agency within its domain of operation. We call this a 'scale of intentionality,' a feature also useful as a design tool in applications such as educational 'intelligent' tutoring software that balances creative user problem solving with system recommendation. (Zhu and Harrell 2008: 2)

Although these experiments are in their initial stages, it is important to note that what motivates the research is the notion that people play games and imagine and dream within social and cultural contexts. These "worlds" are made up of speech communities for which there are language and social and cultural symbolic systems known to members. For computer scientists, the crucial issue is whether it is possible to identify intentional acts and the cultural contexts in which they are produced and then to re-create that process. While it is enticing to think that computer scientists' incorporation of philosophy, art and advanced technology may be able to create a world of intentionality, there is reason for skepticism. Human experience is both predictable and unpredictable. As Duranti argues:

---

[4] It relates, in part, to critical technical practices, a concept introduced by Philip Agre that represents a union between technical research and development, and critical theory.

the predicament of our social ontology is that we cannot be human in general (i.e. in universal terms) without being human in particular, that is, without defining ourselves and being defined by others as particular types of persons, that is, subjects who – under circumstances that are always particular (even though generalizable) – display, for example, compassion or hate, hope or despair, care or indifference toward real or imagined entities. It is this property of human existence that makes its detailed documentation possible and, at the same time, necessary. If we accept that intentionality is a directionality or aboutness (of our thinking, feeling, and doing) that always has both universal and culture-specific manifestations, we do not have to sacrifice the complexity of the human experience. (Duranti 2006: 37)

7.4 IMAGINING AND TRANSLATING SPACE AND PLACE

Internet speech communities are unlike any other in that the entire world has access to the medium of communication in much the same way. This access to speech is often compared to the notion of a public sphere (Habermas (1991, 1992), where private people get together as a public articulating the needs of the society to the state. In the public sphere, people use spaces that are physical, online and sometimes organized to represent their interests and to be heard. Of concern is access to policy and resistance to rules for public speech that are not inclusive of non-dominant groups. While some societies may have access to new developments in technology before others, in general there is equal access to the medium. This access includes the ability to communicate in one's own language(s) as well as to observe others communicate in virtually every language in the world. Internet access allows both local and global access through images, video, chat rooms, etc. where people can write to, see and hear each other. The existence of the Internet can appear in the real world without any active participation.

For instance, what is referred to as a flash mob is organized through social media and e-mail. Flash mobs can only exist in the real world if they begin through technology that identifies a community, provides some social indicator of membership, constructs membership through language and discourse style, and provides information of space and place and time for meeting that all correspond to the social reality of the group. They are not *sudden* in the online community, and are often rehearsed, but the sudden appearance of people in a public place doing the same thing or with the same purpose – thereby redefining the public space – provides the group with the appearance of surprise and power. These mobs generally operate under leadership and direction, and can range from political protest to orchestral playing of the Star Wars theme. What is actually mobbed is the public space – which participants claim, act in and then abruptly exit.

The need to represent social identity and interpret intentionality is fundamental in all aspects of Internet usage. The formation of a group and social network includes recurring evaluations to determine whether participants are members and communicatively competent, or whether participants are frauds. Besides actual participants during chats and exchanges, there are onlookers, referred to as lurkers, who follow forums but never post. There are also anonymous participants, known as trolls, who post intentionally provocative messages. They are Internet bullies for whom there is the acronym DFTT – Don't Feed the Troll (see below).

If we recall the discussions in Chapter 3 above of Hymes (1974a) and the parts of a speech event represented by the acronym SPEAKING, it becomes clear that, for the Internet, there are some modifications to the description. First, the Setting is expanded to include online forums, chat rooms and blogs, as well as the psychological setting and cultural definitions described by Hymes (1974). It may also include public spaces like Internet cafes. Participants may include messengers/speakers, audiences and provocateurs, as well as observers of the interaction. The Ends or purpose of the interaction may include those who are trolling the chat. In that case, the space and place of the Internet community are under constant scrutiny and surveillance, and speech events are relentlessly evaluated. The Act Sequence includes possible forms based on whether communication is a forum, blog, etc. While the Setting, Participants, Ends and Key are essential, it is the remaining components that have additional function in Internet communication. Instrumentalities, Norms and Genre determine the nature of specific online speech communities. The Key refers to the signals that establish and maintain the message and interaction, while the Instrumentalities include the styles and forms of speech. It is through these components that intentionality and indexicality are centered. Norms constantly shift, depending on the design of the online platform and networks. Designs may include rules on word and sentence length, symbols, etc. Finally, the Genre and type of message and interaction within the particular format also construct the speech community.

At the heart of many blogs is an understanding of the social rules for interaction governing a particular speech community. The process of real-world language socialization from adult to child is often reversed as older generations are taught new forms of contact from the young and Internet-savvy. Yet the importance of literacy and language loyalty exist on- and offline. As Crystal (2006) writes, online communities:

> demonstrate their solidarity by evolving (consciously or unconsciously) measures of identity, some of which will be non-linguistic (e.g. shared knowledge, a particular morality) and some linguistic in character. The linguistic features will take time to evolve, especially in a medium where technological facilities change so quickly and where some degree of nonconformity is commonplace among users, but eventually they will provide the community with an occupational dialect that which newcomers will have to learn if they wish to join it. (Crystal 2006: 64)

Issues of the virtual worlds of gaming described above, as well as inter-actions in different forms of social media, rely on "culturally specific, nuanced understandings of how these media shape communication and what kinds of utterances are most appropriately stated through which media" (Gershon 2010: 290). She considers media a channel of commu-nication that can refer to codes, semiotic systems of signification, etc. (cf. Hymes 1974a). Gershon argues that frequent users of technology develop media ideologies about the channels available to construct rel-evant audiences as well as authorship "Media ideologies as a term can sharpen a focus on how people understand both the communicative possibilities and the material limitations of a specific channel, and how they conceive of channels in general" (Gershon 2010: 283).

7.5 LANGUAGE SOCIALIZATION AND SOCIALIZING IN SOCIAL NETWORKS

Social networking platforms exist that represent business, art, dating, etc. and that maintain contacts among groups with shared values and experiences or to let people "see" something about a person. Thus factors like socialization and contextualization cues may shift across network-ing platforms. For example, Jones and Schieffelin found that in their study of instant-messaging talk and use of endquoting "The migration of be + like into IM has contributed to speakers' ability to constitute the type of informal conversations they were already having offline (and of which this particular quotative is an indexical sign) in an online, typewritten medium" (2009: 108–109). Additionally, using data from the Heritage and Identity forums on Asian Avenue, Black Planet and Mi Gente, collected between 1999 to 2006, Byrne found that "online com-munities are giving rise to new collective subjectivities unfolding across local, national, and international lines" (2008: 16).[5] Although activity

---

[5] Byrne was also interested in "how real-world forces, such as the shift in racial tensions post-9/11, contribute to renewed commitments to racial identification and anti-imperialism; and . . . how these discourses accept and reject racial typologies" (2008: 16).

in these communities, as with most social networks, may wane, sites based on an identity and ideology often develop strong communications networks,

> especially through the use of tools such as instant messengers, chat rooms, Weblogs, and discussion boards that, among other things, increase the rapidity of discursive exchange. But this new media publicness and the overwhelming popularity of online communities are unequivocally tied to creating and defining borders, if only symbolically, and publicly laying claims to distinct identities. Signs of territory, and the accompanying rhetorics of "nation building," are more visible than ever. (Byrne 2008: 20–21)

In ongoing work on African American online speech communities and what is called Black Twitter, Morgan (2013) found the migration of expressions, words and speech styles without other contextualization cues like prosody leads to many arguments and accusations of meanness online. Black Twitter is attributed to African American discourse styles and is used throughout many social networks as a recognized style of communication. Farhad Manjoo (2010) of Slate.com tried to explain some of the particular norms of Black Twitter:

> After watching several of these hashtags from start to finish and talking to a few researchers who've studied trends on Twitter, I've got some potential answers to these questions. Black people – specifically, young black people – do seem to use Twitter differently from everyone else on the service. They form tighter clusters on the network—they follow one another more readily, they retweet each other more often, and more of their posts are @-replies – posts directed at other users. It's this behavior, intentional or not, that gives black people – and in particular, black teenagers – the means to dominate the conversation on Twitter . . . One of the leading explanations for these memes [is] the theory that the hashtags are sparked by something particular to black culture. "There's a long oral dissing tradition in black communities," says Baratunde Thurston, the Web editor of the Onion, whose funny presentation at this year's South by Southwest conference, "How To Be Black Online," argued that blacktags were a new take on the Dozens. "Twitter works very naturally with that call-and-response tradition – it's so short, so economical, and you get an instant signal validating the quality of your contribution." (If people like what you say, they retweet it.)

While there is much theorizing of public spheres and urban public spaces, the mechanisms for participating in terms of content, turn-taking, etc. remains problematic. In fact, monitoring borders and sustaining speech communities is exemplified when there is intertextual discourse between varying channels of the Internet. This occurred when

video and online blogs joined in criticism of trolls. Trolls hide their identity and politicians often attempt to prevent online bullying by insisting
that people cannot hide their "real" identity. Yet bloggers who represent progressive thought concerning race and sexuality tend to support
anonymous posting, as well as open access to critique, and discuss comments and communicative strategies that are considered unacceptable
and communicatively incompetent.

For instance, on June 24, 2012, blogger Jay Smooth posted on his video
blog Ill Doctrine: "All These Sexist Gamer Dudes Are Some Shook Ones."
He explained:

> A couple of weeks ago I made a video about how sometimes internet
> trolls are just sad and annoying – and other times internet trolls are
> *still* sad – but also generally destructive and dangerous. And this week
> we've had a great example of that second type of trolling – with the
> sexist gamer dude attack on Anita Sarkeesian. Anita does a web series
> named *Feminist Frequency* . . . and recently she set up a kick starter page
> for a new project looking at the representation of women in video
> games.[6] And after the kick starter page went up a whole bunch of
> gamer dudes decided – even though they haven't heard what her
> opinion is yet – that the mere idea of this woman presuming to form
> an opinion about them at some time in the future is so frightening
> that they had to organize a scorched earth campaign of harassment
> and bullying against her . . . It has still been an intensely ugly spectacle
> that raises a lot of questions about why this happens so often.

On her blog, Feminist Frequency, Anita Sarkeesian (2012) discussed the
aggressive use of symbols and communicative strategies and writes:

> Humorous photoshop manipulation, cartoons and image macros are a
> legitimate and important part of a healthy political discourse online
> especially when used to challenge powerful institutions, leaders or
> regressive social norms . . . It's important to remember though that
> these same tactics can be employed as tools of oppression to lash out at
> or bully members of marginalized groups. There is a difference
> between using ridicule to challenge power and using it as a weapon to
> police the status quo by reinforcing sexism, racism or homophobia.
> The image-based harassment I'm discussing here is not part of any
> legitimate discourse but instead falls squarely into the category of
> misogynist abuse. It's a critical distinction and is evidenced by the fact
> that all of the images are attacking my gender or presumed sexuality
> and rely heavily on pre-existing sexist stereotypes.
> This harassment is best classified as a cyber mob attack as it's a hate
> campaign loosely organized through various internet forums.

[6] A kick starter is a funding platform for such projects as films, games, music, art,
design and technology. Projects are brought to life through the direct financial and
professional support of others.

> Participating harassers will share these images as a way to show off and gain validation from their peers as well as to try and recruit others to join the harassment campaign.
>
> The ultimate goal of this behaviour is to try and intimidate, scare and silence women by creating an online environment that is too hostile, toxic and disturbing to endure.

While explaining the details of the exchange, Jay Smooth also defended free speech and provided an example of how one group responded to trolls and why he does not believe the Internet should get rid of anonymous users.

> "Gay for a Day," the international day against homophobia, came out of a trolling incident. We had a troll . . . who couched his extensive homophobia in what seemed like reasonable language. Because he wasn't screaming profanities, we tried to argue with him, but it didn't make a dent. One of our lurkers, who when motivated had an immensely powerful rhetorical ability, showed up and decimated this guy, and it didn't phase him at all. And so we tried to ignore him, until one of the LGBTQ members of the community confided in someone that the silence felt a lot like agreement.
>
> So one of the women finally posted to this guy, "Well, I'm gay, and I disagree with you." Then I posted the same thing. Then dozens of other people did. Soon we had a whole board flooded with people acting in solidarity. There were a lot of Spartacus jokes too, because, well, we were *Buffy* fans. Meta movie references were kind of our thing. Hardly a major civil rights moment, obviously, but the troll left, and those of us who did it sent a signal to our friends that we wouldn't leave them standing alone against people like that.

7.6 CONCLUSION

At the beginning of this chapter I argued that the freedom of the Internet allows people to connect with communities and create new communities of interlocutors who have redefined our notion of friendship, boundaries, protest, advocacy, education, sharing and communication itself. The growing body of literature on intentionality and how media users incorporate technology into their lives promises to provide insight on how our cultures and speech communities are developing and changing. While this chapter has introduced some of the growing work on online speech communities, it is important to remember that the process of participation is in constant flux. This is especially true when we consider the relationship between language and discourse practices in face-to-face interactions and online interactions that use similar norms and values. For online speech communities, social attitudes toward gender, race, sexuality, nationality and social class are represented, critiqued, attacked and more. Yet bloggers consistently argue for the right to develop communicative strategies and platforms to engage all levels of discourse rather than regulate cyber space. Jay Smooth (2012) best reinforces the ideal of Lessig's (2005) notion of free culture (above) in his commitment against bullying and harassment and to maintain dialogue in his speech community – and conversations across communities – in play.

> Abuse and harassment matters and when it happens in our corner of the Internet we need to treat it like it matters . . . No matter what scene on the Internet is your scene, if you are a dude on the Internet and you see other dudes in your scene harassing women or transgender people or anyone else who's outside of our little privileged corner of the gender spectrum, we need to speak up. We need to treat this like it matters. We need to add some extra humanity into our scene to counteract their detachment from their humanity.

The future of online speech communities depends on the continued inclusion of speakers and users who bring their cultures, rules and critiques to cyberspace and new media and participate in the constant socialization about their speaking and complicated world.

DISCUSSION QUESTIONS

1. Describe the different types of online community.
2. Describe the ways in which representing and determining identity are important online.
3. What are some orthographic and discourse styles common in online communities?
4. How can online communities address bullying?
5. How is place constructed through online communities?
6. Describe ways that people learn how to communicate online.

FURTHER READING

Crystal, D. (2006). *Language and the Internet*. Cambridge University Press.
Gershon, I. (2010). Breaking up is Hard to Do: Media Switching and Media Ideologies. *Journal of Linguistic Anthropology* 20(2): 389–405.

Harrell, D. F. (2010). Toward a Theory of Critical Computing: The Case of Social Identity Representation in Digital Media Applications. CTheory.net. Retrieved from www.ctheory.net/articles.aspx?id=641.

Zhu, J. and Harrell, D. F. (2008). Daydreaming with Intention: Scalable Blending-Based Imagining and Agency in Generative Interactive Narrative. *AAI Press:* 156–162.

8 Language in and out of the classroom

This chapter focuses on language socialization and how nations and educational systems interact with speech communities through formal aspects of language policy. Knowing and learning how to communicate is the essence of social and cultural life for children in any society. They learn how to navigate their speech communities through caretakers who teach children how to speak, when to speak, where to speak and how to think about their speech community and language(s). This chapter describes the relationship between speech community belief and values, and educational policy. It explores youth language in public and urban settings, educational and literacy issues, and controversies including important debates on African American English (AAE) in US schools.

8.1 LANGUAGE STANDARDS

While members of non-dominant speech communities often acknowledge and incorporate the standard language, they seldom have access to the social knowledge associated with it. It is during the teaching of literacy, math, science, art, etc. that educational institutions also institutionalize a language standard as the dominant and prestige variety as it socializes children to the norms of cultural and communicative hegemony (cf. Briggs 1986). Educational institutions not only convey specific and specialized knowledge, but also the assumption that the prestige variety is more valuable than that acquired in the conversations and activities of those who do not characterize the dominant language (e.g. Bourdieu and Passeron 1977; Woolard 1985). In fact, Bourdieu writes: "Integration into a single 'linguistic community', which is a product of the political domination that is endlessly reproduced by institutions capable of imposing universal recognition of the dominant language, is the condition for the establishment of relations of linguistic domination" (1991: 46).

In the US, speech communities have had complicated interactions with educational institutions and programs, and some educational psychologists and sociolinguists have argued that only the middle class share the school speech community ideal. In fact, there have been many studies that consider contrasting views and practices about literacy skills at home and at school (e.g. Ward 1971 and Heath 1983). These studies reveal that working-class children have not had practice in school prestige models. Although the school is often aware of the home speech community and its version of cultural capital, the educational system is designed to replace the home speech community with its own ideology, rather than incorporate other speech communities. The result is that the school language is variously described as representing "the elitist traditions of education" (Adger 1998: 151), where there is only one acceptable variety. In contrast, the home acknowledges and at times incorporates both, and only chooses to abandon dominant discourse at times of civil unrest – or when representation and identity are called into question. As Bourdieu further argues: "Political unification and the accompanying imposition of an official language establish relations *between the different uses of the same language* which differ fundamentally from the theoretical relations ... between different languages, spoken by politically and economically independent groups. All linguistic practices are measured against the legitimate practices, i.e. the practices of those who are dominant" (1991: 53).

While the politics of the linguistic market and the social values of language styles and varieties are constantly negotiated, all speech communities are different yet similar in very specific ways. Every speech community is constructed around at least one language and all of its varieties. However, as mentioned earlier, no particular language norm and analysis can predict the complex ways a speech community might use that language(s) to represent its ideology. Linguists may describe a language as though it is a fixed phenomenon, and language teachers may constantly correct for grammar rules and promote prescriptive and so-called standard-usage practices, but it is people in their daily lives that *work* their language to do what they need done. Control of resources can be simply about who is in power, but the world and social order are constantly shifting, and language shifts with them. Consequently, control is a very complicated issue at every conceivable level of language and society. What we can examine however, is how societies develop and introduce linguistic and discourse options in their speech communities. One illustration of the work individuals will do to represent the social, political and cultural complexities of their speech communities occurs in language planning and language policy-making efforts.

8.2 LANGUAGE POLICY: POWER AND CONTROL IN SPEECH COMMUNITIES

As discussed earlier, language planning often occurs in situations where a group or nation is being formed or reconfigured in some way. The need for reconfiguration can occur as part of an inaugural narrative, political unification and so on. Conflicts regarding language policies and practices can be the result of unresolved issues associated with the cultural and political outcomes of language contact. When this moment occurs, there can be numerous competing speech communities with differing ideologies. The formations of speech communities from these contacts may result in language maintenance or shift, or bilingualism and multilingualism. As Paulston reminds us, "People have rioted and faced death over unpopular choices, frequently in defense of their own language but not necessarily so" (Paulston 2003: 394).

Even when people speak the same language, they may not share the same conventions for interpreting each other's speech. For instance, Suzanne Romaine describes the communicative practices of Papua New Guinea as one where membership is differentiated based on differences that are small from a linguistic perspective: "People in one village or clan insist they speak a different language from the next village, although there is a high degree of mutual intelligibility between them" (2000: 23).

How people respond to and participate in planning may also vary greatly. For instance, in Norway, where many regional dialects are spoken, there are two official, written, standard languages, but no official spoken standard (Haugen 1966). Four centuries of dynastic unification with Denmark had left Norway without its own national language when it became independent in 1814. Norway's founding as a nation-state included long-term negotiations with two opposing views over what should be the language of Norway. One position was that Danish, spoken by the educated city-dwellers, was preferred, while the other argument was that the folk speech of the countryside was more representative of the country. In 1905, the Norwegian state settled on two official written languages: Bokmål, based largely on colonial Danish, and Nynorsk, based on rural dialects (see Haugen 1966). It was also agreed that there be no official spoken standard; and all Norwegians were encouraged to speak their local dialects. As Spolsky reports: "Schoolteachers who taught the written standards were urged not to interfere with their children's spoken variety of Norwegian" (2004: 33).

In spite of this sanctioned language situation, in 2005 a popular radio station in Norway sponsored a National Dialect Popularity contest where citizens could vote for their favorite dialect. Strand (2012) reports that the winner of the contest was the dialect spoken in the rural agricultural community of Valdres – and not the urban center of Oslo. She observes that this dialect was the popular choice even though:

> the language varieties spoken in the relatively densely populated urban areas of Eastern Norway and Oslo, in particular, have functioned as a de facto national (or at least regional)... spoken norm for some time in the sense that they are perceived as unmarked and not popularly seen as "dialectal" in the way that other local and regional varieties are. (Strand 2012: 26)

The enthusiasm for the regional dialect is supported by several theories. One argument is that the contest results are directly related to what the oral and written forms mean to the people who voted. Strand argues that though Norwegians may freely choose between Bokmål and Nynorsk, Bokmål is preferred by a significant majority (Strand 2012: 25). However, Strand also reports that Bokmål and Oslo speech are viewed "as a continuation of Danish (linguistic) imposition" (26). In many respects the vote for Valdres, which came from many regions of Norway, was a patriotic vote for a language ideology that identified Norway as an autonomous nation-state – after all of these years. While Norway represents a national language situation where speech community diversity is supported, this is often not the ideology of national communities toward dialects and languages.

In 1948, the White National Party of South Africa officially established the system of apartheid, severely limiting the freedom of Black Africans. Between 1948 and 1994 the National Party enforced racial segregation through apartheid and considered the Afrikaans language the mother tongue of South Africa, and English and Afrikaans were declared the only official languages.[1] All education was administered in these tongues. The Bantu education system, created in 1953, further stratified education by creating nineteen levels of education (based on color) to determine the degree of access to education. The Afrikaans Medium Decree of 1974 forced all Black schools to use Afrikaans and English in a 50–50 mix as languages of instruction. While neither language was native to the students, Black African high-school students in Soweto protested against the move from English to Afrikaans. The decree was resented deeply by Blacks, as Afrikaans was widely viewed, in the words of Desmond Tutu, as "the language of the oppressor." The National Party's policy of enforced racial segregation included severe

---

[1] Phaswana (2003) quotes McLean: "The basis on which Black people have been stripped of their South African citizenship and forcibly removed to bantustans has been their ethnic identity, of which language has often been the only index" (1992: 152).

restrictions on the rights of the Black majority and the policy of White supremacy. Afrikaans was also rejected by the apartheid government's designated separate states for Black ethnic groups (known as homelands and Bantustans), which chose English and an indigenous African language as official languages. In 1976, hundreds of young Black African students were killed in the Soweto riots in South Africa while protesting the education and language policy. The Black community's opposition to Afrikaans and preference for continuing English instruction were overwhelming, and the government rescinded the policy one month after the uprising. Today, South Africa is no longer an apartheid nation and acknowledges eleven official languages: Afrikaans, English, Ndebele, Northern Sotho, Sotho, Swazi, Tswana, Tsonga, Venda, Xhosa and Zulu.

8.3 MULTILINGUALISM, NATIONALISM AND RACISM

Language policy, planning and control can be explicit and direct, and it can be chaotic and arbitrary. The possible range of language policies and their consequences are especially evident in the US where, beginning in the 1780s, notions of the social and cultural consequences of immigration were popularly referred to as a "melting pot" where diverse cultures, societies and national identities could harmoniously merge as a single, homogenous nation.[2] The melting-pot concept did not include Blacks and Native Americans, and the colonists considered "English Protestant culture as the norm" (Dicker 2003: 42). This notion of "one nation" with a unified identity was also inherent in the ideology of the beginnings of US public schooling, which was conceived as a key socializing agent and resource for individual improvement and economic equality (Dewey 1900).

American European immigration history began during the seventeenth century, and the mid nineteenth century saw mainly an influx from northern Europe. The early twentieth century saw immigration mainly from southern and eastern Europe. Dicker notes: "Large numbers

---

[2] The "melting pot" was a metaphor for the idealized and utopian process of immigration and colonization by which different nationalities, cultures and "races" (a term that could encompass nationality, ethnicity and race) were to blend into a new, virtuous community. "Melting pot" came into general usage in 1908, after the premiere of the play *The Melting Pot* by Israel Zangwill. After 1970, the notion of assimilation and the melting-pot model were challenged by proponents of multiculturalism, who asserted that cultural differences within society are valuable and should be preserved.

of immigrants from Ireland, Germany and Scandinavia arrived in the mid-nineteenth century. Native Americans were herded into reservations, the Civil War emancipated Blacks, and Asians began arriving in the western part of the country. Then the late 1800s and early 1900s saw the massive arrival of Southern and Eastern Europeans" (2003: 43).

Gordon reports that during World War I the overriding force in the cultural reality of the US was an Anglo-Saxon America as part of "a consciously articulated movement to strip the immigrant of his native culture and attachment and make him over into an American along Anglo-Saxon lines" (1966: 99). Linguistically, Anglo-conformity requires the substitution of local or immigrant languages for English. Anglo-conformity ideology is also reflected in contemporary public discourse on the role of Spanish in American society.

There was significant doubt whether these new immigrants could be "melted" into the dominant society, and the concept of Anglo-conformity gained adherence. This seemingly idealistic and fair objective was a policy of assimilation, and, as Lippi-Green reports, "More than a hundred years later, many still consider this concept of one America – an assimilated Anglo-Saxon America and a linguistic Utopia – as possible and desirable" (1997: 248).

While European immigration and settlement in cities are often described as including White ethnic and social-class identity, it was the movement to the suburbs that began the development of the social construction of White identity (McDermott and Samson 2005). Whiteness became part of the standard or norm (Hyde 1995), although many Whites did not see themselves as having race at all (McDermott and Samson 2005: 248). Schooling was part of a policy agenda to increase equitable distribution of life chances irrespective of social class. As the need for a trained labor force increased, public education began preparing the working class to meet the growing and changing needs of business and industry (see Sorokin 1927, Durkheim 1961 [1925]; Bowles and Gintis 1976; Bidwell and Friedkin 1988). In spite of these needs, literacy education in particular was not developed solely to prepare workers to read job manuals and follow instructions. Rather, it also included middle-class designs to increase writing skills, introduce literature, creativity, etc. (see Heath 1983). Although Fishman has argued that in the US English is "an instrumentality ... not an object of love, affection, devotion, emotion" (1981: 516), the arguments for "English only" seem as right and proper to monolingual English speakers as apple pie is to "true Americans."

While the notion of "one America" was challenged during the Vietnam, civil rights, Black Power and women's movements, the ideology of one type of America persists and is often resurrected when considering the notion of the US as a unified speech community with shared values, norms and expectations with regard to American English. There is continuous debate about the need for an official language that reflects both national and local state; ideologies about the US, English and the world (Adams and Brink 1990; Crawford 1992). As Huebner argues, "these debates and the language used to argue them reflect attitudes, beliefs, and ideologies about the nature of language and its role in society ... These attitudes and beliefs buttress more general ideologies encompassing notions of race, ethnicity, nationhood, culture, community, gender and self." (1999: 1–2). According to the 2010 census, the population of the US is estimated at 310 million people. The Native American and Hawaiian populations comprise about 3.2 million people.

Irrespective of the competing goals of language and education, language policy, whether explicit or de facto, is about acting on ideological beliefs about how society and culture are represented through language. It requires that one choose whose variety is the norm, which group has power, and is thus always a part of the social and political context. As Spolsky (2004) explains:

> It may be the choice of a specific sound, or expression, or of a specific variety of language. It may be the choice regularly made by an individual, or a defined group of individuals. It may be discovered in the linguistic behavior ... of the individual or group. It may also be discovered in the ideology or beliefs about language of the individual or group. Finally, it may be made explicit in the formal language management or planning decisions of an authorized body. (Spolsky 2004: 217)

The model and norm for language education and formal socialization became middle-class Americans of European ancestry.

To date, the US has no specifically planned national language policy but instead responds to political and social pressures. Despite public education's egalitarian origins, African Americans originally were systematically excluded from public education, and the system has yet to treat students equitably irrespective of race or social class (Wharton 1947; Bond 1969 [1939]; West 1972). Although the majority of US citizens are the descendants of immigrants, the prevailing language ideology is one that attributes a lack of standard language assimilation to a lack of intelligence, laziness, and a lack of loyalty and patriotism toward the US.

The US Census Bureau uses the name Hispanic to refer to everyone of Spanish-speaking national or ethnic origin. They estimate the population as 15.5 percent, with the probability that Latino ancestry will be 25 percent of the population in 2050. This diverse population often reflects settlement patterns based on the country of origin and includes Cubans residing in southern Florida and metropolitan New York, Mexican-origin population in the southwest, and Puerto Ricans and Caribbean Spanish Dominican Republic speakers in the New York city area and other east coast metropolises.

Ana Celia Zentella (1996) refers to the symbol of Chiquita Banana that was widely used by the United Fruit Company to advertise the South American fruit as the chiquitification of Latinos. The elaborate fruit hat was originally created in 1944 on top of an animated banana with a woman's dress and legs, singing vocals with a stereotypical Spanish accent. In 1987 the banana image was replaced by a woman with a fruit hat that included bananas. Zentella considers this symbol as the homogenization of the Latino cultures and a "one America" version of a form of "one Latino" that results in at least three misconceptions. These include: (1) the idea of a homogeneous "Hispanic community" that refuses to learn English; (2) the belittling of non-Castilian varieties of Spanish; and (3) the labeling of second-generation bilinguals as semi- or alinguals (1996: 1). In many respects, today's call for middle-class language usage for Latinos and Black students, coupled with cries for "just the basics," reflects a contradiction over the purpose of education for African American and Latino children in particular.

Martin's (2009) review of an English Only ordinance in Pahrump, Nevada illustrates the competing ideologies around language, citizenship and speech community membership. She describes how a small town reacted to a national increase in immigration. Martin argues that the national language ideologies surrounding debates of similar English Only policies nationwide created panic among some in the English-speaking population. She describes how, in November of 2006, the town of Pahrump, Nevada enacted an English Only ordinance limiting the use of Spanish in schools and local transactions – even though the town had few Spanish-language speakers. The hostility toward Spanish speakers by those who supported the ordinance was also expressed in quoted written discourse. "The most shocking was the sign in a local Pahrump restaurant that read: 'No dogs or Mexicans allowed' . . . [and] a T-shirt worn by a supporter during one of the public hearings that read: 'Speak English or get the (expletive) out'" (Martin 2009: 98).[3]

---

[3] The ordinance was eventually proved illegal.

8.4 LANGUAGE POLICY AND FRAGMENTED SPEECH COMMUNITIES

While languages may be targeted and stigmatized, in the US there is a tolerance of and even pride about regional dialects of English. As discussed earlier, this is partially due to widespread support for European immigration and the regions in which Europeans settled. In contrast, social dialects like AAE are often attacked and even considered un-American. Until 1954, state laws allowed the establishment of separate public schools for Blacks and Whites. These states often argued that the schools were "separate but equal." The Brown v. Board of Education Supreme Court case of 1954 prevented states from acting independently regarding schooling and stated that "separate educational facilities are inherently unequal," paving the way for integrated public schools. Some states did not immediately follow the new law, and in the 1960s enforcement of the laws through compulsory integration of public schools began in earnest. At the same time, numerous psychological theories about the school performance of African American children surfaced.[4] One influential psychological theory argued that differences in educational achievement between Black working-class and White middle-class children occur because Black children suffer from genetic or cognitive deficiencies (e.g. Bereiter and Engelman 1966; Jensen 1969). These deficit theories ignored social class and racial inequality, arguing that inherent characteristics are the true culprit, and they attacked the cultural and social environment of African American children (cf. Deutsch, Katz and Jensen 1968). Deprivation theories are repeatedly given credence by other sociological theories that consider middle-class family values and childhood experiences to be normative (Brodkin 1994). Middle-class life is then compared with the social life of those from different racial groups and social classes. In 1994, Hernstein and Murray attempted to resurrect these theories. But as Fischer et al. write in their convincing debunking of Hernstein and Murray: "Research has shown that nature determines neither the level of inequality in America nor which Americans in particular will be privileged or disprivileged; social conditions and national policies do. Inequality is in that sense designed" (Fischer et al. 1996: xi).

The response of linguistic scholars to deficit and deprivation social-psychological approaches has been aggressive and thorough. Detailed descriptions of language and verbal style and the system and structure of AAE have been conducted (e.g. Stewart 1969; Wolfram 1969; Kochman

---

[4] In fact, it was partly the infamy of the deficit theories that jeopardized the Oakland proposal (discussed below), which included arguments of genetic links between African languages and AAE.

1972; Labov 1972a; Mitchell-Kernan 1972a; Baratz 1973; Smitherman 1977; Baugh 1983a,b; Brooks 1985; Morgan 1994a). Many linguists and education theorists have directly addressed this particular issue by detailing White working-class and African American working-class varieties and the plight of African Americans within public education (e.g. Ogbu 1978; Baugh 1981; Smitherman 1981a,b; Labov 1982; Morgan 1994b; Rickford and Rickford 1995). In addition, linguists and language educators have been consistent, if not always united, in their recognition of the necessity to contribute to educators' understanding of AAE. Some linguists and communication specialists developed language programs that were designed to use the child's home language as a vehicle to learn school-specific activities and middle-class varieties of English.

Language education plans specifically designed to address the needs of African American children began in the early 1970s under the name Standard English as a Second Dialect (SESD) instruction. SESD was introduced into the school curricula of most major metropolitan areas, including Los Angeles, Chicago, Washington DC, Detroit, Gary, Indiana and Brooklyn. These programs emerged at the height of the Black Power, civil rights and African liberation support movements. This period was an extremely creative, intense and fluid time when identity was being redefined throughout the Black community. In fact, many Black Power advocates argued that African Americans should speak both Standard English and Swahili! Some proponents of these beliefs began an alternative school movement that focused on African history and African languages, and that attacked the public educational system. It was also a period when community representatives focused on the right of African Americans to the same-quality education afforded middle-class Whites.

Within this climate, the mission of SESD programs was to improve the life chances of African American children by introducing Standard English norms into their verbal repertoire while respecting the child's home dialect. Criticism of these programs evolved around what was considered respecting the home dialect and how parents perceived the function of literacy education.

The SESD approach focused on structural language learning methods and communicative competence models.

> It was felt, moreover, that there should be incorporated some of the sociological knowledge which led many practitioners of the newly developed sociolinguistics to believe that "Your Language is Good Language," while a noble slogan, did not take sufficiently into account the social problems which might be encountered by one holding to the first language variety which he happened to have learned as a child. (Dillard 1978: 300)

Yet Dillard's own discussion of language education programs and issues illustrates the difficulty of reconciling how schooling works in America with linguistic and educational policy-making and the rights and interests of African American parents and their children. While using terminology like "the language of the classroom" and "the language of the community" few theorists actually studied the discourse about language in either the classroom or community. There was no development of an assessment instrument to determine whether a student's knowledge of AAE causes problems with learning and whether he or she could benefit from the program. What's more, administrators of SESD programs did little to explain these programs to parents and inform them about the dialect materials and how they would be used in the teaching of standard literacy. Nor did they train teachers about stereotypes, racism and the relationship between language and culture, or historical and language-loyalty issues. This failure to inform both parents and teachers had dire effects on all SESD programs.

For example, African American parents reproached one program conducted in Florida that included dialect-reading material about a young Black boy who repeatedly skipped school. In his article "Teaching Blacks to Read against Their Will," William Stewart (1975) condemned the parents for rejecting the program and, ironically, charged them with having middle-class values. He argued that they suffered from self-hate because they didn't want their children to bring home "realistic" reading material written in AAE grammatical style (Morgan 1994a). His assessment suggests that African American homes do not contain families who care about their children's literacy education and can participate in it. Unsurprisingly, Stewart's program was not the only one to be rejected. Nearly every city that had an AAE program saw it rejected by parents, and its proponents were accused of attempting to mis-educate Black children.

This was also the fate of one of the more innovative programs to emerge during this SESD period. The Bridge Program (Simpkins, Holt and Simpkins 1977) was designed for students in grades 7–12 and differed from many other programs in that it incorporated grammatical, verbal play and discourse styles into the body of literature read by the children (Rickford and Rickford 1995). It included African American folk tales and experiences with transitional grammatical exercises, and was written in a variety of AAE and standard school grammar. Because Bridge incorporated culturally relevant materials that included respect for oral traditions and that made dialect-shifting logical, as opposed to a simple structural exercise, many thought it would have great success (e.g. Smitherman 1977). Yet it ran into problems similar to those of other SESD approaches which were attributed to parental resistance to dialect readers in the school. That is, although effective at every level of educational assessment, parents and many students did not accept the argument that it was the best way to attain General English (GE) literacy. As one community college teacher told me who was unsuccessful in using it in junior high, Bridge is "fantastic for older students" who understand what the texts are teaching and who don't have to explain their assignments to parents.

Yet closer examination reveals two key factors about the African American speech community that actually shaped the controversy during the 1970s. First, parental complaints focused on cultural attitudes toward literacy, literacy standards, social status and formal education. That is, the questions parents raised about the SESD approach was not whether AAE existed, but the cultural and political implications of programs that did not highlight the social functions of literacy (Baugh 1981; Wolfram 1991; Rickford and Rickford 1995; Gee 1996; Gilyard 1996). Their questions were about the nature and purpose of education for all children and for their children in particular. For example, in at least two programs (Chicago and Florida) parents could see the following types of materials that their children brought home: a) dialect stories and folk tales, some developed for the purpose of SESD exercises; b) grammatical exercises that reviewed AAE structure exclusively; c) grammatical exercises that tested GE structure exclusively; and d) contrastive exercises that included both forms.

It is not surprising that reaction to SESD was overwhelmingly hostile, in spite of numerous studies showing the success of dialect readers (Simpkins and Simpkins 1981; Rickford and Rickford 1995). But these readers were an innovation that actually contradicted everything that the community – and most Americans – expected to happen in a classroom. No one had been socialized with regard to dialect readers or the notion that a quality education included them – especially when integrated educational institutions had worked so hard to exclude Black children culturally. So even during the Black Power movement, when all aspects of Black culture were celebrated, dialect readers were a problem, to the families who viewed public schooling as a socializing agent in preparation for an equal chance and full citizenship for their children too. It is not difficult to imagine what parents must have thought as their children shared their materials, practiced AAE grammar and read to them dialect versions of schoolbooks and classics!

Although the controversy concerning the use of non-prestige dialects in literacy education is rife with misinformation and prejudice, it is not about racial prejudice alone. Disputes over educational practices include social class differences and values about the function and style of home literacy appropriate to a child's preparation for school literacy. Both Martha Ward (1971) and Shirley Brice Heath (1983) conducted ethnographic studies of language learning in poor and working-class African American homes. Heath's study of a Black and a White community in the Piedmont Carolinas revealed that attitudes toward the value of home reading differed between the two, although the amount of reading and writing and the motivations were similar. In the Black community of Trackton, Heath described reading as a public, group affair and writes that for young people "reading alone . . . marks an individual as someone who cannot make it socially" (1983: 191). Consequently, quiet reading times, a process valued in middle-class education, is not always made available to children. Instead, for African American children, reading activities that facilitate social action or that are instrumental are encouraged.

Heath's findings supported Labov's (1972a) earlier work in New York City, where he identified those who pursued education as lames. Heath's work suggests that the middle-class homework practices that schools follow may be disruptive to working-class households because they are child-centered, focusing on the value of the individual child rather than all members of the family.

Contrasts with the White working-class community is significant not in outcome, but in the overall attitude toward literacy activities associated with schooling. In the White working-class community of Roadville, reading is "a frequently praised ideal" (Heath 1983: 231). In spite of this, it usually occurs in order to complete a task. It should be noted that, for working-class families, children often have household responsibilities that take precedence over reading for pleasure. Similarly, in my observations of young people from working-class families in urban areas, private time is allowed for writing among peers, although parents are not as supportive of writing as a private activity at home.[5] Yet, it is clear that irrespective of the nature of these literacy activities, "Neither community's ways with the written word

---

[5] There are some practical reasons that working-class parents are less than enthusiastic about reading and writing that are not directly related to school, since it means the child is not available to help with other children or household activities. Reading and writing in the home are probably high for working-class families who have an Afrocentric focus and for those youth interested in writing rap music and graffiti. In the first case, children's books, literature and home education in general are very important. In the case of hiphop, writing skills are individually practiced, and all writers must learn some aspect of history and social science, as well as popular culture.

prepares it for the school's ways" (235). It is within this problematic construction of the working-class household as semi-literate and uncaring that social psychological theories about literacy and race have taken shape.

Unfortunately, since working-class children's home literacy practices are not ideally suited to the middle-class language education norms, working-class parents are regularly viewed as bad parents and indifferent toward education. Consequently, the school often conducts literacy education with the assumption that parents either will not be involved or cannot because of ignorance. This mismatch is not benign but a reflection of an education system that does not support diverse views of the importance and function of literacy education, or does so uneasily. It is the unspoken dirty secret of public education: to receive a middle-class education you must criticize working-class and African American cultural practices. This creates a crisis of identity and loyalty for students who want to excel academically without sacrificing membership in their community. In order to avoid a crisis, they must concentrate on creating a balance in order to maintain a positive social face and avoid becoming the most tragic character described by the African American community. In 1930 Carter G. Woodson described this stance in his book *The Mis-Education of the Negro*, in which he called educated Blacks who "have the attitude of contempt toward their own people" educated fools.

The consequences of highlighting and supporting AAE and its young speakers were highlighted on December 18, 1996 when the Oakland, California Unified School District Board of Education approved a language education policy for speakers of AAE (Ebonics) that, they argued, affirmed Standard English language development for all children.[6] The media responded with an eruption of dialect language jokes and Ebonics renditions of classics like *The Night before Christmas* and soliloquies from Shakespeare's plays that ranged from the hysterical to the bigoted. As Patricia Williams observed in the *New York Times*: "there is no greater talisman of lower or underclass accent status than the Black accent . . . Whether in *The Dartmouth Review* or "The Lion King," Black

---

[6] The Ann Arbor legal case on Black English in education was settled in 1979. In *Martin Luther King Junior Elementary School vs. Ann Arbor School District Board* (1979), school officials were charged with placing African American children in learning-disabled and speech pathology classes and holding them at low grade levels because of AAE. The King case was won largely because linguists argued successfully that AAE has systemic features that are not all related to English. (See Martin Luther King Junior Elementary School Children et al. vs. Ann Arbor School District Board.1979. US Dist. Court East. Dist. Mich., South. Div. No. 77186.)

English is the perpetual symbolic code for ignorance, evil and jest, the lingo of the hep cats and hyenas" (P. Williams 1996).[7]

Although the speech of African Americans was the subject of public ridicule throughout this period, in the midst of the hoopla two critically different views emerged regarding language and literacy education. One view was that Black people speak AAE because they don't want to participate in American society in the same way as Whites. This perspective considers AAE to be a language variety that children consciously choose to speak rather than one that reflects culture, historical contact, social class, etc. The educational policy articulated with this view is that children should be taught basic, "no frills" skills that will prepare them for what amounts to non-career employment. For Black children, preparation for a non-career employment track includes the requirement that they speak middle-class varieties of American English (cf. P. Williams 1996; Morgan 2002). The opposing view that emerged during the debate was that Black people speak AAE for cultural and historical reasons, and because of race and class discrimination. Proponents of this view argued that literacy education should include basic skills as well as other areas in order to prepare individuals to choose any employment path they desire.

The nearly exclusive association of public school education with low-level employment opportunities rather than careers or higher education persisted, even though the majority of the students targeted by the resolution, as well as those shown in the media, were young children. This is particularly alarming because Black children value education precisely because they believe it might lead to lucrative careers (see below). At the same time, there were fundamental political and ideological differences based on racial and class lines about the nature of social dialects in general and AAE in particular. Perhaps it was predictable that in the midst of the public debate an ideological split developed among educators and linguists over the policy implications of language education theories, as well as the programs that began in the 1970s (e.g. R. Williams 1975; Tolliver-Weddington 1979). The conflict among linguists and educators has persisted since the advent of public education and is particularly problematic because it foregrounds the mismatch between literacy goals and education for the working class in general

---

[7] For example, after the Oakland resolution was made public, Jay Leno, the host of the late-night talk show *The Tonight Show*, introduced a comedy routine titled "The Ebonics Plague," and a local Los Angeles radio station introduced a skit named "Hooked on Ebonics" modeled after a reading program "Hooked on Phonics."

and African Americans in particular. This split concerns the purpose of education for minority and working-class children and how language education programs address overall social class and minority issues.[8]

Once the media began its "spin" on the Oakland resolution, debates and opinions about the value of African American speech patterns and Ebonics circulated throughout the country. In the Black community, these discussions eventually gave way to near unanimous agreement that all children should speak "good English" in order to improve career opportunities. This trend was repeated in Black-oriented publications and other media throughout the country. In all reports and television interviews, those claiming to represent the African American community focused on the importance of White, middle-class varieties of English in achieving academic and later financial success. Only after the necessity of Standard English was clearly articulated did African Americans discuss AAE's cultural value. Moreover, many community leaders argued for the teaching of code-switching or style-shifting – processes that they maintained are not made available to some adolescents and working-class students.

In contrast, with few exceptions, non-African American communities responded to the Oakland proposal with charges of "going too far" in order to achieve political correctness and special privileges. On talk radio programs and many Internet sites, little or no attention was paid to cultural, political, historical or social differences and the idea that African American children do not have equal chances in life. As one caller said to me when I was a guest on a radio show, "Why can't you people just be like us and stop complaining? You've gotten enough!"

The public debate was well into its second week before linguists were able to introduce theories about language norms, standards and dialects into public debate. Many sociolinguists who researched African American language and discourse attempted to address the media coverage and draw relationships between White, working-class dialects and other situations in the world through appearances on talk shows, in newspaper editorials, etc. For the most part, linguistic arguments about the significance of AAE fell on deaf ears. Thus a racist, "genetic" argument that Black people do not master educated English norms because they are biologically incapable of it and because African Americans want to receive special treatment was circulated without effective rebuttal for nearly a week.

---

[8] In fact Smith (1997) accused SESD supporters of ignoring and often contributing to failures in language education programs.

This striking polarization by African American and non-African American speech communities of popular interpretations of what actually happened and what it was about reflects and is partially due to social psychological theories about literacy, race and social class in research and educational policy.

8.5 CONCLUSION

The language socialization and literacy education of African American children in the US provides an insight into the workings and politics of dominant speech communities and the power and complexities of marginalized speech communities. The attempt to incorporate social dialect programs in school raises hard questions about literacy education, politics and the effects of race on social life. While the need to recognize and incorporate social dialect diversity in school has been recognized by linguists and educators (e.g. Stewart 1969; Labov 1972a,b; Smitherman 1977, 1981a,b; Baugh 1987; Rickford and Rickford 1995), resistance often arises due to a lack of communication and doubt that dialect literacy enhances language education. This problem is compounded by a conflict between notions of literacy education for learning ideas on the one hand and for earning potential on the other. In either case, proponents believe that they have the interests of African American children at heart. Yet, it seems unreasonable to expect linguists and language specialists to develop plans based primarily on the occupational concerns of society. In this respect, educational planners are often at odds with societal demands. Research and descriptions of unsuccessful schooling, especially for Black children, reveal that many educators and politicians have carried this notion too far (cf. Ogbu 1978; Jaynes and Williams 1989). In that sense, literacy education for African American children regularly involves addressing social and political issues within the planning itself.

While the Language Development Program for African American Students has been widely supported since it began in 1988, the furor surrounding the Oakland resolution has subjected it to intense scrutiny and evaluation. Throughout this process, it has continued to incorporate parent, community and teacher input into the overall program. Literacy means more than reading and writing. It is a powerful tool of expression and identity. The development and implementation of language and literacy policies that teach without compromising the identity and integrity of all children is the language education challenge of this century.

DISCUSSION QUESTIONS

1. Most societies have some form of language standards. What are some of the problems that may arise from enforcing standards?
2. What are some examples of how multilingual communities approach language learning?
3. Speech communities do not always agree over language policy. Provide examples of disagreement.
4. What is the relationship between language and social identity?
5. What is and what is not mutable about language, specifically about phonology (accent)?
6. Do individuals have language rights?
7. Who claims the authority to make these decisions?

FURTHER READING

Garcia, O. and Bartlett, L. (2007). A Speech Community Model of Bilingual Education: Educating Latino Newcomers in the USA. *International Journal of Bilingual Education and Bilingualism* 10(1): 1–25.

Heath, S. B. (1983). *Ways with Words: Language, Life and Work in Communities and Classrooms.* Cambridge University Press.

Heller, M. (2008). Language and the Nation-State: Challenges to Sociolinguistic Theory and Practice. *Journal of Sociolinguistics* 12(4): 504–524.

Labov, W. (2012). *Dialect Diversity in America: The Politics of Language Change.* Charlottesville, VA: University of Virginia Press.

Solsky, B. (2004). *Language Policy.* Cambridge University Press.

9 Performance and play in speech communities

Chapelle: I'm not saying I don't like police. I'm saying I'm just scared
of them. Some times we want to call them too. Somebody broke
into my house once – but I didn't want to call the police, Uhhh
uhhh. [My] house was too nice! And in a real nice house – they'd
never believe I lived in it!

Police: "He's still here! Thump! Ohhh my God! Open and shut case
Johnson! I saw this once before when I was a rookie. Apparently
this ni**ga broke in and hung pictures of his family everywhere.
Well ... let's sprinkle some crack on him and get out of here."

(Dave Chapelle 2000)

In 2000, when Dave Chapelle performed a comedy routine depicting
his imagined arrest by police who thought he had broken into his own
house and hung photographs of his family on the wall, those outside of
the African American speech community may have thought that it was
a brilliant comedic representation of police abuse, but an impossible
one. Yet nine years later, the Cambridge, Massachusetts police arrested
Harvard University professor Henry Louis Gates Jr. for breaking and
entering his own home – with pictures of his family and one of himself
alongside Nelson Mandela on the wall![1]

---

[1] As an example of the ironic humor that followed Gates' arrest and meeting with
President Obama, the site www.democraticunderground.com posted the following
by Political Heretic on July 31, 2009:

> BREAKING NEWS: WASHINGTON – Upon arriving late to his meeting with President
> Barack Obama and famed African-American intellectual Henry Louis Gates, Cambridge
> police officer James Crowley once again detained the distinguished Harvard scholar after
> failing to recognize the man he had arrested just two weeks earlier, White House sources
> reported Thursday. "When I entered the Oval Office, I observed an unidentified black
> male sitting near Mr. Obama, and in the interest of the president's safety, I attempted
> to ascertain the individual's business at the White House," Crowley said in a sworn
> statement following the arrest. "The suspect then became uncooperative and verbally
> abusive. I had no choice but to apprehend him at the scene for disorderly conduct."
> Witnesses said that Sgt. Crowley, failing to recognize Gates on their flight to Logan
> Airport, arrested the tenured professor in midair, once again at the baggage claim, and
> twice during their shared cab ride back to Cambridge.

This chapter focuses on how humor, irony, sarcasm, etc. are framed in speech communities. It is concerned with the importance of communicative performance and performativity (Butler 1993) as a social activity that is intended for members of particular speech communities. The analysis of discourse in performance is of particular interest in modern society as political arguments and the representation of social identity are often embedded in satirical and comedic performances that include indirection, irony, sarcasm, etc. Following Don Kulick, performance is something a subject does and performativity is the process through which the subject emerges (2009: 494). This chapter also explores these concepts in literary and film criticism, where race, ethnicity, gender, sexuality, social class, etc. are constructed through the notion of speech community. It also considers Kulick's cautionary observation that "Performance is one dimension of performativity. But performativity theory insists that what is expressed or performed in any social context is importantly linked to that which is not expressed or cannot be performed. Hence, analysis of action and identity must take into account what is not or cannot be enacted" (494). The concept of speech community is always in crisis when it is being referred to with humor and satire. That is because members are aware that there is a critique, something missing, and that there is the possibility of losing social face and being suspected of not being a full member of a speech community, or of being incompetent in some way.

9.1 PERFORMATIVITY: BETWEEN POLITENESS AND SOCIAL FACE

Performatives create the state of affairs that they appear to refer to (Lee 1997: 50) and can enact identities (Butler 1993). As Dorinne Kondo argues, "they are the product of constitutive constraints that create identities . . . elicited under duress" (1997: 7). Within contexts of communication between those with unequal power, especially regarding race, class and gender, there is also the possibility of resignification (Butler 1997) and change that may transform the previous meanings by either expanding the concepts or by including a range of other meanings within them. One way to resignify is to frame the sign by indirection. A frame defines the packaging of an element of rhetoric in such a way as to encourage certain interpretations and to discourage others. In fact, it is the indirection frame that actualizes the schema of interpretations and stereotypes and our subjective involvement in them (see Goffman 1974: 10).

While there are many African American terms that are emblematic of the tension between subtlety and non-subtlety and indirect speech, perhaps the most widespread cultural concept of social face that both critiques and symbolizes the tension is the contrast between being "cool" and acting "a fool." As discussed in Chapter 4, a cool social face is the ability to respond to indirectness and directness, as well as symbolic incidents and subtle varieties of cultural practice, with eloquence, skill, wit, patience and precise timing. While performance itself requires knowledge of the social, discursive and cultural forces (see Derrida 1982; Bauman 1992; Pennycook 2007), for African Americans the social and communicative process of maintaining a cool social face includes braving and witnessing verbal assaults and innuendos. It is not enough for a speaker to claim that he or she has successfully prevented an attack on his or her positive social face. The audience (as witness) must also weigh in on the success of the interaction. Consequently, maintaining a cool face is often difficult, especially in interactions, because indirect discourse requires that all participants (including hearers/witnesses) constantly assess and address potential meanings within and across contexts.

Because these conventions are so widely disseminated, their use and misuse can both reveal and mask intentionality and appear as both a means to provide straightforward communication and as a means of deception and embarrassment. As reviewed in Chapter 3, Brown and Levinson (1987) have argued that the contrast between positive and negative politeness was the difference between constructive relationship and one of deference where a speaker's agency may be threatened. Yet what is called positive politeness need not be constructive when considering how indexicality and intentionality are framed in humor. In fact, politeness toward a subject may index that the subject is a target of humor.

Through politeness, indirectness can be exploited, shared background and common understanding can be challenged, and joking and humor can be framed. For instance, Brown and Levinson point out that in Western societies "joking is a basic positive-politeness technique" for putting hearers at ease, and "jokes may be used to stress that shared background or those shared" (1987: 124). While this is true, it is also true that jokes can directly ridicule and can in addition be used as a frame through which to indirectly critique and challenge social face. That is, one can introduce the frame and code that we all share the same background knowledge and discourse conventions in order to highlight the ways that we don't.

The question considered here is how individuals participate and maneuver within the communication process as they set the stage for a kind of information game – "a potentially infinite cycle of concealment, discovery, false revelation, and rediscovery" (Goffman 1959: 8). As Goffman argues, the effort of appearing to be unintentional is seldom invisible, and thus "The witness has the advantage over the actor" (9). That is, the actor may be unaware that the witness suspects she is up to something. Therefore individual actors and witnesses project definitions of situations and social contexts throughout interactions as part of the information game. The problem (and question) is whether everyone knows they are in fact playing. To further paraphrase Goffman, participants establish an appearance of consensus, facilitated by each participant suppressing his or her feelings so that the other can find the interaction satisfactory. There is an unspoken agreement to minimize information on things not immediately important to others in the conversation (8–10). Thus there is a working consensus or real agreement "concerning the desirability of avoiding an open conflict of definitions of the situation" (10).

9.2 LEARNING TO PLAY WITH IRONY

The notion of "play" differentiates the real from the serious (Abrahams 1970, 1975; Goffman, 1974; Kochman, 1983, 1986) by focusing on that which is socially and/or culturally significant (e.g. relatives, sexuality, physical appearance, political figures, class and economic status) and placing it in implausible contexts. Adolescents play games of indirection as part of social, cultural and language socialization (cf. Schieffelin and Ochs 1986; Goodwin 1988, 1990; Morgan 2002). Both males and females participate in ritualized and episodic verbal disputes that focus on the tension between *play* and *getting played*. To play is to participate in activities that result in pleasurable feelings. To *get played* is to be made a fool because one did not realize one was simply an object of playful pleasure. African American *culture* employs numerous expressions to refer to this notion. A related word of significance to play is *game* and the expression "*game recognize game.*" One is said to "*have game*" when one has the ability to persuade and at times mislead others to do what one wants.

Childhood verbal games of indirection like signifying and sounding are concerned with learning the difference between play and being played (Morgan 2002). Whether a context is plausible or implausible is culturally determined and socially ratified. For example, a signifying episode that begins with a non-judgmental, non-stereotypical media report of a young African American male wanted by police would be considered an improbable context. The media simply do not refer to Black males in an unbiased way. On the other hand, adult jokes and humor often imply signification that relies on just this local knowledge. For example, a current popular joke goes, "If a Black and a Mexican are in the back of a car, who's driving?" "The police!" The irony of the joke, at least according to numerous adults and several youth I spoke to, is that it is a critique of the reality show *Cops*. In this show, whenever there is a Black or Latino male, he is being placed into the back of a police car. So it is a comment on racist representations, as well as surveillance, and the way in which the communities share the problem of racist treatment and representation.

In its form as verbal play, signifying or snapping is mainly performed by adolescent males, although it also occurs among adult males and females involved in competitive activities (e.g. sports, stock trading). Percelay, Monteria and Dweck (1994) introduce seventeen adjectival categories of snaps, including: fat, stupid, sexy and ugly. "Playing the dozens" is the term often used for signifying sequences that include the noun phrase "your mother" or "yo mama." While playing the dozens may be an important part of adolescent male activity, members also recognize it as a language socialization activity (cf. Schieffelin and Ochs 1986; Goodwin 1988, 1990), especially for conversational signifying (discussed below).

As Percelay, Monteria and Dweck (1994) suggest, "your mother" (or "yo mama") statements both highlight and subvert the notion that mothers are sacred (see also Smitherman 1977). These statements should not be misunderstood to relate specifically to someone's particular mother, since that is not a requirement to participate. "Your mother" statements are a device to practice and perform verbal skill, and this practice often occurs in the presence of family members, including mothers, who help judge their effectiveness and comment on the wit or irony in the statements, often offering other examples which they deem more impressive.

Along with being constituted through African American cultural contexts, "your mother" statements are also grammatically constituted. They are usually marked by both African American English (AAE) and General English (GE) prescriptive grammatical practices that are juxtaposed in terms of both the linguistic level and the system of indirection being employed. That is, there is a tendency to use AAE and GE categorically within linguistic levels but not across levels. This tendency is apparent in what Hutcherson, a stand-up comic and comedy writer, argues is the anatomy of a mother joke. He describes it as beginning with "Your mother so" followed by an adjective that will be the straight line of the joke. He argues that it is also acceptable to begin with "That's why your mother" even if what follows is not an explanation (1993: 52). Derrick Fox (1992: 20) provides the following example:" Your mother is so old that when she read(s) the Bible she reminisces." In this example, the age of the mother is related to when the Bible was written, so that the mother is as old as the Bible and some of the events reported there might be childhood memories. When one considers the above examples, it seems clear that with "the dozens" prescriptive or regularized grammatical norms may actually allow the audience to pay attention to the level(s) of indirection present. What makes the above cases signifying with the dozens, and not simply indirection, is the combination of grammatical structure and form and the level of deconstruction of the characteristics and attributes of the adjectival – the logic. Cases of signifying like "playing the dozens" or "your mother" statements are constructed through the interaction of both grammar and speech event. Moreover, this verbal genre is but one aspect of a multilevel grammatical system that is constructed through AAE and GE linguistic and pragmatic systems.

Once a "your mother" sequence is launched, it is usually acknowledged as "in play" within an interactive episode when another person responds with a statement, and is therefore in competition with the initiator (Abrahams 1962; Labov 1972a, b; Kochman 1983). The episode continues until someone delivers enough witty, acerbic and indirect statements that the audience or participants determine the winner. As Warren Hutcherson (1993) explains, the true essence of the dozens is the relationship between choice of signs and the "logic" of the implausibility. For Hutcherson, this "logic" is culturally loaded and refers to African American local theories (cf. Geertz 1983; Lindstrom 1992) that include knowledge of cultural celebrations as well as US racism, bigotry, injustice, etc.[2]

The childhood practices of signifying, the dozens, he-said-she-said and instigating described above and in previous chapters are not discarded in adulthood. Instead, they socialize youth into a language ideology that requires long-term observation, participation, criticism, analysis,

---

[2] After Gates' arrest described above, the arresting officer, James Crowley, wrote that he told Gates that he (Crowley) was leaving his residence and that if Gates wanted to continue discussing the matter, Crowley would speak to him outside. Gates allegedly replied, "Yeah, I'll speak with your mama outside." Gates denied ever saying this, and, based on the general use of these statements in the African American speech community, it is highly unlikely that it was said. Cambridge Police Incident Report #9005127.

and punishments and rewards. They are reconstructed in adult conversations and narratives that increase in complexity and subtlety, and take into consideration possible hearers, and the speaker's intentionality and social face. These practices also incorporate knowledge of grammar and attitudes toward speakers of AAE.

Those who possess coolness are current and trend-setting, calm, detached, yet in control – in any situation (cf. Major 1994; Smitherman 1994). In this sense, a cool social face is not only about identity, but also about a performativity that requires witnesses who corroborate the status of one's social face. Within this framework, having "no cool" is akin to having a negative social face and no self-awareness of social identity, and it is to be avoided at all costs.

The 2008 US presidential campaign provided numerous examples of the complexity involved in framing indirectness as a performative and signifier of coolness. The presidential election was, on the one hand, a case of a competition for the highest political office. On the other hand, it was a campaign that tactically engaged and often encouraged discourses about race, racism, stereotypes, hate, etc. Obama's campaign for the presidency recognized that bigotry and racial stereotyping about him and Black people in general would be a constant occurrence. One charge for and against him that emerged during the campaign was that he always maintained his cool. In fact, one particular performative was widely critiqued in multiple ways by the African American community, the press, and throughout public culture.

In April 2008, during the democratic primary, when Hillary Clinton was campaigning against Barack Obama, Clinton began arguing (as Sarah Palin did later) that she stood for what *Newsweek* magazine referred to as "hard-working, White Americans" (D. A. Thomas 2008). Obama ran on a political platform that he represented all Americans and bristled at the notion that pandering to racism and racial differences should be a part of the campaign. Shortly after Clinton's statement, Obama told a crowd in Raleigh, NC:

> "When you're running for president, then you've got to expect it, and you've kind of got to let it . . . " He paused, shrugged and made a brushing motion with his right hand, as if flicking some dust off his right shoulder, then his left. The crowd, which included many African-Americans, burst into surprised laughter and applause, and many stood to cheer as Obama gave a self-satisfied smile and an exaggerated nod, and then said, "That's what you gotta do."

Both the Clinton and McCain campaigns were outraged at Obama's actions, which they described as arrogant. In contrast, the African American community and many young people of other ethnicities saw it as a nod to them to have confidence that he could handle the criticism and stereotyping that was constant during the campaign – that he possessed, and could perform with, a cool social face. By metaphorically brushing the dirt off his shoulders, he referenced generations of male hiphop artists like Rakim and Jay-Z who flick their shoulders to show they are in control of the rhetoric on the mic in spite of overwhelming obstacles and haters. Much more than disrespect and arrogance, his main constituents considered it a positive performance.

9.3 PERFORMING IDENTITY

Humor that probes social conditions and that questions authority and social identity also exposes how discourse and pragmatic principles of language work within and across speech communities. Political humor, in particular, treats the identification and recognition of social context as the major indication of which speech community one has membership, as well as one's status in that community. Within comedic performances, the choice of which contexts are depicted as linguistically encoded and which language-specific styles, dialects, etc. reveal status, attitude and various subjectivities exposes ruptures in the social fabric. Dorinne Kondo (2000) examines the work of the theatrical comedy troupe Culture Clash. Culture Clash is a male Chicano-Latino trio formed on Cinco de Mayo (May 5) 1984 and known for its largely skit-based satire on Chicano themes.[3] Their satirical focus is on stereotype as well as on cultural practices, and how the culture relates and refers to the dominant culture. Kondo describes their previous work:

> *The Mission* depicted three Latino actors in the Mission district of San Francisco who concoct a scheme to kidnap Julio Iglesias in order to gain national attention; *A Bowl of Beings*, their second play, comprised a series of skits including a satiric opera based on Christopher Columbus's invasion of the Americas, a parody of the film *Stand and Deliver*, and a classic piece in which a Berkeley Chicano activist conjures the ghost of Che Guevara, who in turn is shocked to discover the current plight of the left under Reagan and Bush. (Kondo 2000: 89)

Culture Clash is determined not to promote Zentella's (1996) chiquitafication of Latin Americans under the "one America" ideology described in Chapter 8. Instead, they identify Latino/a culture by contrasting the diversity of the community and also by focusing on the social and political contexts that reveal the discriminatory

---

[3] The members are Richard Montoya, Ricardo Salinas and Herbert Siguenza.

treatment of Latinos/as in the US context in general. In *Radio Mambo* and *Culture Clash in Bordertown*, Culture Clash uses interviews to construct their plays about Latino/a life in Miami, Florida and San Diego, California respectively. Kondo argues:

> *Mambo* and *Bordertown* represent a development in Culture Clash's work, an opening to more serious consideration of issues of sexuality and gender, global capitalism and class, though race remains a central line of critique. Montoya's statement is about penetrating a veneer of politesse and exposing its underlying contradictions. Here the therapeutic metaphor is apt: it stands for speaking the unspoken, so that stories can "bubble forward." They strive to flush out the debris of the "stories that have been hidden under years of dust and dirt." (Kondo 2000: 91)

To make their political point even more explicit regarding the encoded meaning of both context and language, Culture Clash created a character, Sidewinder Sam, who introduces two of San Diego's eminent citizens, the capitalists Horton and Spreckels.[4] Below is an excerpt from the play.

> Sidewinder Sam: Ladies and Gentlemen, damas y caballeros, I'm
>   Sidewinder Sam and this is my sidekick Gus. We're here to tell you
>   why San Diego is the city of tomorrow . . . Ladies and gents, please
>   meet one of our most cherished citizens . . . Alonzo Erastus Horton!
>   (*A large, old-fashioned, narrow banner unfurls from the rafter bearing the
>   likeness of "Father" Horton. The assistant plays a drum roll.*)
> Sidewinder Sam: . . . There is only one other fella that can even
>   compare with Father Horton . . . please meet Mr. John D. Spreckels.
>   (*A large narrow banner of Mr. Spreckels unfurls.*) Spreckels and Horton,
>   God bless our city fathers! No one has done more for the city of
>   San Diego, why I'm getting a bit teary-eyed about the whole
>   affair . . . (*Just then a Mexican Bandido steps onstage with his gun
>   drawn.*) . . .
> Bandido: Read the note, gringo.
> Bandido: READ THE GODDAMN NOTE, GABACHO! . . .
> Sam: (*Reading note*) Spreckels and Horton were just two men of means
>   who were opportunists who bought their way into city
>   government and made the place Republican . . . What is this
>   sheepshit? (*Bandido points gun.*)

Kondo reports that Culture Clash refused to address what motivated Spreckels and Horton. She refers to this view as the "multiplicity of the colonizer": That is, in the face of political critique, those who inhabit

---

[4] A sidewinder is a small, pale desert rattlesnake that thrusts in a series of flat S-shaped curves. Thus it can't follow the 'straight and narrow'. Horton and Spreckels are considered American forefathers of San Diego, though the area was originally part of Mexico.

sites of privilege may desire to focus on the complexities of that position. This in turn implicitly refocuses attention on the subjectivity of the colonizer, implicitly equating their position with the situation of those who are far more disempowered" (2000: 93–94). While Culture Clash preferred to remain silent regarding the motivation for the Spreckels character, the interaction between Sidewinder Sam and Bandido identify the injustices within the social and historical context. Moreover, this interaction pays special attention to the contrast of code-switching styles and motivation and intentionality in the use of Spanish by the two characters.

9.4 HUMOR AND SATIRE

Whether African-American humor is seen as a folk expression or an art form, it challenges the critic to acknowledge that humor and creativity may also come from victims of unspeakable acts of injustice and brutality. In *Laughing Fit to Kill*, Glenda Carpio (2008) illustrates how Black comedians, writers and artists have deftly deployed various modes of comedic framing and indirection to expose and critique the absurd, the grotesque and the strategic expression of racial stereotypes. In doing so, they redress not only the past injustices of slavery and racism in America, but also their legacy in the present. This framing is accomplished in the presence of critical onlookers, speech community participants and powerful outsiders. The laugh encompasses the injustice, pain, irony, defiance and hope of the speech community.

Of course, within the act of discourse, the real life activity of representation and social standing are witnessed, scrutinized, maintained and constructed. This is even more apparent when personal and political discourse is delivered through media and technology – where discourses of both truth and theater (see Hill 2000) are endlessly evaluated. Public interactions and comments, especially those witnessed by audiences and pundits, can involve pitfalls and pratfalls where one's social face and sense of oneself is potentially in jeopardy. Yet, even these public discourses are influenced by norms and conventions of public and private discourse.

In many respects, comedic performances complicate the public sphere with indirect discourse about racism in the public sphere. They describe the frame, code and social context and break rules of consensus. At issue are instances where race and racism are publicly discussed and where evidence of its social construction is indirectly indexed. In this sense, in dominant culture race can represent both injustice and identity, and is thus constantly being manipulated and exposed in order to represent the complex of social meanings (see Omi and Winant 1994). While everyday interaction is not a staged presentation, it is public, and it involves the representation, negotiation and performance of self within and across various social contexts and interlocutors.

Woolard researched joking in Catalan in the winter and spring of 1980, a politically tense time in Barcelona, Spain. It was during this period that the comedian Eugenio was extremely popular as he told what Woolard described as "standard set pieces of the 'Did you hear the one about...' variety" (1987: 107). She reports that code-switching and -mixing of Catalan and Castilian was the feature of his performance that stood out in most people's minds in accounting for Eugenio's comic appeal. Catalan and Castilian are closely related languages that share syntax and vocabulary. Their main difference is in phonetics and phonology. Woolard reports that due to political constraints on language learning, many Catalan speakers use non-standard forms greatly influenced by contact with Castilian. Yet, she found that many people reported that what was appealing about his style was that "you can't tell what language he's speaking." She argues that Eugenio's code-switching was not situational, and did not index certain topics or social realms and a specific language. Nor was it metaphorical code-switching, where the use of a particular language adds a connotation of e.g. intimacy, distancing, mitigation or authority to the switched utterance itself. In the material analyzed here, the social message is not one that exploits the social contrasts between two languages or language groups to achieve rhetorical effects. What was humorous was that the audience had an unequal distribution of knowledge of the two languages and knew that it was unequal, and "an increasingly anomic vision of the social distribution of the two languages, the relatively predictable distribution of codeswitching across the narrative structure of the joke interacts with this distribution of the languages across social groups to produce in a more indirect way the social meaning of the codeswitching event" (119). Thus the speech communities were addressed in a way that indexed the irony and profound difficulty of the situation:

> The symbolic social message, that the two languages and thus language communities can co-exist and interact peacefully, is indeed contained in the whole event rather than specifically in any of its switched parts. But it is very much a product of those specific parts, and the same social effect would not result from a different distribution of the two languages. (Woolard 1987: 119)

The use of indirectness can enact race and racist situations. Comedian Chris Rock explicitly exposed "You are articulate" as an indirect insult masquerading as a compliment, in 1996. In a widely publicized routine about whether Colin Powell, then Secretary of State, would run for president, Chris Rock describes the "code" as he goes into a tirade over the indirect racist implications of what he believes many Whites may consider a compliment – "*He speaks so well*".[5]

> Chris Rock: "How do you feel about Colin Powell?"
> White Citizen: ((*in a whispery voice*)) "He speaks so we::ll!" "He's so well spo:::ken." ... "He speaks so we:::ll." "I mean he **really** speaks we:::ll." "He speaks so we:::ll." ((*audience laughs*))

Rock's criticism focuses on embedded language ideology as he challenges speakers' intentionality. He provides the explicit and directed discourse necessary to expose the depth of the insult of the offensive statement framed as a *compliment*. Rock uses multiple intonation to contrast voices of '*speaks so well*' including breathless, sincere, insincere, normal to loud voice and screaming. He is outraged! He explains that typically the expression is only appropriate in reference to a grown person if he or she is disabled in some way. Then, he excoriates the audience/speakers for making such a statement. Finally, he imagines the educated and previous US Army General and Secretary of State Colin Powell using a stereotypical variety of AAE including phrase reduction *Ahmma* – (*I am going to*), stative copula *be* and mispronuncation "*I be pre-so-dent*." He then ends his routine with an accusatory question: "What voice did you **expect** to come out of his mouth? What did you **expect** him to sound like?" The audience/witnesses roar with laughter as the speech communities' differing language ideologies are exposed.

Chris Rock's tirade about intentionality and indirectness continued, and the audience/witnesses laughed and applauded. Rock provides the explicit and directed discourse necessary in order to clarify for the uninformed how deep an insult the compliment actually is. He uses a direct insincere voice (Morgan 2002) to say "Colin Powell speaks so well" five times. Rock then moves from screaming, to loud voice, to normal voice and then back to a screaming voice. He is outraged! His discourse style is directed and explicit as he describes the intentions behind the statement. First, he explains that it is only appropriate to use the expression in reference to a grown person if he or she is disabled in some way. Then he excoriates the White audience/speakers for making such a statement.

---

[5] Chris Rock. 1996. *Bring the Pain*. This performance won an Emmy and was one of the most viewed stand-up performances on HBO. In addition, the video/dvd was a best-seller.

Finally, he imitates Colin Powell using a stereotypical variety of AAE. This variety includes phrase reduction (*Ahmma* – *I am going to*), stative copula *be*, and a form of hypocorrection (Baugh 1992) and mispronunciation (*pre-so-dent* – *president*). He then ends with an accusatory question, "What did you *expect* him to sound like?" The audience/witnesses now roar with laughter, confirming that the true intention is exposed and racism is revealed.

In *Laughter out of Place* (2003), Donna Goldstein studies women in a shantytown in Rio de Janeiro where they use laughter as they deal with tragedies, impossible situations and desperation. Goldstein argues that laughter "reveals the fault lines in social relations" (2003: 35). Yet this laughter also reframes the situation and provides a discourse of power. For example, as discussed in Chapter 7, after Hurricane Katrina devastated New Orleans in 2005 there were many instances where race and racism were raised as an explanation for government inaction and lack of aggressive response. Much of the accusations were in the form of numerous instances of both direct and indirect representations of American cultural and societal beliefs and policies about race and social class. These cases require collaboration, indexing of local knowledge and other discursive strategies. In fact, indirectness in discourse is not present unless it is indexed through symbols that represent contexts that in turn represent plausible ideologies, memories and so on.

Shortly after Kanye West made the statement "George Bush doesn't like Black people" described above, an e-mail appeared about Kanye West suggesting that he was in a car accident. It came under the heading: "Subject: FM: KANYE WEST in ANOTHER CAR ACCIDENT". This subject heading actually indirectly reminds everyone that Kanye West was in a previous accident before he became successful, and he nearly died. People are aware of this because he talked, rhymed and sang about it on numerous occasions. The e-mail skillfully presents Kanye West as from Chicago (a place he raps about) who adored his mother (a person he also raps about).[6] The actual message is as follows:

> In the midst of all the controversy in regards to Kanye West's comment towards George Bush, he's got another problem on his hands. Mr. West was in another car accident late yesterday afternoon, just outside of Chicago.

> Witnesses say it was a hit and run incident, involving a white pick up truck. Mr. West was struck while crossing a street adjacent to his mother's home. Luckily, a bystander at the scene managed to snap a picture of the white truck. Police have released this picture below.

[6] Tragically, his mother died of complications from surgery in November 2007.

After reading the text, one must scroll down to actually see a photo of the suspect doing a "drive-by" in the white truck. They find President George Bush at the wheel. The white truck contains a smiling President George Bush and President Vladimir Putin of Russia during Putin's visit to the president's ranch in Crawford, Texas. On the side of the van is a famous hiphop phrase: "How ya like me now?" Above the photo is West's statement: "George Bush doesn't care about Black people." The caption below the photo reads: "If you or anyone you know recognize the individual in the attached picture, please contact the Illinois State Police at X.XXX.XXX.XXXX."

How Ya Like Me Now? is the title of a 1987 album from the hiphop MC Kool Moe Dee. It is one of the best-known signifying lines in hiphop and signaled the end of an epic lyrical battle. Kool Moe Dee ends a verbal whipping of his opponent (LL Cool J) with the following:

> [I'll] Whip him good, then I'll make him sweat / [He's] Talkin' about battles and never had a battle yet / But if we ever did how could you beat me? /You're so petrified – Even scared to meet me / My word's the law / That's why you don't beef / You're nothing but a punk, track star, and a thief / So I'm puttin' you on punishment / Just like a child / Never touch another mic / How ya like me now? / How ya like me now?

The Internet audience response to Kanye West's timid but directed discourse was to strategically produce a text where a Kanye West audience that knows about his hometown (Chicago), his love for his mother, his auto accident, etc. is thoughtfully constructed. This is followed by at least some relief that the perpetrators of the crime are identified. Then we find that Kanye was right. George Bush, with Putin as his wingman, has run over Kanye and has claimed "How ya like me now?"

9.5 CONCLUSION

Our participation as actors in our everyday lives includes the local and general knowledge required in identifying and interpreting power and social actors and actions on a day-to-day basis. Illocutionary force is considered within the framework of social context and perlocutionary effect. On the one hand, we can perform our lives on stage with witnesses and, on the other, we can do so without the stage and widespread witnessing. Political campaigns and hurricanes come and go, and sometimes in their aftermath there are discourses of power, privilege, outrage and compassion. In American dominant society, indirectness is often indispensable as a method to reveal what people – especially the poor, people of color and women – mean and believe without them suffering severe consequences. This seems to be true in many societies. The consequences are not quick and severe, because the larger society often refuses to accept or believe the indexicality and its signifiers. The other extreme is the powerful, who also use indirectness with phrases like "articulate" and "magic Negros," and are being indirectly racist by perpetuating stereotypes – whether they know it or not. Our public discourse includes performers, observers, witnesses and numerous participants who may wish the interaction rituals to be a circus for entertainment and not an occasion for bigotry and impatience for multiple and new ideas. To paraphrase Erving Goffman, even in comedy as in life, participation in social life requires "real techniques – the same technique by which everyday persons sustain their real social situations" (1959: 255). While the language of discourse may produce knowledge, it does so within a system of signs and symbols that produces meaning.

This chapter has been concerned with how performers and audiences interpret intentionality and indirection to determine humor. These devices require hearers and the audiences to agree on what the speaker actually means by what is said. The contrast and tension inherent in constructing humor with these devices are made more evident in that both Dave Chapelle and Chris Rock left their highly successful television shows, which were viewed by millions of young Americans of all ethnicities, because they believed the audience was laughing at the wrong things. As Chapelle explained to Oprah Winfrey: "I know the difference of people laughing with me and people laughing at me – and it was the first time I had ever gotten a laugh that I was uncomfortable with" (Winfrey 2006). Generations have learned about power, racism and injustice through the representation of the irony of discourse. Recently, comedian Dave Chappelle reported that he went to vote in the 2008 primary election, and the election poll workers, upon seeing him, said, "Another vote for Barack Obama." He reported that he was offended. He didn't know "White people could read Black people's mind like that." He considered the automatic assumption a racial insult. Dave Chapelle also confirmed that he did, indeed, vote for Barack Obama, but he objected to the illocutionary force of the poll workers' statement because he knew full well that hundreds of years of the bigoted perlocutionary force was behind it.

DISCUSSION QUESTIONS

1. What is the difference between performance and performativity?
2. What is the relationship between politeness and humor?

3. What political and social factors make discourse racist or xeno-phobic?
4. How does humor protect positive social face?

FURTHER READING

Aarons, D. (2012). *Jokes and the Linguistic Mind*. New York: Routledge.

Brown, P. and Levinson, S. (1987). *Politeness: Some Universals in Language Usage*. Cambridge University Press.

Goffman, E. (1967). *Interaction Ritual: Essays in Face to Face Behavior*. Garden City, NY: Doubleday.

Kondo, D. (2000). (Re)Visions of Race: Contemporary Race Theory and the Cultural Politics of Racial Crossover in Documentary Theater. *Theater Journal* 52: 81–107.

Kulick, D. (2009). No. In Duranti (ed.), 1997, pp. 493–503.

Morgan, M. (2009b). The Presentation of Indirectness and Power in Everyday Life. *Journal of Pragmatics* 42(2): 283–291.

Watkins, M. (1994). *On the Real Side: Laughing, Lying and Signifying*. New York: Simon and Schuster.

10   Power, ideology and prejudice

This chapter is concerned with identity and ideological positions that develop within speech communities. It explores the concept of language ideology in terms of dominance, resistance, representation, power and control. It is concerned with language loyalty, identity, and how these are ratified across different formations of speech communities. More directly, this chapter focuses on the role of the speech community in the critique of power relationships and interactions where bigotry and injustice are suspected. It will explore the relationship between power and powerful speech through reviews and critiques of theories of language, culture, and identity as they relate to ethnicity, race, gender, and nationalism.

10.1 THE GLOBAL SPEECH COMMUNITY

While it is true that one can be a member of multiple speech communities, it is also true that the extent of participation may vary depending on what one knows and understands about the norms that might shape the discursive practices unique to each community. The task is to grasp the intertextuality between and within speech communities in order to unpack the knowledge that makes a speech community member competent. This challenge is illustrated in the words and images of *Le Bien, Le Mal* – *The Good, The Bad*, a hiphop song by the late US hiphop artist Guru and the French hiphop artist MC Solaar. In Morgan (2001) the global reach of what is often called "The Hiphop Nation" is explored through the song's linguistic, musical and spatial merging of Paris and New York/Brooklyn. The prelude to the Guru-Solaar music video collaboration *Le Bien, Le Mal* includes a mobile phone call from MC Solaar – in Paris and speaking French to Guru – in Brooklyn and speaking English. They are not simply speaking French and English but rather MC Solaar's French includes *verlan* – urban French vernacular

that incorporates movement of syllables and deletion of consonants.[1]
Guru's English is laced with Hiphop terminology and African American
English (AAE) as he talks to MC Solaar. Yet in spite of these obvious differ-
ences they communicate 'perfectly' and arrange to meet in a Paris/New
York space that can only be Hiphop.

Paris

MC Solaar: C'est longtemps depuis qu'on a vu Guru Gangstarr.[2]
(It's been a long time since we've seen Guru from Gangstarr.)
C'est pas cool, s'il venait a Paris?
(It will be fly if he comes to Paris.)
Friend: Ouais.
(Yeah)
MC Solaar: On essait de l'appler
(Let's give him a call.)

New York

Guru *(on phone)*: Hello – Who dis? Solaar! What up Man? Yeah! No I'm
comin' man. I know I'm late Yo! Hold up for me al(r)ight. Baby! I'm
on my way now al(r)ight! Peace!

At the end of the conversation, Guru leaves to meet MC Solaar and
descends stairs into a New York subway. When he ascends the subway,
he is in Paris! Then the two begin their song about the contradictions of
life in respective cities and shared speech community.[3]

In their tribute to the hiphop global community MC Solaar and Guru
present a speech community in which they share the same style of speaking, method of grammatical innovation, lexical creativity and more –
but not the same linguistic system. In the case of these hiphop artists,
the speech community is not linguistically and physically located but is
bound by politics, culture, social condition and norms, values and attitudes about language use that those of African descent in Paris and New
York presumably share. As detailed in Chapter 1, speech communities
that are partially constructed through transnationalism, technology,
music and politically and socially marginalized youth were treated as
subordinate in earlier descriptions of speech community if they were

---

[1] For example, "blouson", the French word for jacket would be 'zomblou'. Verlan is
used widely in the suburbs of Paris and also incorporates Arabic slang as well.
[2] Of course Solaar not only speaks French slang, but is an innovator.
[3] *Le Bien, Le Mal.* 1993. Guru with MC Solaar. Jazzmatazz. Chrysalis Records (EMI) New
York.

considered at all. While the previous chapters have explored the strategies members use to represent their identities within and across communities, the notion of the fluent, ever competent and expert mem-
ber/gatekeeper has not been treated as the norm. Rather the focus has
been on how membership is practiced, and depending on the medium
and social and cultural context, how it is negotiated.

10.2 SPEECH COMMUNITIES IN CONFLICT

For many speech communities discursive practices can symbolize and
index the existence of multiple identities and areas of cultural
and social unity and conflict. This is true of a dispute that I witnessed
and analyzed in Morgan (2009) of an African American community in Los
Angeles that became suspicious of youth who participated in a hiphop
workshop called Project Blowed. The conflict resulted in the Los Angeles
police riot squad entering and temporarily closing the establishment.
This police action occurred even though no person was ever identified
or admitted to accusing youth or the owners of the venue of any wrong-
doing. Yet the police reported in a series of community meetings that
I attended afterwards that, "We received a lot of complaints." Older
African American residents of the community continue to deny this
statement. Yet the issue here is not so much what someone actually
said, but what discourse and pragmatic devices might have been used
in conversations with the police that they might have perceived as a real
threat – and whether members of the speech community might have
known how it would be interpreted.

Project Blowed began as the Good Life Cafe, a Health Food Center.[4]
It offered a workshop-like atmosphere for aspiring hiphop MCs, poets
and musicians to hone their craft on Thursday nights in the Crenshaw
area of Los Angeles. When disputes developed with the owners over the
method of audience and artist collaboration and critique, the artists
(under the name Project Blowed) moved to Leimert Park and the KAOS
Network studio owned by Ben Caldwell.[5] On January 4, 1996 around
11 pm, police helicopters began flying low around Project Blowed. The
helicopter spotlights rippled across the quiet middle class neighborhood of Leimert Park as they hovered, rounding up groups of youth

---

[4] This was promoted by owner B. Hall and her son R. Kain Blaze. See Morgan (2009c)
for culture and freestyle that developed at The Good Life.
[5] This occurred around 1994. See Morgan (2009c) for interview with Good Life and
DuVernay (2009).

and intruding on adults enjoying a late night of jazz in a neighboring club.

Leimert Park Village is located in the Crenshaw district of Los Angeles. It boasts one of the highest concentrations of African American owned and/or operated businesses in the US. It is the site of various Afrocentric and Black cultural events and celebrations including: Kwanzaa, the Martin Luther King Day Parade, Blues and Jazz Festivals, the African Film Festival and is adjacent to the annual fall African Marketplace. Leimert Park businesses are mainly a series of small shops and stores that contain hard-to-find gems of African American history, culture, and art. During the 1990s, the selection of businesses included African themed clothing stores, as well as stores featuring comprehensive yet eclectic collections of Black memorabilia. It also featured dance and artist studios, soul food, Mexican restaurants, as well as other eateries, theater, performance spaces, artist's studio, jazz and poetry performance spaces and so on. Even though Leimert Park has a long history and has enjoyed its status as the center of African American culture and arts in Los Angeles, youth throughout LA also consider it the center of their own cultural movement. Moreover, unlike many of the businesses in the Leimert Village area, KAOS is well known for collaborating with community artists and young people in developing their own projects. As KAOS Network and Project Blowed's popularity grew, the surrounding businesses noticed. Slowly rumors began to spread about the presence of youth from other neighborhoods and increased graffiti.

The unraveling of the intergenerational speech community occurred through a series of discursive strategies in the form of complaints and rumors that had predictable implications. The complaints were shared both publicly and informally among merchants and in some cases with the police. Complaints are part of the elaborate talk and verbal genres typical in African American communities described in Chapter 4 that are crafted within a system of indirect discursive practices that both index and address racism and discrimination, especially at the level of stereotype. These discursive practices include insult, rumor, and signifying. Within the African American community in the US, verbal acts also function to save face as they address multiple audiences, some aware and some unaware, through ambiguity and camouflaging. Intentionality and responsibility are viewed as both socially situated and constituted so that speakers and audience collaborate in determining what is meant by what is said (Duranti, 1993; Irvine, 1993). Thus, as described in Chapter 4, speakers who use indirectness actually mean to target certain individuals and they mean to do so indirectly. Of course, indirection, with its nuanced use of local knowledge and symbols is learned through practice and one is socialized as to the rules of usage. Thus, while signifying is a verbal game of indirection and form of play for adolescents, when adults signify in conversations, it is seldom purely a form of play (Morgan 1993). In fact adults often make a point of saying – to whoever may be listening: "I don't play."

Because signifying complaints from adults typically index to the speech community that a serious point is being made, it is not necessary that complaints be based on truth, evidence or specific instances. Rather, complaints in the African American speech community are associated with intentionality and represent the speaker's attitude and how the speaker feels about the particular target in general. The complaints attributed to Project Blowed that emerged through interviews and interactions were that the business community believed,

1. They lost business because the youth kept adults away.
2. Youth caused trash on the street.
3. Project Blowed was actually a club without a license.
4. The youth used and sold drugs.
5. The youth placed graffiti on private property

While Ben Caldwell and Project Blowed worked to address the merchants' accusations, many of which were not true, the complaints actually masquerade the general grievance among the merchants that the youth did not show them their proper respect. This lack of respect was not in the form of particular disrespectful acts. Rather, they considered the youth to be engaged in a discourse of disrespect. While merchants complained about youth vocabulary that they didn't understand, profanity and the use of the "N word," their main grievance was that young people largely ignored them. They did not greet and use respectful address, and refused to participate in what the merchants considered meaningful discourse. In fact I observed Project Blowed members use respectful language toward the merchants on many occasions, only to be told by the merchant later that the person disrespected him. To youth, the energy and future of Leimert Park rested with them and the merchants strongly disagreed. The merchants believed that the youth intentionally showed them disrespect and did not acknowledge the merchants' values and role in the community. As Ben Caldwell explains:

> It was bad. It was bad. It was bad. It was too bad! One of the things that was happening was Blowed was starting to rise up on one level. And the kids were getting cocky – and, they were kids!... Another thing

that was happening – I was going to sell my building. The building was going to sell... The guy who was really interested in buying this facility was starting to work the community... and they didn't want hiphop in the mix you know. So, I was being talked about very badly you know. They were really kind of, dissing me, a lot, mainly because of the youth. It was a rough and ready element and they, they were a little bit frightened by the kids, even though they had never really done anything. It was nothing really tangible. It was just their own fear.

Many of the proprietors represent traditional middle class African American values of respect of elders and property as well as beliefs that lack of respect is an indication of absence of African American culture – and good home training. Many of them also maintained a strong Afrocentric identity that included the respect of elders above anything else. These community proprietors' identities did not necessarily include advocating for the youth. So they complained.

Complaining in African American speech communities is often indirect and a form of signifying. It is accomplished through both direct discursive practices as well as a deeply entangled indirect style based on local knowledge. For example, a direct complaint like "You play your music too loud." when one hears loud music, is regularly interpreted as an accusation and command to turn the music down. That is, it is interpellated and the reaction or lack thereof is considered in relation to dominant discourse ideology (Althusser 1972). The listener, target and speech community member each has the responsibility to determine intentionality and interpret the meaning and potential meaning of what is being said. Thus while it is a direct statement, it is also one that embeds a request/demand for action. One cannot respond by saying "thank you," but one can discursively act by saying: "Too bad." "So what." This particular style is in contrast to complaint signifying where upon hearing the intrusive music, someone says, "I love to hear my favorite song." Or even "I've heard that song ten thousand times already!" "So all you know is Jay Z?" All questions and statements recognize that the playing is loud enough to hear, but neither requires immediate and direct response. It is the speaker that generates the implicature (Grice 1975, Levinson 1983), and by commenting on something not inherent in the logic of the statement, the speaker has introduced the complaint discourse. Consequently, the target/offender appears guilty if he or she argues with the implicature – The music is too loud!

Complaints often mask the social and cultural basis of the conflict; though within the speech community the masking is highly marked.

That is, it is indexical in terms of social meaning (Blom and Gumperz 1972, Kroskrity 1993) in that a move to indirection signals that a problem exists, but not the nature of the problem that must be determined through local knowledge. Because one must be aware of speech community norms, it is possible to provide a 'normal' signifying complaint and others not understand it as such as well as provide a directed one. The question arises when the complaint is directed to an unambiguous symbol of state power like the police – especially in the African American community. At issue is not whether one intends for the police to interpret the complaint as a request to act; it is well within the realm of possibility. Rather, the issue is whether a member of a speech community can reasonably argue that an indirect complaint to the police about young Black men in America could possibly be interpreted as a discursive strategy rather than an indirect request for action. This question holds even if the police are members of the African American community since they must choose the speech community ideology that will direct their action. These signifying complaints occurred during the height of criminalization of the urban Black male and were reckless and indexed the merchants distance from the youth of Project Blowed.

In fact, the police defended the raid by alleging that they had complaints regarding gang activity and overcrowding, complaints never mentioned among discussions with merchants or residents. Thus, the police did not interpret complaints about loss of business, increased trash, and graffiti as a manipulation of and reference to public, negative, and stereotypical symbols of Black urban youth. There was no indication that the LAPD considered that the merchants might have used those symbols as signifying weapons with which to chide the youth. Instead, they referred to the complaints as indicative of gang activity. Likewise, the suggestion that Ben Caldwell was operating a club without a license suggested overcrowding to the LAPD rather than potential jealousy or competitiveness from merchants.

It is not surprising that a group whose discursive practices represent its identity as a speech community apply its system of analysis and representation into other areas of social reality. In fact, Black political thought has historically reflected lively critique and contestation regarding the nature of political power and representation and has been framed around "competing visions of freedom and the means to gain that freedom" (Dawson 2001: 2). With the introduction of hiphop lyrics and activities, an enigmatic political ideology spread among youth in Black communities that contested both the visions and strategies to achieve freedom previously developed as a defining force among Black political ideology.

> These ideologies, and the discourses around them, form the core of
> Black political thought, which historically has not only captured the
> range of political debate within the Black community, but has also
> produced one of the most trenchant critiques of the theory and
> practice of American "democracy." (Dawson 2001: 2)

The notion that indirection may be used to represent political and
ideological positions is evident in debates surrounding recent legal opinions. In May 2005, the Federal Court of Appeals, Seventh Circuit, heard
a case concerning an informant who supplied testimony at an earlier
trial and whether any legal procedures had been violated. A footnote in
the opinion of the case referred back to the original trial and raised the
question of an indirect racial insult.[6]

> The trial transcript quotes Ms. Hayden as saying Murphy called her a
> snitch bitch "hoe." . . . We think the court reporter, unfamiliar with rap
> music (perhaps thankfully so), misunderstood Hayden's response. We
> have taken the liberty of changing "hoe" to "ho," a staple of rap music
> vernacular as, for example, when Ludacris raps "You doin' ho activities
> with ho tendencies."

Lawyers involved in civil rights law became interested in the intentionality of the footnote reference. Was it intended as a racial insult? Was
the clerk who wrote this 'clarification' a misguided fan of hiphop? Was
this an attempt at humor for a reference that will appear in law books
for decades? Are sex, race, and class-based humor appropriate in formal
legal writing? How did the clerk or judge come by the Ludacris reference? Do they intend to insult women and Black women in particular
with the quote?

These types of questions are also raised in the 2013 trial of George
Zimmerman, who killed a young Black man named Trayvon Martin
and was found not guilty. One of his most important witnesses was a
young woman named Jentel who used African American English and
signifying indirection. Zimmerman's defense attorney and many news
outlets ridiculed her speech and suggested that it, the style of talk, was
not capable of being truthful.

---

[6] In the United States Court of Appeals For the Seventh Circuit _____ Nos. 04–
2032, 04–2293 & 04–2309 UNITED STATES OF AMERICA, Plaintiff-Appellee, Cross-
Appellant, v. DARRON J. MURPHY, SR., Defendant-Appellant, Cross-Appellee, and
JENNIFER BAKER, Defendant, Cross-Appellee. _____ Appeals from the United
States District Court for the Southern District of Illinois. No. 03 CR 30137—G. Patrick
Murphy, Chief Judge. _____ ARGUED JANUARY 13, 2005—DECIDED MAY
4, 2005 _____ Before ROVNER, EVANS, and SYKES, Circuit Judges. EVANS,
Circuit Judge. A jury found Darron Murphy, Sr. Page 2 footnote 1.

The Leimert Park merchants and older generation, spoke negatively about the youth in the presence of the police and their agents, though not necessarily directly to them. Yet, they were very aware of the stereotyping of youth and regular attacks on them and the aggressive history of the LAPD. The merchants who participated in this type of complaint knew that when Emmett Till was lynched in Mississippi, it was after White supremacists "overheard" Black men talking about him whistling at a White woman while at the local grocery store. They talked about this in a situation where they knew they could be overheard. The White supremacists that heard that story lynched Emmett Till in a fashion even savage for the time. The Leimert Park merchants may have wanted something to happen, but they had no control over what actually happened. But they understood very well what could happen.

10.3 CONCLUSION

Speech communities remain fundamental to the way we organize our social lives across mediums, space, places and social networks. What is important to both speech and community is that a system of interaction and symbols is shared, learned and taught and participants and members are aware that they share these symbols. Yet as the world both grows and becomes smaller, our need to operate in speech communities may become greater. Clearly we are not people who will always share the same norms about language use across life spans and social, political and technological contexts. Yet we consistently identify and seek the networks, ideas, practices, beliefs, etc. that make it possible. Linguists have a vast and changing world of language attitudes and uses to explore so that we continue to increase our understanding of what it means to be human – and so that we always find a way to keep talking to each other.

DISCUSSION QUESTIONS

1. Describe ways in which global speech communities may cause conflicts within nations and across cultures.
2. Using examples from this chapter and others, explain how conflicts within speech communities can lead to a political response from other speech communitites.

3. How do concepts like indexicality, intentionality and indirectness help us to understand power, conflict and miscommunication?

4. Project Blowed is an example of how language and discourse styles within and across speech communities may lead to unintended consequences. Issues like social context and language ideology along with other factors may be incorporated into how one understands intentionality and what one means. Please provide an example of a situation where conflicts occurred through different interpretations of speech community norms.

FURTHER READING

Bourdieu, P. (1997 [1977]). *Language and Symbolic Power*. G. Raymond and M. Adamson, trans., J. Thompson, ed. Cambridge, MA: Harvard University Press.

Grimshaw, A. (ed.). (1990). *Conflict Talk: Sociolinguistic Investigations of Arguments in Conversations*. Cambridge University Press.

Kroskrity, P. (1993). *Language, History and Identity: Ethnolinguistic Studies of the Arizona Tewa*. Tucson, AZ: University of Arizona Press.

Morgan, M. (2002). *Language, Discourse and Power in African American Culture*. Cambridge University Press.

Morgan, M. (2009b). The Presentation of Indirectness and Power in Everyday Life. *Journal of Pragmatics* 42(2): 283–291.

Bibliography

Aarons, D. (2012). *Jokes and the Linguistic Mind*. New York: Routledge.

Abrahams, R. (1962). Playing the Dozens. *Journal of American Folklore* 75: 209–218.

(1970). *Deep Down in the Jungle*. Chicago: Aldine Publishing Co.

(1974). Black Talking on the Streets. In R. Bauman and J. Sherzer (eds.), *Explorations in the Ethnography of Speaking* (pp. 240–262). Cambridge University Press.

(1975). Negotiating Respects: Patterns of Presentation among Black Women. *Journal of American Folklore*, 88: 58–80.

Abrahams, R. and Szwed, J. (1983). *After Africa: Extracts from the British Travel Accounts and Journals of the Seventeenth, Eighteenth and Nineteenth Centuries Concerning the Slaves, Their Manners and Customs in the British West Indies*. Hartford: Yale University Press.

Abu-Lughod. (2000). *Veiled Sentiments: Honor and Poetry in a Bedouin Society*. Berkeley, CA: University of California Press.

Adams, K. and Brink, D. (1990). *Perspectives on Official English: The Campaign for English as the Official Language of the USA*. Berlin/New York: Mouton de Gruyter.

Adero, M. (ed.). (1993). *Up South: Stories, Studies and Letters of African American Migrations*. New York: The New Press.

Adger, C. T. (1998). Register Shifting and Dialect Resources in Instructional Discourse. In S. M. Hoyle and C. T. Adger (eds.), *Kids Talk: Strategic Language Use in Later Childhood* (pp. 151–169). Oxford University Press.

Adger, C. T., Wolfram, W. and Christian, D. (2007). *Dialects in Schools and Communities*. 2nd. edn. Mahwah, New Jersey: Lawrence Erlbaum.

Adorno, T. and Horkheimer, M. (1979). *Dialectic of Enlightenment*. London: Verso.

Agre, P. E. (1997). *Computation and Human Experience*. Cambridge University Press.

Ahearn, C. (1983). *Wild Style*. Rhino Theatrical.

Ahearn, L. M. (2011). *Living Language: An Introduction to Linguistic Anthropology*. 1st edn. Hoboken, New Jersey: Wiley-Blackwell.

Alexander, M. J. and C. T. M. (ed.). (1997). *Feminist Genealogies, Colonial Legacies, Democratic Futures*. New York and London: Routledge.

Alim, H. S. (2006). *Roc the Mic Right: The Language of Hip Hop Culture* New York: Routledge.

(2011a). Hip Hop and the Politics of Ill-Literacy. In B. A. U. Levinson and M. Pollock (eds.), *A Companion to the Anthropology of Education* (pp. 232–246). Hoboken, New Jersey: Wiley-Blackwell.

(2011b). Global Ill-Literacies: Hiphop Cultures, Youth Identities, and the Politics of Literacy. *Review of Research in Education* 35(1): 120–146.

Alim, H. S. and Smitherman, G. (2012). *Articulate While Black: Barack Obama, Language, and Race in the US.* Oxford University Press.

Alim, H. S., Ibrahim, A. and Pennycook, A. (2008). *Global Linguistic Flows: Hip Hop Cultures, Youth Identities, and the Politics of Language.* 1st edn. London, New York: Routledge.

Alim, H. S., Lee, J. and Carris, L. M. (2011). Moving the Crowd, "Crowding" the Emcee: The Coproduction and Contestation of Black Normativity in Freestyle Rap Battles. *Discourse & Society* 22(4): 422–439. doi:10.1177/0957926510395828

Alleyne, B. (2002). An Idea of Community and its Discontents: Towards a More Reflexive Sense of Belonging in Multicultural Britain. *Ethnic and Racial Studies* 25(4): 607–627.

Alleyne, M. C. (1980). *Comparative Afro-American: An Historical-Comparative Study of English-Based Afro-American Dialects of the New World.* Ann Arbor: Karoma.

(1989). *Roots of Jamaican Culture.* London: Pluto Press.

Althusser, L. (1972). Ideology and Ideological State Apparatuses (Notes toward an Investigation). In L. Althusser, *Lenin and Philosophy, and Other Essays.* New York: Monthly Review Press.

Anderson, B. (1983). *Imagined Communities: Reflections on the Origin and Spread of Nationalism.* London, New York: Verso.

Androutsopoulos, J. and Scholz, A. (2002). On the Recontextualization of Hip-Hop in European Speech Communities: A Contrastive Analysis of Rap Lyrics. *Philologie im Netz* 19: 1–42.

Angogo, R. (1978). Language and Politics in South Africa. *Studies in African Languages* 9(2): 211–221.

Askew, K. and Wilk, R. R. (eds.). (2002). *The Anthropology of Media.* Oxford: Blackwell Publishing.

Archambault, J. S. (2013). Cruising through Uncertainty: Cell Phones and the Politics of Display and Disguise in Inhambane, Mozambique. *American Ethnologist* 40(1): 88–101.

Atkins, E. T. (2001). *Blue Nippon: Authenticating Jazz in Japan.* Durham, NC: Duke University Press.

Austin, J. L. (1961). *Philosophical Papers.* Oxford University Press.

(1962). *How to Do Things with Words.* Cambridge, MA: Harvard University Press.

Bakhtin, M. M. (1981). *The Dialogic Imagination: Four Essays* (C. Emerson and M. Holquist, trans.). Austin: University of Texas Press.

(1986). *Speech Genres and Other Late Essays.* Austin: University of Texas Press.

Baldwin, J. (1986). James Baldwin's National Press Club Speech (December 10). Available online at: www.youtube.com/watch?v=qDNkT4xH3YE& feature=youtube_gdata_player).

Baratz, J. (1973). Language Abilities of Black Americans. In M. Dreger (ed.), *Comparative Studies of Blacks and Whites in the United States* (pp. 125–183). New York: Seminar Press.

Barnes, J. (1954). Class and Committees in a Norwegian Island Parish. *Human Relations* 7: 39–58.

Basu, D. and Lemelle, S. (eds.). (2006). *The Vinyl Ain't Final: Hip Hop and the Globalization of Black Popular Culture.* London: Pluto Press.

Baugh, J. (1981). Design and Implementation of Language Arts Programs for Speakers of Nonstandard English: Perspectives for a National Neighborhood Literacy Program. In B. Cronell (ed.), *The Linguistic Needs of Linguistically Different Children* (pp. 17–43). Los Alamitos, CA: South West Regional Laboratory (SWRL).

(1983a). A Survey of Afro-American English. *Annual Review of Anthropology* 12: 335–354.

(1983b). *Black Street Speech: Its History, Structure and Survival.* Austin: University of Texas Press.

(1987). The Situational Dimension of Linguistic Power. *Language Arts* 64: 234–240.

(1988). Discourse Function for "Come" in Black English Vernacular. *Texas Linguistics Forum* 31: 42–49.

(1992). Hypocorrection: Mistakes in Production of Vernacular African American English as a Second Dialect. *Language Community* 12(3/4): 317–326.

(1999). *Out of the Mouths of Slaves.* Austin: University of Texas Press.

Bauman, R. (ed.). (1992). *Folklore, Cultural Performances, and Popular Entertainments: A Communications-Centered Handbook.* New York: Oxford University Press.

(2004). *A World of Others' Words: Cross-Cultural Perspectives on Intertextuality.* Malden, MA: Blackwell.

Bauman, R. and Briggs, C. (1990). Poetics and Performance as Critical Perspectives on Language and Social Life. *Annual Review of Anthropology* 19: 59–88.

Bell, A. (2001). Back in Style: Reworking Audience Design. In Eckert and Rickford (eds.), pp. 139–169.

Benjamin, J. (1997). *Shadow of the Other: Intersubjectivity and Gender in Psychoanalysis.* 1st edn. New York: Routledge.

Bennett, A. and Peterson, R. A. (eds.). (2004). *Music Scenes: Local, Translocal and Virtual.* Nashville: Vanderbilt University Press.

Bennett, D. (2012). Imagination Communities: Hiphop's Creative Labor. Paper presented at the Hiphop and Globalization Conference, Harvard University. Cambridge, MA: Hiphop Archive.

Bereiter, C. and Engelman, S. (1966). *Teaching Disadvantaged Children in the Preschool.* Englewood Cliffs, NJ: Prentice Hall.

Berger, P. and Luckman, T. (1966). *The Social Construction of Reality*. Middlesex: Penguin Books.

Berry, M. F. and Blassingame, J. (1982). *Long Memory: The Black Experience in America*. Oxford University Press.

Best, S. and Hartman, S. (2005). Fugitive Justice. *Representations* 92(1): 1–15.

Béthune, C. (1999). *Le rap: une esthétique hors la loi*. Paris: Editions Autrement.

Bhabba, H. (1994). *The Location of Culture*. London: Routledge.

(2000). *On Cultural Choice*. In M. Garber and R. Walkowitz (eds.), *The Turn to Ethics* (pp. 181–200). New York, London: Routledge.

Bidwell, C. E. and Friedkin, N. E. (1988). The Sociology of Education. In N. J. Smelser (ed.), *Handbook of Sociology* (pp. 449–471). Newbury Park, CA: Sage.

Block, P. (2009). *Community: The Structure of Belonging*. San Francisco: Berrett-Koehler Publishers.

Blom, J.-P. and Gumperz, J. J. (1972). Social Meaning in Linguistic Structures: Code Switching in Northern Norway. In Gumperz and Hymes (eds.), *Directions in Sociolinguistics*, pp. 407–434.

Bloomfield, L. (1933). *Language*. University of Chicago Press.

(1935). *Language*. London: Allen & Unwin.

Bloomquist, J. (2009). "People Say I Speak Proper, but Girl, I'm Ghetto!": Regional Dialect Use and Adaptation by African American Women in Pennsylvania's Lower Susquehanna Valley. In Lanehart (ed.), pp. 165–183.

Bobo, L. and Hutchings, V. L. (1996). Perceptions of Racial Group Competition: Extending Blumer's Theory of Group Position to a Multiracial Social Context. *American Sociological Review* 61: 951–972.

Bond, H. M. (1969 [1939]). *Negro Education in Alabama: A Study in Cotton and Steel*. New York: Atheneum.

Bourdieu, P. (1991 [1977]). *Language and Symbolic Power*. (G. Raymond and M. Adamson, trans., J. Thompson, ed.). Cambridge, MA: Harvard University Press.

Bourdieu, P. P. and Passeron, Jean-Claude (1977). *Reproduction in Education, Society, and Culture*. London: Sage.

Bowles, S. and Gintis, H. (1976). *Schooling in Capitalist America: Educational Reform and the Contradictions of Economic Life*. New York: Basic Books.

Bragg, M. (2004). *The Adventure of English: The Biography of a Language*. New York: Arcade.

Briggs, C. (1986). *Learning How to Ask: A Sociolinguistic Appraisal of the Role of the Interview in Social Science Research*. Cambridge University Press.

Briggs, C. L. and Bauman, R. (2009). Genre, Intertextuality and Social Power. In Duranti (ed.), *Linguistic Anthropology*, pp. 214–244.

Briggs, C. and Mantini-Briggs, C. (2004). *Stories in the Time of Cholera: Racial Profiling during a Medical Nightmare*. Berkeley: University of California Press.

Brodkin, K. (1994). How Did Jews Become White Folks? In S. Gregory and R. Sanjek (eds.), *Race*. New Brunswick, NJ: Rutgers University Press.

Brooks, C. K. (ed.). (1985). *Tapping Potential: English and Language Arts for the Black Learner*. Urbana, IL: National Council of Teachers of English.

Brown, P. and Levinson, S. C. (1987). *Politeness: Some Universals in Language Usage*. Cambridge University Press.

Brown, T. (2006). "Keeping it Real" in a Different Hood: (African) American-ization and Hip Hop in Germany. In D. Basu and S. J. Lemelle (eds.), *The Vinyl Ain't Final: Hip Hop and the Globalization of Black Popular Culture* (pp. 137–150). London: Pluto.

Bryce-Laporte, R. S. (1971). The Slave Plantation: Background to Present Conditions of Urban Blacks. In P. Orleans and W. R. Ellis Jr. (eds.), *Race Change and Urban Society* (pp. 257–284). Beverly Hills: Sage.

Bucholtz, M. (1996). Black Feminist Theory and African American Women's Linguistic Practice. In V. L. Bergvall, J. M. Bing and A. F. Freed (eds.), *Rethinking Language and Gender Research: Theory and Practice* (pp. 267–290). London, New York: Longman.

(1999). Language and Identity Practices in a Community of Nerd Girls. *Language in Society* 28(2): 203–223.

(2009). From Stance to Style: Gender, Interaction, and Indexicality in Mexican Immigrant Youth Slang. In A. Jaffe (ed.), *Stance: Sociolinguistic Perspectives* (pp. 146–170). Oxford University Press.

Bucholtz, M. and K. H. (eds.). (1995). *Gender Articulated: Language and the Socially Constructed Self*. New York: Routledge.

Bucholtz, M. and Hall, K. (2004). Language and Identity. In A. Duranti (ed.), *A Companion to Linguistic Anthropology* (pp. 369–394). Hoboken, NJ: Wiley Blackwell.

Butler, J. (1990). *Gender Trouble: Feminism and the Subversion of Identity*. London, New York: Routledge.

(1993). *Bodies that Matter on the Discursive Limits of "Sex."* Abingdon, Oxon; New York: Routledge.

(1997). *Excitable Speech: A Politics of the Performative*. New York: Routledge.

(1999). On Speech, Race, and Melancholia. *Theory, Race, Culture, and Society* 16(2): 163–74.

Byrne, D. (2008). The Future of (the) "Race": Identity, Discourse, and the Rise of the Computer-Mediated Public Spheres. In A. Everett (ed.), *Learning Race and Ethnicity: Youth and Digital Media* (pp. 15–38). Cambridge, MA: MIT Press.

Caldeira, T. P. D. R. (2000). *City of Walls: Crime, Segregation, and Citizenship in São Paulo*. Berkeley: University of California Press.

Cameron, D. (2007). *The Myth of Mars and Venus: Do Men and Women Really Speak Different Languages?* Oxford University Press.

Cameron, D. and Coates, J. (1989). Some Problems in the Sociolinguistic Explanation of Sex Differences. In Coates and Cameron (eds.), pp. 13–26.

Cameron, D. and Kulick, D. (2003). *Language and Sexuality*. Cambridge University Press.

Carby, H. (1987). *Reconstructing Womanhood: The Emergence of the Afro-American Woman Novelist.* Oxford University Press.

Carpio, G. (2008). *Laughing Fit to Kill: Black Humor in the Fictions of Slavery.* Oxford University Press.

Celayo, A. and Shook, D. (2008). In Darkness We Meet: A Conversation with Junot Diaz. *World Literature Today* 82(2): 12–17.

Chang, J. (2005). *Can't Stop Won't Stop: A History of the Hip Hop Generation.* New York: St Martin's Press.

Chappelle, Dave (2000). *Killin' Them Softly.* HBO.

Chomsky, N. (1965). *Aspects of the Theory of Syntax.* Cambridge, MA: MIT Press.

Christenson, P. and Roberts, D. (1998). *It's Not Only Rock & Roll: Popular Music in the Lives of Adolescents.* Cresskill, NJ: Hampton Press.

Chuck, D. and C. R. and Jah, Y. (1998). *Fight the Power: Rap, Race and Reality.* New York: Dell Publishing.

Coates, J. (1996). *Women Talk.* Oxford: Blackwell.

   (1998). *Language and Gender: A Reader.* Malden, MA: Blackwell.

Coates, J. and Cameron, D. (eds.). (1989). *Women in Their Speech Communities.* London: Longman.

Cohen, A. P. (1985). *Symbolic Construction of Community.* London: Routledge.

Collins, P. H. (1990). *Black Feminist Thought: Knowledge, Consciousness, and the Politics of Empowerment.* New York: Routledge.

Condry, I. (2006). *Hip-Hop Japan.* Durham, NC: Duke University Press.

Connor, M. K. (1995). *What is Cool? Understanding Black Manhood in America.* New York Crown Publishers.

Coombe, R. J. (1998). *The Cultural Life of Intellectual Properties: Authorship, Appropriation, and the Law.* Durham, NC.

Crawford, J. (ed.). (1992). *Language Loyalties: A Source Book on the Official English Controversy.* University of Chicago Press.

Crystal, D. (2006). Language and the Internet. Cambridge University Press.

Dandy, E. (1991). *Black Communications: Breaking down the Barriers.* Chicago: African American Images.

Danet, B. and Herring, S. C. (eds.). (2007). *The Multilingual Internet: Language, Culture, and Communication Online.* Oxford University Press.

Davis, A. (1981). *Women, Race and Class.* New York: Vintage.

   (1998). *Blues Legacies and Black Feminism: Gertrude "Ma" Rainey, Bessie Smith and Billie Holiday.* New York: Pantheon.

Davis, O. (2006 [1967]). The English Language is My Enemy. In O. Davis and R. Dee (eds.), *Life Lit by Some Large Vision: Selected Speeches and Writings by Ossie Davis* (Foreword by Ruby Dee) (pp. 9–18). New York: Aria Books.

Dawson, M. (1997). *Structure and Ideology: The Shaping of Black Public Opinion.* Chicago: Department of Political Science, University of Chicago.

   (2001). *Black Visions: The Roots of Contemporary African-American Political Ideologies.* University of Chicago Press.

Derrida, J. (1982). *Margins of Philosophy.* University of Chicago Press.

Descartes, R. (1996). *Descartes: Meditations on First Philosophy: With Selections from the Objections and Replies* (J. Cottingham, ed.) Cambridge University Press.

Deutsch, M., Katz, I. and Jensen, A. (eds.). (1968). *Social Class, Race, and Psychological Development*. New York: Holt, Rinehart and Winston.

Dewey, J. (1900). *The School and Society*. University of Chicago Press.

Dicker, S. J. (2003). *Languages in America: A Pluralist View*. Clevedon: Multilingual Matters.

Dill, B. T. (1994). Fictive Kin, Paper Sons, and Compradrazgo: Women of Color and the Struggle for Family Survival. In M. B. Zinn and B. T. Dill (eds.), *Women of Color in US Society* (pp. 149–170). Philadelphia: Temple University Press.

Dillard, J. L. (1972). *Black English: Its History and Usage in the United States*. New York: Random House.

(1978). Bidialectal Education: Black English and Standard English in the United States. In B. Spolsky and R. L. Cooper (eds.), *Case Studies in Bilingual Education* (pp. 293–311). Rowley, MA: Newbury House.

Drake, St. Clair and Cayton, H. R. (1945). *Black Metropolis: A Study of Negro Life in a Northern City*. New York: Harcourt, Brace & World.

Du Bois, W. E. B. (1975 [1920]). *Dark Water: Voices from within the Veil*. Millwood, NY: Krauss International.

(1990). *The Souls of Black Folk*. Chicago: A. C. McClurg.

Durand, A.-P. (2002). *Black, Blanc, Beur: Rap Music and Hip-hop Culture in the Francophone World*. Lanham, MD: Scarecrow Press.

Duranti, A. (1986). The Audience as Co-Author: An Introduction. *Text – Interdisciplinary Journal for the Study of Discourse* 6(3): 239–247.

(1993). Truth and Intentionality: An Ethnographic Critique. *Culture Anthropology* 8(2): 214–245.

(1997). *Linguistic Anthropology*. Cambridge University Press.

(2004). *A Companion to Linguistic Anthropology*. Hoboken, NJ: Wiley-Blackwell.

(2006). The Social Ontology of Intentions. *Discourse Studies* 8(1): 31–40.

(2009). *Linguistic Anthropology: A Reader*. 2nd edn. Oxford: Blackwell.

(2011). Ethnopragmatics and Beyond: Intentionality and Agency across Languages and Cultures. In C. Baraldi, A. Borsari and A. Carli (eds.), *Hybrids, Differences, Visions: On the Study of Culture* (pp. 151–168). Aurora, CO: The Davies Group.

Duranti, A. and Black, S. (2011). Language Socialization and Verbal Improvisation. In A. Duranti, E. Ochs and B. Schieffelin (eds.), *Handbook of Language Socialization*. Malden, MA: Hoboken, NJ: Wiley-Blackwell.

Duranti, A. and Brenneis, D. (1986). The Audience as Co-Author: An Introduction. *Text Special Issue* 6(3): 239–347.

Durkheim, E. (1961 [1925]). *Moral Education*. Glencoe, IL: Free Press.

DuVernay, A. (2009). *This is the Life*. Film.

Eckert, P. (2000). *Linguistic Variation as Social Practice: The Linguistic Construction of Identity in Belten High*. Hoboken, NJ: Wiley-Blackwell.

Eckert, P. and McConnell-Ginet, S. (2003). *Language and Gender*. Cambridge University Press.

Eckert, P. and Rickford, J. (eds.). (2001). *Style and Sociolinguistic Variation*. Cambridge University Press.

Edwards, J. (2009). *Language and Identity*. Cambridge University Press.

Edwards, V. and Kaatbamna, S. (1989). The Wedding Songs of British Gujarati Women. In Coates and Cameron (eds.), pp. 158–174.

Eglash, R. (2002). Race, Sex, and Nerds: From Black Geeks to Asian American Hipsters. *Social Text* 71 20(2): 49–64.

Eltis, D. and Richardson, D. (2007). The Trans-Atlantic Slave Trade Database. *The Trans-Atlantic Slave Trade Database*. Retrieved from www.slavevoyages.org/tast/index.faces

Ensslin, A. (2010). "Black and White": Language Ideologies in Computer Game Discourse. In Milani and Johnson (eds.), pp. 202–222.

Etter-Lewis, G. (1993). *My Soul is My Own: Oral Narratives of African American Women in Professions*. New York: Routledge.

(1996). From the Inside Out: Survival and Continuity in African American Women's Oral Narratives. In G. Etter-Lewis and M. Foster (eds.), *Unrelated Kin: Race and Gender in Women's Personal Narratives* (pp. 169–182). New York: Routledge.

Everett, A. (2002). The Revolution Will Be Digitized: Afrocentricity and the Digital Public Sphere. *Social Text* 71 20(2): 125–146.

Everett, A. and Watkins, C. (2008). The Power of Play: The Portrayal and Performance of Race in Video Games. In *The Ecology of Games: Connecting Youth, Games, and Learning* (pp. 141–164). Cambridge, MA: MIT Press.

Fairclough, N. (2001). *Language and Power*. London: Longman.

Fanon, F. (1967). *Black Skin, White Masks*. New York: Grove Weidenfeld.

Fantz, A. (2012). "N**gas in Paris": A Winning Campaign Ad or Offensive "Ethnic" Marketing? *CNN*. Retrieved July 19, 2013 from www.cnn.com/2012/04/27/world/europe/france-politician-uses-offensive-song/index.html.

Fasold, R. (1972). *Tense Marking in Black English: A Linguistic and Social Analysis*. Arlington, VA: Centre for Applied Linguistics.

Fields, B. J. (1985). *Slavery and Freedom on the Middle Ground: Maryland during the Nineteenth Century*. New Haven, CT: Yale University Press.

Fikes, K. (2009). *Managing African Portugal: The Citizen–Migrant Distinction*. Durham, NC: Duke University Press.

Firth, R. (1972). Verbal and Bodily Rituals of Greeting and Parting. In J. S. La Fontaine (ed.), *The Interpretation of Ritual: Essays in Honor of A.I. Richards* (pp. 1–38). London: Tavistock.

Fischer, C., Hout, M., Jankowksi, M. S., Swidler, A. and Lucas, S. R. (1996). *Inequality by Design: Cracking the Bell Curve Myth*. Princeton University Press.

Fischer, D. E. (2007). *Kobushi Agero (Pump Ya Fist): Blackness, Race and Politics in Japanese Hiphop*. Gainesville: University of Florida.

Fisher, L. (1976). Dropping Remarks and the Barbadian Audience. *American Ethnologist* 3(2): 227–242.

Fishman, J. (1981). Language Policy: Past, Present, and Future. In C. A. Ferguson and S. B. Heath (eds.), *Language in the USA* (pp. 516–526). New York: Cambridge University Press.

Fix, S. (2010). Representations of Blackness by White Women: Linguistic Practice in the Community versus the Media. *University of Pennsylvania Working Papers in Linguistics* 16(2): 56–65.

Folb, E. (1980). *Runnin' Down Some Lines: The Language and Culture of Black Teenagers.* Cambridge, MA: Harvard University Press.

Fonarow, W. (2006). *Empire of Dirt: The Aesthetics and Rituals of British Indie Music.* Middletown, CT: Wesleyan University Press.

Forman, M. (2000). Race, Space and Place in Rap Music. *Popular Music* 19(1): 65–90.

(2002). *The 'Hood Comes First: Race, Space, and Place in Rap and Hip-Hop.* Middletown, CT: Wesleyan University Press.

Forman, M. and Neal, M. A. (eds.). (2004). *That's the Joint! The Hip-Hop Studies Reader.* New York: Routledge.

Foster, M. (1989). "It's Cookin' Now": A Performance Analysis of a Black Teacher in an Urban Community College. *Language in Society* 18(1): 1–29.

(1995). "Are you with me?" Power and Solidarity in the Discourse of African American Women. In K. Hall and M. Bucholtz (eds.), *Gender Articulated: Language and the Socially Constructed Self* (pp. 329–350). New York: Routledge.

Foucault, M. (1972). *The Archaeology of Knowledge and the Discourse on Language.* New York: Pantheon.

Fought, C. (2006). *Language and Ethnicity.* Cambridge University Press.

Fox, D. (1992). Punchline. July. *The Source* 20.

Franklin, J. H. and Moss, A. (1988). *From Slavery to Freedom: A History of Negro Americans.* New York: McGraw-Hill.

Fujita, T. (1996). *Tokyo Hip Hop Guide.* Tokyo: Ohta Publishing Company.

Gal, S. (1991). Between Speech and Silence: The Problematics of Research on Language and Gender. In M. D. Leonardo (ed.), *Gender at the Crossroads of Knowledge: Feminist Anthropology in the Post Modern Era* (pp. 175–203). University of Chicago Press.

Garcia, O. and Bartlett, L. (2007). A Speech Community Model of Bilingual Education: Educating Latino Newcomers in the US. *International Journal of Bilingual Education and Bilingualism* 10(1): 1–25.

Garner, T. (1983). Playing the Dozens: Folklore as Strategies for Living. *Quarterly Journal of Speech* 68: 41–47.

Garrett, P. B. and Baquedano-López, P. (2002). Language Socialization: Reproduction and Continuity, Transformation and Change. *Annual Review of Anthropology*, 31: 339–361.

Gates, H. L. (1988). *The Signifying Monkey: A Theory of African-American Literary Criticism.* New York: Oxford University Press.

(2013a). How Many Slaves Came to America? Fact vs. Fiction. *The Root*. Retrieved March 23, 2013 from www.theroot.com/views/ 100-amazing-facts-about-negro-0.

(2013b). Middle Passage: Slaves Weren't Just Forced across the Atlantic. *The Root*. Retrieved March 23, 2013 from www.theroot.com/views/ there-was-more-1-middle-passage.

Gee, J. P. (1996). *Social Linguistics and Literacies: Ideology in Discourses*. London: Taylor and Francis.

Geertz, C. (ed.). (1973). *The Interpretation of Cultures*. New York: Basic Books.

(1983). *Local Knowledge: Further Essays in Interpretive Anthroplogy*. New York: Basic Books.

Gershon, I. (2010). Breaking up is Hard to Do: Media Switching and Media Ideologies. *Journal of Linguistic Anthropology* 20(2): 389–405.

Giddens, A. (1991). *Modernity and Self-Identity*. Stanford University Press.

Gilligan, C. (1982). *In a Different Voice: Psychological Theory and Women's Development*. Cambridge, MA: Harvard University Press.

Gilroy, P. (1994). After the Love Has Gone: Biopolitics and Etho-poetics in the Black Public Sphere. *Public Culture* 7: 49–76.

Gilyard, K. (1996). *Let's Flip the Script: An African American Discourse on Language, Literature and Learning*. Detroit: Wayne State University Press.

Goffman, E. (1959). *The Presentation of Self in Everyday Life*. New York: Anchor.

(1961). *Asylums: Essays on the Social Situation of Mental Patients and Other Inmates*. New York: Anchor.

(1967). *Interaction Ritual: Essays in Face to Face Behavior*. Garden City, NY: Doubleday.

(1971). *Relations in Public: Microstudies of the Public Order*. New York: Basic Books.

(1974). *Frame Analysis*. New York: HarperCollins.

(1981). *Forms of Talk*. Oxford: Blackwell.

(1982). *Interaction Ritual – Essays on Face-to-Face Behavior*. New York: Pantheon, 1982.

Goldstein, D. M. (2003). *Laughter out of Place: Race, Class, Violence, and Sexuality in a Rio Shantytown*. Berkeley: University of California Press.

Goodwin, M. H. (1988). Cooperation and Competition across Girls' Play Activities. In S. Fisher and A. Todd (eds.), *Gender and Discourse: The Power of Talk* (pp. 55–94). Norwood, NJ: Ablex.

(1990). *He-Said-She-Said: Talk as Social Organization among Black Children*. Bloomington: Indiana University Press.

(2003). The Relevance of Ethnicity, Class, and Gender in Children's Peer Negotiations. In Holmes and Meyerhoff (eds.), pp. 229–251.

(2006). *The Hidden Life of Girls: Games of Stance, Status, and Exclusion*. Oxford: Blackwell.

Gordon, M. M. (1966). *Assimilation in American Life: The Role of Race, Religion, and National Origins*. New York: Oxford University Press.

Gramsci, A. (1971). *Selections from the Prison Notebooks* (Q. Hoare and G. N. Smith, eds.) New York: International Press.

(1996). *Prison Notebooks, Volume II* (J. Buttigieg, trans.). New York: Columbia University Press.

Green, L. (2002). *African American English: A Linguistic Introduction.* Cambridge University Press.

Green, L. and Coner, T. (2009). Rhetorical Markers in Girls' Developing African American Language Use. In Lanehart, pp. 91–109.

Grice, P. (1975). Logic and Conversation. In P. Cole and J. L. Morgan (eds.), *Syntax and Semantics, Volume III: Speech Acts.* New York: Academic Press.

Grimshaw, A. (ed.). (1990). *Conflict Talk: Sociolinguistic Investigations of Arguments in Conversations.* Cambridge University Press.

Gumperz, J. (1968). The Speech Community. In David L. Sills and Robert K. Merton (eds.), *International Encyclopedia of the Social Sciences* (pp. 381–386). New York: Macmillan.

(1972). Introduction. In J. Gumperz & D. Hymes (eds.), *Directions in Sociolinguistics: The Ethnography of Communication* (pp. 1–25). New York: Holt, Rinehart, & Winston, Inc.

(1982a). *Discourse Strategies.* Cambridge University Press.

(1982b). *Language and Social Identity.* Cambridge University Press.

Gumperz, J. (1983). *Language and Social Identity.* 2nd edn. Cambridge University Press.

(1992). Contextualization and Understanding. In A. Duranti and C. Goodwin (eds.), *Rethinking Context: Language as an Interactive Phenomenon* (pp. 229–252). Cambridge University Press.

Gumperz, J. and Cook-Gumperz, J. (1982). Introduction: Language and the Communication of Social Identity. In Gumperz (ed.), *Language and Social Identity* (pp. 1–21).

Gumperz, J. and Hymes, D. (1972). *Directions in Sociolinguistics: The Ethnography of Communication.* New York: Holt, Rinehart and Winston, Inc.

Guthrie, G. (2013). *Ain't Nothin' Goin' on but the Rent.* Polydor. Retrieved from http://en.wikipedia.org/w/index.php?title=Ain%27t_Nothin%27_Goin%27_on_But_the_Rent&oldid=545986170

Gutierrez, K., Baquedano-Lopez, P. and Alvarez, H. (2000). The Crisis in Latino Education: The Norming of America. In C. Tejeda, Z. Leonardo and C. Martinez (eds.), *Charting New Terrains in Chicano(a) and Latina(o) Education* (pp. 213–232). Creskill, NJ: Hampton Press.

Guy, G. (1989). Language and Social Class. In F. J. Newmeyer (ed.), *Linguistics: The Cambridge Survey, Volume IV: Language: The Socio-cultural Context* (pp. 37–63). Cambridge University Press.

Gwaltney, J. (1993). *Drylongso: A Self-Portrait of Black America.* New York: The New Press.

Habermas, Jürgen (1991). *The Structural Transformation of the Public Sphere: An Inquiry into a Category of Bourgeois Society* (T. Burger, trans.). Cambridge, MA: MIT Press.

(1992). Further Reflections on the Public Sphere. In Calhoun (ed.), *Habermas and the Public Sphere* (pp. 421–461).

Hall, S. (1996a). Introduction: Who Needs Identity? In Hall and du Gay (eds.), pp. 1–17.

(1996b). The West and the Rest: Discourse and Power. In Hall, Held, Hubert and Thompson (eds.), pp. 185–227.

(1997). The Local and the Global: Globalization and Ethnicity. In A. M. Anne McClintlock and Ella Shohat (eds.), *Dangerous Liaisons: Gender, Nation, and Postcolonial Perspectives* (pp. 173–187). University of Minneapolis Press.

Hall, S. and Gay, P. du (eds.). (1996). *Questions of Cultural Identity*. London: Sage.

Hall, S., Held, D., Hubert, D. and Thompson, K. (eds.). (1996). *Modernity: An Introduction to Modern Societies*. Oxford: Blackwell.

Halliday, M. A. K. (1973). *Explorations in the Functions of Language*. London: Edward Arnold.

(1978). *Language as Social Semiotic – The Social Interaction of Language and Meaning*. London: Edward Arnold.

Hanks, W. F. (1996). *Language and Communicative Practices*. Boulder, CO: Westview.

(2001). Indexicality. In A. Duranti (ed.), *Key Terms in Language and Culture* (pp. 119–121). Malden, MA: Blackwell.

(2010). Toward a Theory of Critical Computing: The Case of Social Identity Representation in Digital Media Applications. CTheory.net. Retrieved from www.ctheory.net/articles.aspx?id=641.

Harrell, D. F. (2010). Toward a Theory of Critical Computing: The Case of Social Identity Representation in Digital Media Applications. CTheory. net. Retrieved from www.ctheory.net/articles.aspx?id=641.

Harris, C. I. (1996). Finding Sojourner's Truth: Race, Gender and the Institution of Property. *Cardozo Law Review* 18: 309–409.

Harris, R. and Rampton, B. (eds.). (2003). *The Language, Ethnicity and Race Reader*. London: Routledge.

Harris-Perry, M. (2011). *Sister Citizen: Shame, Stereotypes, and Black Women in America*. Cambridge, MA: Harvard University Press.

Hassa, S. (2010). Kiff my zikmu: Symbolic Dimensions of Arabic, English and Verlan in French Rap Texts. In M. Terkourafi (ed.), pp. 44–66.

Hatala, E. (1976). Environmental Effects on White Students in Black Schools. Unpublished manuscript, Philadelphia.

Haugen, E. (1966). *Language Conflict and Language Planning: The Case of Modern Norway*. Cambridge, MA: Harvard University Press.

Heath, S. B. (1983). *Ways with Words: Language, Life and Work in Communities and Classrooms*. Cambridge University Press.

(2012). *Words at Work and Play: Three Decades in Family and Community Life*. Cambridge University Press.

Heller, M. (1993). Code-Switching and the Politics of Language. In L. Milroy and P. Muysken (eds.), pp. 158–174.

(2008). Language and the Nation-State: Challenges to Sociolinguistic Theory and Practice. *Journal of Sociolinguistics* 12(4): pp. 504–524.

Henley, N. (1995). Ethnicity and Gender Issues in Language. In H. Ladrine (ed.), *Bringing Cultural Diversity to Feminist Psychology: Theory, Research and Practice* (pp. 361–396). Washington, DC: American Psychological Association.

Herring, S. C. (2005). Gender and Power in Online Communication. In T. Heubner and K. Davis (eds.), *Sociopolitical Porspectives on Language Policy and Planning in the USA* (pp. 1–16). Amsterdam: John Benjamins.

Hey, V. (2006). The Politics of Performative Resignification: Translating Judith Butler's Theoretical Discourse and its Potential for a Sociology of Education. *British Journal of Sociology of Education* 27(4): 439–457.

Higginbotham, E. B. (1993). *Righteous Discontent: The Women's Movement in the Black Baptist Church, 1880–1920*. Cambridge, MA: Harvard University Press.

Hill, J. H. (2000). Read My Article: Language Ideology and the Over-Determination of "Promising" in American Presidential Politics. In P. V. Kroskrity (ed.), *Regimes of Language: Ideologies, Polities and Identities* (pp. 259–292). Santa Fe: SAR Press.

   (2008). *The Everyday Language of White Racism*. Chichester, UK; Malden, MA: Wiley-Blackwell.

Hine, C. (2000). *Virtual Ethnography*. London: Sage.

Holmes, J. and Meyerhoff, M. (eds.). (2005). *The Handbook of Language and Gender*. Oxford: Blackwell.

Hooks, B. (1993). Ice Cube Culture: A Shared Passion for Speaking Truth. *Spin* April.

   (1994). *Outlaw Culture: Resisting Representations*. New York: Routledge.

Houston, M. and Davis, O. (2001). *Centering Ourselves: African American Feminist and Womanist Studies of Discourse*. Creskill, NJ: Hampton Press.

How Many Slaves Came to America? Fact vs. Fiction. (n.d.). *The Root*. Retrieved March 23, 2013, from www.theroot.com/views/100-amazing-facts-about-negro-0

Huang, E. (2013). *Fresh off the Boat: A Memoir*. New York: Spiegel & Grau.

Hudson, B. (2001). *African American Female Speech Communities: Varieties of Talk*. Westport: Bergin & Garvey.

Hudson, R. A. (1980). *Sociolinguistics*. Cambridge University Press.

Huebner, T. (1999). Sociopolitical Perspectives on Language Policy, Politics and Praxis. In T. Huebner and K. Davis (eds.), *Sociopolitical Perspectives on Language Policy and Planning – the USA* (pp. 1–16). Amsterdam: John Benjamins.

Hurston, Z. N. (1937). *Their Eyes were Watching God*. New York: HarperCollins.

Hutcherson, W. (1993). Dr. Hutcherson's Guide to Mother Jokes. *Source* 4: 52.

Hyde, C. (1995). The Meaning of Whiteness. *Qualitative Sociology* 18: 87–95.

Hymes, D. (1964). *Language in Culture and Society: A Reader in Linguistics and Anthropology*. New York: Harper and Row.

   (1972). On Communicative Competence. In J. B. Pride and J. Holmes (eds.), *Sociolinguistics* (pp. 269–293). Harmondsworth: Penguin.

(1974a). *Foundations in Sociolinguistics: An Ethnographic Approach*. Philadelphia: University of Pennsylvania Press.

(1974b). Ways of Speaking. In R. Bauman and J. Sherzer (eds.), *Explorations in the Ethnography of Speaking* (pp. 433–451). Cambridge University Press.

Ice Cube. (1996). *Bow Down*. Lench/Priority.

Ice Cube and Davis, A. Y. (1992). Nappy Happy. *Transition* 58: 174–192.

Inoue, M. (2002). Gender, Language, and Modernity: Toward an Effective History of Japanese Women's Language. *American Ethnologist* 29(2): 392–422.

(2006). *Vicarious Language: Gender and Linguistic Modernity in Japan*. Berkeley: University of California Press.

Irvine, J. (1974). Strategies of Status Manipulation in Wolof Greeting. In R. Bauman and J. Sherzer (eds.), *Explorations in the Ethnography of Speaking* (pp. 167–191). Cambridge University Press.

(1989). When Talk Isn't Cheap: Language and Political Economy. *American Ethnologist* May 16(2).

(1993). Insult and Responsibility: Verbal Abuse in a Wolof Village. In J. H. Hill and J. T. Irvine (eds.), *Responsibility and Evidence in Oral Discourse* (pp. 105–135). Cambridge University Press.

(2001). "Style" as Distinctiveness: The Culture and Ideology of Linguistic Distinctiveness. In Eckert and Rickford (eds.), pp. 21–43.

Irvine, J. and Gal, S. (2000). Language Ideology and Linguistic Differentiation. In P. Kroskrity (ed.), *Regimes of Language: Ideologies, Polities and Identities* (pp. 35–84). Santa Fe: SAR Press.

Jackson, B. (2004 [1974]). *Get Your Ass in the Water and Swim Like Me: African-American Narrative Poetry from the Oral Tradition*. London: Routledge.

Jackson, J. (1974). Language Identity of the Colombian Vaupés Indians. In R. Bauman and J. Sherzer (eds.), *Explorations in the Ethnography of Speaking* (pp. 50–64). Cambridge University Press.

(1983). *The Fish People: Linguistic Exogamy and Tukanoan Identity in Northwest Amazonia*. Cambridge University Press.

(1995). Preserving Indian Culture: Shaman Schools and Ethno-Education in the Vaupés, Colombia. *Cultural Anthropology* 10(3): 302–329.

Jacobs, H. A. (2001). *Incidents in the Life of a Slave Girl*. Mineola, NY: Dover Publications.

Jacobs-Huey, L. (1997). Is There an Authentic African American Speech Community: Carla Revisited. *University of Pennsylvania Working Papers* 4(1).

(2006). *From the Kitchen to the Parlor: Language and African American Women's Hair Care*. Oxford University Press.

Jakobson, R. (1960). Closing Statement: Linguistics and Poetics. In T. A. Sebeok (ed.), *Style in Language* (pp. 398–429). Cambridge, MA: MIT Press.

Jam, B. (2010, July 22). The Gospel of Hip Hop According to KRS ONE, Part III – Spellings & Definitions of Hip Hop. *AMOEBLOG*. Retrieved from www.amoeba.com/blog/2010/07/jamoeblog/the-gospel-of-hip-hop-according-to-krs-one-part-iii-spellings-definitions-of-hip-hop.html.

Jaynes, G. D. and Williams, J. (1989). The Schooling of Black Americans. In G. Jaynes and R. W. Jr. (eds.), *A Common Destiny* (pp. 329–390). Washington, DC: National Academy Press.

Jensen, A. (1969). How Much Can We Boost IQ and Scholastic Achievement? *Harvard Educational Review* 39(1): 1–123.

Jespersen, O. (1992 [1964]). *Language: Its Nature, Development and Origin.* London: Allen & Unwin.

Johnson, C. (1982). *Oxherding Tales.* New York: Grove Weidenfeld.

Johnson, D. and Campbell, R. (1981). *Black Migration in America.* Durham, NC: Duke University Press.

Johnson, W. (1999). *Soul by Soul: Life Inside the Antebellum Slave Market.* Cambridge, MA: Harvard University Press.

Jones, D. (1988). Towards a Native Anthroplogy. In J. Cole (ed.), *Anthroplogy for the Nineties* (pp. 30–41). New York: The Free Press.

Jones, G. M. and Schieffelin, B. B. (2009). Enquoting Voices, Accomplishing Talk: Uses of be + like in Instant Messaging. *Language and Communication* 29(1): 77–113.

Keating, E. and Sunakawa, C. (2010). Participation Cues: Coordinating Activity and Collaboration in Complex Online Gaming Worlds. *Language in Society* 39(03): 331–356.

Kelley, R. D. G. (1996). Kickin' Reality, Kickin' Ballistics: Gangsta Rap and Postindustrial Los Angeles. In Perkins (ed.), pp. 117–158.

(1997). *Yo' Mama's dysfunctional! – Fighting the Culture Wars in Urban America.* Boston: Beacon Press.

Kennedy, J. (2010). IFPI Digital Music Report 2010: Music How, When, Where You Want It. (Recording). IFPI Digital Music.

Keyes, C. L. (2004). *Rap Music and Street Consciousness.* Urbana: University of Illinois Press.

Kiesling, S. (2077). Men, Masculinities and Language. *Language and Linguistic Compass* 1(6): 653–673.

Kiesling, S. and Schilling-Estes, N. (1998). Language Style as Identity Construction: A Footing and Framing Approach. Paper presented at the NWAVE 27.

Kikuzawa, S. (1929). Fujin no kotobano tokucho ni tsuite (On the Characteristics of Women's Language). *Kokugo Kyoiku* 14(3): 66–75.

Kincaid, J. (1988). *A Small Place.* New York: Farrar, Straus and Giroux.

K'naan (2005). What's Hardcore? (Recording.) On The Dusty Foot Philosopher: BMG Music.

Kochman, T. (ed.). (1972). *Rappin' and Stylin' Out: Communication in Urban Black America.* Urbana: University of Illinois Press.

(1981). *Black and White Styles in Conflict.* University of Chicago Press.

(1983). The Boundary between Play and Nonplay in Black Verbal Dueling. *Language and Society* 12(3): 329–337.

(1986). Strategic Ambiguity in Black Speech Genres: Cross-Cultural Interference in Participant–Observation Research. *Text* 6(2): 153–170.

Kondo, D. (1990). *Crafting Selves: Power, Gender, and Discourses of Identity in a Japanese Workplace*. London: Routledge.

(1997). *About Face: Performing Race in Fashion and Theater*. London: Routledge.

(2000). (Re)Visions of Race: Contemporary Race Theory and the Cultural Politics of Racial Crossover in Documentary Theatre. *Theatre Journal* 52: 81–107.

Kool Herc. (2005). Introduction. In Chang (ed.), pp. xi–xii.

Krims, A. (2000). *Rap Music and the Poetics of Identity*. New York: Cambridge University Press.

Kroskrity, P. (1993). *Language, History and Identity: Ethnolinguistic Studies of the Arizona Tewa*. Tucson, AZ: University of Arizona Press.

(2004). Language Ideologies. In Duranti (ed.), pp. 496–517. Hoboken, NJ: Wiley-Blackwell.

KRS-One. (2009). *The Gospel of Hip Hop: First Instrument*. Brooklyn, NY: Power-House Books.

Kulick, D. (2003). Language and Desire. In J. Holmes and M. Meyerhoff (eds.), *The Handbook of Language and Gender* (pp. 119–141). Malden, MA: Blackwell.

(2009). No. In Duranti (ed.), 1997, pp. 493–503.

Labov, W. (1969). Contraction and Deletion and Inherent Variability of the English Copula. *Language* 45: 715–762.

(1972a). *Language in the Inner City: Studies in the Black English Vernacular*. Philadelphia: University of Pennsylvania Press.

(1972b). *Sociolinguistic Patterns*. Philadelphia: University of Pennsylvania Press.

(1980). Is There a Creole Speech Community? In A. Valdman and A. Highfield (eds.), *Theoretical Orientations in Creole Study* (pp. 369–388). New York: Academic Press.

(1982). Objectivity and Commitment in Linguistic Science: The Case of the Black English Trial in Ann Arbor. *Language in Society* 11: 165–202.

(1998). Co-existent Systems in African-American Vernacular English. In S. S. Mufwene, J. R. Rickford, G. Bailey and J. Baugh (eds.), *African-American English: Structure, History and Use* (pp. 110–153). London, New York: Routledge.

(2001). The Anatomy of Style-Shifting. In Eckert and Rickford (eds.), pp. 85–108.

(2008). Unendangered Dialects, Endangered People. In K. King and N. Schilling-Estes (eds.), *Sustaining Linguistic Diversity: Endangered and Minority Languages and Language Varieties* (pp. 219–238). Washington, DC: Georgetown University Press.

(2012). *Dialect Diversity in America: The Politics of Language Change*. Charlottesville, VA: University of Virginia Press.

Labov, W. and Harris, W. (1986). De facto Segregation in Black and White Vernaculars. In D. Sankoff (ed.), *Diversity and Diachrony* (pp. 1–24). Amsterdam: John Benjamins.

Labov, W., Cohen, P., Robins, C. and Lewis, J. (1968). *A Study of the Non-standard English of Negro and Puerto Rican Speakers in New York City, Volume I* (US Regional Survey Final Report, Cooperative Research Project 3288). Philadelphia: US Regional Survey.

Labov, W., Yaeger, M. and Steiner, R. (1972). *A Quantitative Study of Sound Change in Progress*. Philadelphia: US Regional Survey.

Lakoff, R. T. (1975). *Language and Woman's Place*. New York: Harper and Row.
    (2004). Author's Introduction: Language and Woman's Place Revisited. In M. Bucholtz (ed.), *Language and Woman's Place: Text and Commentaries* (pp. 15–38). New York: Oxford University Press.

Lamphere, L., Regoné, H. and Zavella, P. (eds.). (1997). *Situated Lives: Gender and Culture in Everyday Life*. New York: Routledge.

Lanehart, S. L. (2002). *Sista, Speak!: Black Women Kinfolk Talk About Language and Literacy*. Austin: University of Texas Press.
    (ed.). (2009a). *African American Women's Language: Discourse, Education and Identity*. Newcastle: Cambridge Scholars Publishing.
    (2009b). *Sista, Speak! Black Women Kinfolk Talk about Language and Literacy*. Austin: University of Texas Press.

Lathan, S. (1984). *Beat Street*. (Movie.)

Lave, J. and Wenger, E. (1991). *Situated Learning: Legitimate Peripheral Participation*. Cambridge University Press.

Lazuta, J. (2013). Report: Mobile Phones Transform Lives in Africa. *VOA*. Retrieved March 27, 2013, from www.voanews.com/content/wold-bank-reports-says-mobile-phones-transform-lives-in-developing-africa/1592270.html.

Lee, B. (1997). *Talking Heads: Language, Metalanguage, and the Semiotics of Subjectivity*. Durham, NC: Duke University of Press.

Lefebvre, H. (1991). *The Production of Space* (D. Nicholson-Smith, trans; first published as *La production de l'espace* [1974]. Cambridge: Blackwell.
    (2003). *The Urban Revolution*. Minneapolis: University of Minnesota Press.
    (2008). *Critique of Everyday Life: Volume I*. London: Verso.

LePage, R. B. and Tabouret-Keller, A. (1985). *Acts of Identity: Creole-Based Approaches to Language and Ethnicity*. Cambridge University Press.

Lessig, L. (2005). *Free Culture: The Nature and Future of Creativity*. Harmondsworth: Penguin.

Levinson, S. (1983). *Pragmatics*. Cambridge University Press.
    (2002). Contextualizing "Contextualization Cues." In S. Eerdmans, C. Prevignano and P. Thibault (eds.), *Language and Interaction: Discussions with John Gumperz* (pp. 31–39). Amsterdam: John Benjamins.

Lindstrom, L. (1992). Context Contests: Debatable Truth Statements on Tanna (Vanuatu). In A. Duranti and C. Goodwin (eds.), *Rethinking Context: Language as an Interactive Phenomenon* (pp. 101–124). Cambridge University Press.

Lippi-Green, R. (1997). *English with an Accent: Language, Ideology, and Discrimination in the United States*. London, New York: Routledge.

Lipsitz, G. (1994). *Dangerous Crossroads: Popular Music, Postmodernism and the Poetics of Place*. London, New York: Verso.

Lucy, J. A. (1993). *Reflexive Language: Reported Speech and Metapragmatics*. Cambridge University Press.

Lyons, J. (1981). *Language and Linguistics: An Introduction*. Cambridge University Press.

Maartens, J. (1998). Multilingualism and Language Policy in South Africa. In G. Extra and J. Maartens (eds.), *Multilingualism in a Multicultural Context: Case Studies on South Africa and Western Europe* (pp. 15–36). Tilburg University Press.

Major, C. (1994). *Juba to Jive: A Dictionary of African-American Slang*. New York: Penguin Books.

Makoni, S. (2003). From Misinvention to Disinvention of Language: Multilingualism and the South African Constitution. In S. Makoni, G. Smitherman, A. Ball and A. Spears (eds.), *Black Linguistics: Language, Society and Politics in Africa and the Americas* (pp. 132–152). London: Routledge.

Males, M. A. (1996). *The Scapegoat Generation: America's War on Adolescents*. Monroe, ME: Common Courage Press.

(1999). *Framing Youth: 10 Myths about the Next Generation*. Monroe, ME: Common Courage Press.

Manjoo, F. (2010). How Black People Use Twitter. *Slate*. Retrieved August 10, 2010 from www.slate.com/articles/technology/technology/2010/08/

Marks, C. (1989). *Farewell – We're Good and Gone: The Great Black Migration*. Bloomington/Indianapolis: Indiana University Press.

Martin, R. (2009). "No Dogs or Mexicans Allowed": Discourses of Racism and Ideology in Pahrump, Nevada. *Explorations in Anthropology* 9(1): 91–105.

Massey, D. and Denton, N. (1993). *American Apartheid: Segregation and the Making of the Underclass*. Cambrige, MA: Harvard University Press.

McCann, E. J. (1999). Race, Protest, and Public Space: Contextualizing Lefebvre in the US City. *Antipode* 31(2): 163–184.

McConnel-Ginet, S. (1988). Language and Gender. In F. J. Newmeyer (ed.), *Linguistics: The Cambridge Survey* (pp. 75–99). Cambridge University Press.

McCrum, R., MacNeil, R. and Cran, W. (1986). *The Story of English* (3rd rev. edn.). Harmondsworth: Penguin.

McDermott, M. and Samson, F. (2005). White Racial and Ethnic Identity in the United States. *Annual Review of Sociology* 31(1): 245–261.

McIntosh, J. (2010). Mobile Phones and Mipoho's Prophecy: The Powers and Dangers of Flying Language. *American Ethnologist* 37(2): 337–353.

McMillan, D. W. and Chavis, D. M. (1986). Sense of Community: A Definition and Theory. *Journal of Community Psychology* 14(1): 6–23.

Mercer, K. (1994). *Welcome to the Jungle: New Positions in Black Cultural Studies*. New York, London: Routledge.

Meyerhoff, M. (2002). Communities of Practice. In J. K. Chambers, P. Trudgill and N. Schilling-Estes (eds.), *Handbook of Language Variation and Change* (pp. 526–548). Oxford: Blackwell.

Milani, T. M. and Johnson, S. (2010). Critical Intersections: Language Ideologies and Media Discourse. In Johnson and Milani (eds.), pp. 3–16.

Milroy, L. (1980). *Language and Social Networks*. 2nd edn. Hoboken, NJ: Wiley-Blackwell.

(1987). *Observing and Analyzing Natural Language*. Oxford: Blackwell.

Milroy, L. and Milroy, J. (1992). Social Network and Social Class: Toward an Integrated Sociolinguistic Model. *Language in Society* 21; 1–26.

Milroy, L. and Muysken, P. (eds.). (1995). *One Speaker, Two Languages: Cross-Linguistic Perspectives on Code-Switching*. Cambridge University Press.

(1973). Signifying. In A. Dundes (ed.), *Mother Wit from the Laughing Barrel*. (pp. 310–328). New York: Garland Publishing.

Mitchell, T. (1996). *Popular Music and Local Identity: Rock, Pop and Rap in Europe and Oceania*. Leicester University Press.

Mitchell, T. (ed.). (2001). *Global Noise: Rap and Hip-Hop outside the USA*. Middletown, CT: Wesleyan University Press.

Mitchell-Kernan, C. (1971). *Language Behavior in a Black Urban Community* (Working Paper 23). Berkeley CA: Language Behavior Research Laboratory.

(1972a). On the Status of Black English for Native Speakers: An Assessment of Attitudes and Values. In C. Cazden, V. P. John and D. Hymes (eds.), *Functions of Language in the Classroom*. New York: Teachers College Press.

(1972b). Signifying, Loud-Talking, and Marking. In Kochman (ed.), pp. 315–335.

Morgan, M. (1991). Indirectness and Interpretation in African American Women's Discourse. *Pragmatics* 1(4): 421–451.

(1993). The Africanness of Counterlanguage among Afro-Americans. In S. Mufwene (ed.), *Africanisms in Afro-American Language Varieties* (pp. 423–435). Athens, GA: University of Georgia Press.

(ed.). (1994a). *Language and the Construction of Identity in Creole Situations*. Los Angeles: UCLA Center for Afro-American Studies.

(1994b). The African American Speech Community: Reality and Sociolinguistics. In Morgan (ed.), 1994a, pp. 121–148).

(1996). Conversational Signifying: Grammar and Indirectness among African American Women. In E. Ochs, E. Schegloff and S. Thompson (eds.), *Interaction and Grammar* (pp. 405–433). Cambridge University Press.

(1998). More Than a Mood or an Attitude: Discourse and Verbal Genres in African-American Culture. In S. S. Mufwene, J. R. Rickford, G. Bailey and J. Baugh (eds.), *African-American English: Structure, History, and Use* (pp. 251–281). London/New York: Routledge.

(1999). "No Woman No Cry": Claiming African American Women's Place. In M. Bucholtz, A. C. Liang and Laurel A. Sutton (ed.), *Reinventing Identities: From Category to Practice in Language and Gender* (pp. 27–45). Oxford University Press.

(2001). "Ain't Nothin' But A G Thang": Grammar, Variation and Language Ideology in Hip Hop Identity. In S. L. Lanehart (ed.), *Sociocultural and Historical Contexts of African American English* (pp. 185–207). Philadelphia: John Benjamins.

(2002). *Language, Discourse and Power in African American Culture*. Cambridge University Press.

(2003). Signifying Laughter and the Subtleties of Loud-Talking: Memory and Meaning in African American Women's Discourse. In M. Farr (ed.), *Ethnolinguistic Chicago: Language and Literacy in Chicago's Neighborhoods* (pp. 51–76). Mahwah, NJ: Lawrence Erlbaum.

(2004a). "I'm Every Woman": Black Women's (Dis)placement in Women's Language Study. In M. Bucholtz (Ed.), *Robin Tolmach Lakoff, Language and Woman's Place: Text and Commentaries* (2 edn., pp. 252–259). Oxford University Press.

(2004b). Speech Community. In Duranti (ed.), pp. 3–22.

(2005). Hip-Hop Women Shredding the Veil: Race and Class in Popular Feminist Identity. *The South Atlantic Quarterly* 104(3): 424–444.

(2009a). Foreword: "Just Take Me as I Am." In Lanehart (ed.), pp. xiii–xxiv.

(2009b). The Presentation of Indirectness and Power in Everyday Life. *Journal of Pragmatics* 42(2): 283–291.

(2009c). *The Real Hiphop: Battling for Knowledge, Power, and Respect in the LA Underground*. Durham, NC: Duke University Press.

(2013). *Black Twitter: Strategies in Talking Black and Talking Back*. In press.

Morgan, M. and Bennett, D. (2006). Getting off of Black Women's Backs: Love Her or Leave Her Alone. *The Du Bois Review* 3(2): 1–18.

(2011). Hip-Hop and the Global Imprint of a Black Cultural Form. *Deadalus* 140(2): 176–196.

Morgan, M. and Fischer, D. E. (2010). Hiphop and Race: Blackness, Language and Creativity. In H. R. Markus and P. L. Moya (eds.), *Doing Race: 21 Essays for the 21st Century*. New York: Norton Press.

Morrison, T. (1987). *Beloved*. New York: Knopf.

(1994). *The Nobel Lecture In Literature, 1993*. New York: Knopf.

Motley, C. M. and Henderson, G. R. (2008). The Global Hip-Hop Diaspora: Understanding the Culture. *Journal of Business Research* 61(3): 243–253.

Mullings, L. (1994). Images, Ideology, and Women of Color. In M. B. Zinn and B. T. Dill (eds.), *Women of Color in US Society* (pp. 265–289). Philadelphia: Temple University Press.

Myers-Scotton, C. (1998). *Codes and Consequences: Choosing Linguistic Variables*. Oxford University Press.

N. W. A. (1988). Fuck tha Police. In *Straight Outta Compton*. (Recording.) Priority/Ruthless.

Nakamura, L. (2008). *Digitizing Race: Visual Cultures of the Internet*. Minneapolis: University of Minnesota Press.

Neal, M. A. (2002). *Soul Babies: Black Popular Culture and the Post-Soul Aesthetic*. New York: Routledge.

Neate, P. (2006). AfroReggae: Rio's Top Hip-Hop Band. *The Independent*. February 24.

Nelson, A. and Tu, T. L. N. (eds.). (2001). *Technicolor: Race, Technology and Everyday Life*. New York University Press.

Nichols, P. C. (1983). Linguistic Options and Choices for Black Women in the Rural South. In B. Thorne, C. Kramerae and N. Henley (eds.), *Language, Gender and Society* (pp. 54–68). Rowley, MA: Newbury House.

(1998 [1982]). Black Women in the Rural South: Conservative and Innovative. In Coates (ed.), pp. 55–63.

Ntarangwi, M. (2009). *East African Hip Hop: Youth Culture and Globalization*. University of Urbana Press.

Ochs, E. (1992). Indexing Gender. In A. Duranti and C. Goodwin (eds.), *Rethinking Context: Language as an Interactive Phenomenon*. University of Cambridge Press.

Ochs, E. and Schieffelin, B. (1984). Language Acquisition and Socialization: Three Developmental Stories. In R. Shweder and R. LeVine (eds.), *Culture Theory: Essays on Mind, Self and Emotion* (pp. 276–320). Cambridge University Press.

Ogbu, J. (1978). *Minority Education and Caste*. Orlando, FL: Academic Press.

Omi, M. and Winant, H. (1994). *Racial Formation in the United States: From the 1960s to the 1990s*. New York: Routledge.

Omoniyi, T. (2009). "So I Choose to Do Am Naija Style": Hip Hop Language, and Postcolonial Identities. In Alim, Ibrahim and Pennycook (eds.), pp. 113–138.

Osumare, H. (2008). *The Africanist Aesthetic in Global Hip-Hop: Power Moves*. New York: Palgrave Macmillan.

Palfrey, J. and Gasser, U. *Born Digital: Understanding the First Generation of Digital Natives*. New York: Basic Books.

Pardue, D. (2004). Writing in the Margins: Brazilian Hip-Hop as an Educational Project. *Anthropology and Education Quarterly* 35(4): 411–432.

Paris, D. (2011). *Language across Difference: Ethnicity, Communication, and Youth Identities in Changing Urban Schools*. Cambridge University Press.

Patrick, P. (2002). The Speech Community. In J. K. Chambers, P. Trudgill and N. Schilling-Estes (eds.), *Handbook of Language Variation and Change* (pp. 573–597). Oxford: Blackwell.

Paugh, A. L. (2012). *Playing with Languages: Children and Change in a Caribbean Village*. New York: Berghahn Books.

Paulston, C. B. (2003). Linguistic Minorities and Language Policies. In C. B. Paulston and G. R. Tucker (eds.), *Sociolinguistics: The Essential Readings* (pp. 394–407). Oxford: Blackwell.

Peirce, C. S. (1960a). *Collected Papers of Charles Sanders Peirce, Volume II* (H. Charles and P. Weiss, trans.) New York: Harvard University Press.

(1960b). *Philosophical Writings of Peirce*. New York: Dover Publications.

Peirce, C. S. and Buchler, J. (1955). *Philosophical Writings of Peirce*. New York: Dover.

Pennay, M. (2001). Rap in Germany: The Birth of a Genre. In Mitchell (ed.), pp. 111–133. Middletown, CT: Wesleyan University Press.

Pennycook, A. (2007). *Global Englishes and Transcultural Flows*. London: Routledge.

Pennycook, A. and Mitchell, T. (2009). Hip Hop as Dusty Foot Philosophy: Engaging Locality. In Alim, Ibrahim and Pennycook (eds.), pp. 25–42. New York: Routledge.

Percelay, J., Monteria, I. and Dweck, S. (1994). *Snaps*. New York: Quill.

Perkins, W. E. (ed.). (1995). *Droppin' Science: Critical Essays on Rap Music and Hip Hop Culture*. Philadelphia: Temple University Press.

Perry, I. (2004). *Prophets of the Hood: Politics and Poetics in Hip Hop*. Durham, NC: Duke University Press.

Phaswana, N. (2003). Contradiction or Affirmation? The South African Language Policy and the South African National Government. In S. Makoni, G. Smitherman, A. Ball and A. Spears (eds.), *Black Linguistics: Language, Society and Politics in Africa and the Americas* (pp. 117–130). London: Routledge.

Philips, S. U. (1972). Participant Structures and Communicative Competence: Warm Springs Children in Community and Classroom. In C. B. Cazden, V. P. John and D. Hymes (eds.), *Functions of Language in the Classroom* (pp. 370–394). Long Grove, IL: Waveland.

(1974). Warm Springs "Indian Time": How the Regulation of Participation Affects the Progression of Events. In R. Bauman and J. Sherzer (eds.), *Explorations in the Ethnography of Speaking* (pp. 92–109). Cambridge University Press.

(1983). *The Invisible Culture: Communication in Classroom and Community on the Warm Springs Indian Reservation*. Long Grove, IL: Waveland.

Pichler, P. and Coates, J. (eds.). (2011). *Language and Gender: A Reader*. Oxford: Blackwell.

Pirandello, L. (1995). *Six Characters in Search of an Author and Other Plays* (M. Musa, trans.). London: Penguin.

Pitt, D. (1989). Jogger's Attackers Terrorized at Least 9 in 2 Hours. *New York Times*. 22 April.

Pollard, V. (1983). The Social History of Dread Talk. In L. Carrington (ed.), *Studies in Caribbean Language* (pp. 46–62). St Augustine, Trinidad: Society for Caribbean Linguistics.

Pomerantz, A. (1984). Agreeing and Disagreeing with Assessments: Some Features of Preferred/Dispreferred Turn Shapes. In J. M. Atkinson and J. Heritage (eds.), *Structures of Social Action* (pp. 57–101). Cambridge University Press.

Potter, R. A. (1995). *Spectacular Vernaculars: Hip Hop and the Politics of Postmodernism*. New York University Press.

Pough, G. D. (2004). *Check it While I Wreck it: Black Womanhood, Hip Hop Culture, and the Public Sphere*. Boston: Northeastern University Press.

Powell, K. (2003). An Interview with Kevin Powell on Hip Hop. Race and Politics. *Davey D.* Retrieved from www.daveyd.com/interviewkevinpowell.html

Pratt, M. L. (1992). *Imperial Eyes: Travel Writing and Transculturation.* London: Routledge.

Pratto, F. (2005). The Bases of Gendered Power. In A. H. Eagly, A. E. Beall and R. J. Sternberg (eds.), *The Psychology of Gender* (pp. 242–268). New York: Guilford.

Price, E. G. (2006). *Hip Hop Culture.* ABC-CLIO.

Pryor, R. (1976). *Bicentennial Nigger.* Retrieved from http://en.wikipedia.org/w/index.php?title=Bicentennial_Nigger&oldid=530445511

Public Enemy (Writer) and T. B. Squad (Director) (1989). Fight the Power, *Do The Right Thing*: Tamia.

Putnam, R. (2000). *Bowling Alone: The Collapse and Revival of American Community.* New York: Simon Schuster.

Ralli, T. (2005). Who's a Looter? In Storm's Aftermath, Pictures Kick Up a Different Kind of Tempest. September 5. *New York Times.*

Rampton, B. (1998). Speech Community. In J. O. Jeff Vershueren, J. Blommaert and C. Bulcaen (eds.), *Society and Language Use: Handbook of Pragmatics* (pp. 274–303). Amsterdam: John Benjamins.

  (2005). *Crossing: Language and Ethnicity among Adolescents.* 2nd. edn. Manchester: St Jerome Publishing.

  (2006). *Language in Late Modernity: Interaction in an Urban School.* New York: Cambridge University Press.

Ramsey, J. and Guthrie, P. (2003). *Race Music: Black Cultures from Bebop to Hip-Hop.* Berkeley: University of California Press.

Richardson, E. (2006). *Hiphop Literacies.* New York, London: Routledge.

Rickford, J. (1975). Carrying the New Wave into Syntax: The Case of Black English *bin*. In R. W. Fasold and R. W. Shuy (eds.), *Analyzing Variation in Language* (pp. 162–183). Washington, DC: Georgetown University Press.

  (1985). Ethnicity as a Sociolinguistic Boundary. *American Speech* 60: 99–125.

  (1997). *Language in Society* 26: 161–197.

Rickford, J. R. and McNair-Knox, F. (1993). Addressee and Topic-Influenced Style Shift: A Quantitative Sociolinguistic Study. In D. Biber and E. Finegan (eds.), *Perspectives on Register: Situation Register Variation within Sociolinguistics* (pp. 235–276). Oxford University Press.

Rickford, J. and Rickford, A. (1976). Cut-Eye and Suck Teeth: African Words and Gestures in New World Guise. *Journal of American Folklore* 89(353): 194–309.

  (1995). Dialect Readers Revisited. *Linguistics and Education* 7: 107–128.

Rickford, J. R. and Rickford, R. J. (2000). *Spoken Soul: The Story of Black English.* New York: John Wiley & Sons.

Robertson, R. (1995). Glocalization: Time–Space and Homogeneity-Heterogeneity. In M. Featherstone, S. Lash and R. Robertson (eds.), *Global Modernities* (pp. 24–44). Thousand Oaks, CA: Sage Publications.

Rohter, L. (2007). Brazilian Government Invests in Culture of Hip-Hop, *New York Times*. March 14.

Romaine, S. (1994). Language Standardization and Linguistic Fragmentation in Tok Pisin. In Morgan (ed.), *Language in Creole Situations* (pp. 19–41).

(2000). *Language in Society: An Introduction to Sociolinguistics*. 2nd edn. Oxford University Press.

Rosaldo, M. (1974). Women, Culture and Society: A Theoretical Overview. In M. Z. Rosaldo and L. Lamphere (eds.), *Woman, Culture, and Society* (pp. 17–42). Stanford University Press.

(1982). The Things We Do with Words: Ilongot Speech Acts and Speech Act Theory in Philosophy. *Language in Society* 11: 203–237.

Rose, T. (1994). *Black Noise: Rap Music and Black Culture in Contemporary America*. Hanover, NH: Wesleyan University Press.

Rosina, L. (2012). *English with an Accent: Language, Ideology and Discrimination in the United States*. 2nd edn. New York: Routledge.

Ruddick, S. (1996). Constructing Difference in Public Spaces: Race, Class, and Gender as Interlocking Systems. *Urban Geography* 17(2): 132–151.

Sacks, H., Schegloff, E. and Jefferson, G. (1974). A Simplest Systematics for the Organization for Turn-Taking in Conversation. *Language* 50(4): 696–735.

Said, E. (1978). *Orientalism*. New York: Pantheon.

Salzberg, A. (2012). Jay-Z, Kanye West, and the French Presidential Campaign. *Alysa Salzberg's Blog: Fiction and Even Stanger Truths*. Retrieved from http://open.salon.com/blog/alysa_salzberg/2012/04/26/the_french_presidential_campaign_feat_jay-z_and_kanye_west

Santos, J. (2012). "The Meaning of Blackness in Brazilian Hiphop." Paper presented at the W. E. B. Du Bois Institute, Harvard University.

Sapir, E. (1921). *Language: An Introduction to the Study of Speech*. New York: Harcourt, Brace and World.

Sarkeesian, A. (2012). Image-Based Harassment and Visual Misogyny. *Feminist Frequency*. Retrieved July 23. from www.feministfrequency.com/2012/07/image-based-harassment-and-visual-misogyny/

Savigliano, M. (1995). *Tango and the Political Economy of Passion*. Boulder, CO: Westview Press.

Schieffelin, B. B. and Ochs, E. (1986). *Language Socialization across Cultures*. New York: Cambridge University Press.

Searle, J. R. (1969). *Speech Acts: An Essay in the Philosophy of Language*. Cambridge University Press.

(1976). The Classification of Illocutionary Acts. *Language in Society* 5(1): 1–23.

(1983). *Intentionality: An Essay in the Philosophy of Mind*. Cambridge University Press.

Shelby, T. (2005). *We Who Are Dark: The Philosophical Foundations of Black Solidarity*. Cambridge, MA: Harvard University Press.

Shelemay, K. (2011). Musical Communities: Rethinking the Collective in Music Author(s). *Journal of American Musicological Society* 64(2): 349–390.

Sidanius, J. and Pratto, F. (2001). *Social Dominance: An Intergroup Theory of Social Hierarchy and Oppression.* New York: Cambridge University Press.

Silverstein, M. (1976). Shifters, Linguistic Categories, and Cultural Descriptions. In K. Basso and H. Selby (ed.), *Meaning in Anthropology* (pp. 11–55). Albuquerque, NM: University of New Mexico Press.

(1979). Language Structure and Linguistic Ideology. In P. R. Clyne, W. F. Hanks and C. L. Hofbauer (eds.), *The Elements: A Parasession on Linguistic Units and Levels* (pp. 193–247). Chicago Linguistic Society.

(2003). Indexical Order and the Dialectics of Sociolinguistic Life. *Language and Communication* 23: 193–229.

Simpkins, G. A., Holt, G. and Simpkins, C. (1977). *Bridge: A Cross-Cultural Reading Program.* Boston, MA: Houghton Mifflin.

Simonsen, T. (1986). *You May Plow Here: The Narrative of Sara Brooks.* New York: Simon and Shuster.

Smith, E. (1997). *The Historical Development of African-American Language: The Transformationalist Theory.* San Francisco: Aspire Books.

Smitherman, G. (1977). *Talkin and Testifyin: The Language of Black America.* Boston: Houghton Mifflin.

(1981a). *Black English and the Education of Black Children and Youth: Proceedings of the National Invitational Symposium on the King Decision.* Detroit: Harpo Press.

(1981b). What Go Round Come Round: King in Perspective. *Harvard Educational Review* 1: 40–56.

(1991). What is Africa to Me? Language, Ideology and African American. *American Speech* 66: 115–132.

(1994). *Black Talk: Words and Phrases from the Hood to the Amen Corner.* New York: Houghton Mifflin.

(1998). Word from the Hood: The Lexicon of African American English. In S. S. Mufwene, J. Rickford, G. Bailey and J. Baugh (eds.), *African-American English: Structure, History, and Use* (pp. 203–225). London; New York: Routledge.

(1999). *Talkin' That Talk: Language, Culture and Education in African America.* London: Routledge.

Smooth, J. (2012). All These Sexist Gamer Dudes Are Some Shook Ones (June 24). Available online at: www.illdoctrine.com.

Solsky, B. (2004). *Language Policy.* Cambridge University Press.

Sorensen, A. (1967). Multilingualism in the Northwest Amazon. *American Anthropologist* 69(6): 670–682.

Sorokin, P. (1927). *Social and Cultural Mobility.* New York: Harper.

Spady, J. G., Samy Alim, H. and Samir Meghelli. (2006). *Tha Global Cipha: Hip Hop Culture and Consciousness.* Philadelphia: Black History Museum.

Spears, A. (1982). The Semi-Auxiliary "come" in Black English Vernacular. *Language* 58: 850–872.

(2001). Directness in the Use of African American English. In S. Lane-hart (ed.), *Sociocultural and Historical Contexts of African American English* (pp. 239–259). Amsterdam, Philadelphia: John Benjamins.

(2009). Theorizing African American Women's Language: Girl as a Discourse Marker. In Lanehart (ed.), pp. 76–90.

Spolsky, B. (2004). *Language Policy.* Cambridge University Press.

Squires, C. R. (2002). Rethinking the Black Public Sphere: An Alternative Vocabulary for Multiple Public Spheres. *Communication Theory* 12(4): 446–468.

Stanback, M. H. (1986). Language and Black Woman's Place: Evidence from the Black Middle Class. In P. A. Treichlet, C. Kramare and B. Stafford (eds.), *For Alma Mater: Theory and Practice in Feminist Scholarship* (pp. 177–196). Urbana: University of Illinois Press.

Stevenson, B. E. (1996). *Life In Black and White: Family and Community in the Slave South.* New York: Oxford University Press.

Stewart, W. (1969). Historical and Structural Bases for the Recognition of Negro Dialect. In J. Alatis (ed.), *School of Languages and Linguistics Monogram. Series No. 22* (pp. 215–225). Washington, DC: Georgetown University Press.

(1975). Teaching Blacks to Read against Their Will. In P. A. Luelsdorff (ed.), *Linguistic Perspectives on Black English* (pp. 107–132). Regensburg: Verlag Hans Carl Regensburg.

Strand, T. (n.d.). Winning the Dialect Popularity Contest: Mass-Mediated Language Ideologies and Local Responses in Rural Valdres, Norway. *Journal of Linguistic Anthropology* 22(1): 23–43.

Talbot, M. M. (2010). *Language and Gender.* Cambridge: Polity Press.

Tannen, D. (1994). *Gender and Discourse.* Oxford University Press.

(2012). Contextualization in Digital Discourse. Paper presented at the American Anthropological Association, November 14–18.

Tarski, A. (1956). *Logic, Semantics, Metamathematics.* Oxford: Clarendon Press.

Terkourafi, M. (ed.). (2010). *Languages of Global Hip Hop.* London: Continuum.

Thomas, D. A. (2004). *Modern Blackness: Nationalism, Globalization, and the Politics of Culture in Jamaica.* Durham, NC: Duke University Press.

Thomas, Euan, 2008. Chapter 1: Going into Battle. November 17. *Newsweek Magazine.*

Thomas, J. (1995). *Meaning in Interaction: An Introduction to Pragmatics.* London: Longman.

Thorne, B., Kramarae, C. and Henley, N. (1983). Language, Gender and Society: Opening a Second Decade of Research. In B. Thorne, C. Kramarae and N. Henley (eds.), *Language, Gender and Society* (pp. 7–24). Rowley, MA: Newbury House.

Tolliver-Weddington, G. (1979). Introduction: Ebonics (Black English): Implications for Education. *Journal of Black Studies* 9(4): 364–366.

Toop, D. (1992). *Rap Attack #2.* 2 edn. London, New York: Serpent's Tail.

Troutman, D. (2001). African American Women: Talking that Talk. In S. Lanehart (ed.), *Sociocultural and Historical Contexts of African American English* (pp. 211–238). Amsterdam, Philadelphia: John Benjamins.

Trudgill, P. (1972). Sex, Covert Prestige, and Linguistic Change in the Urban British English of Norwich. *Language in Society* 1: 179–195.

Turner, V. (1982). *From Ritual to Theater: The Human Seriousness of Play*. Baltimore, MA: PAJ Publications/The Johns Hopkins University Press.

Urciuoli, B. (1996). *Exposing Prejudice: Puerto Rican Experiences of Language, Race, and Class*. Boulder, CO: Westview Press.

Urla, J. (2001). "We are all Malcolm X!" Negu Gorriak, Hip Hop and the Basque Political Imaginary. In Mitchell (ed.), pp. 171–193.

Van Dijk, T. (2008). *Discourse and Power*. New York: Palgrave Macmillan.

Walker, A. (1982). *The Color Purple*. New York: Harcourt Brace Jovanovich.

Ward, M. C. (1971). *Them Children*. New York: Holt, Rinehart and Winston.

Watkins, C. (2009). *The Young and the Digital: What the Migration to Social Network Sites, Games, and Anytime Anywhere Media Means for our Future*. Boston: Beacon Press.

Watkins, M. (1994). On the Real Side: *Laughing, Lying, and Signifying*. New York: Simon and Schuster.

Weiss, B. (2009). *Street Dreams and Hip-Hop Barbershops: Global Fantasy in Urban Tanzania*. Bloomington, IN: Indiana University Press.

West, C. (1993). *Race Matters*. Boston: Beacon Press.

West, E. H. (1972). *The Black American and Education*. Columbus, OH: Charles E. Merrill.

Wharton, V. L. (1947). *The Negroes in Mississippi 1865–1890*. Chapel Hill, NC: University of North Carolina Press.

Wheeler, E. (1992). "Most of My Heroes Don't Appear on No Stamps": The Dialogics of Rap Music. *Black Music Research Journal* 11(2): 193–216.

Whitfield, S. (1992). *A Death in the Delta: The Story of Emmett Till*. Baltimore: The Johns Hopkins University Press.

Williams, B. (2001). Black Secret Technology: Detroit Techno and the Information Age. In Nelson and Tu (eds.), pp. 154–176.

Williams, P. (1996). Op-Ed. December 29. *The New York Times*.

Williams, R. (ed.). (1975). *Ebonics: The True Language of Black Folks*. St Louis: Institute of Black Studies.

Williams, S. A. (1986). *Dessa Rose*. New York: Berkeley Books.

Wilson, W. J. (1978). *The Declining Significance of Race*. University of Chicago Press.

(1987). *The Truly Disadvantaged*. University of Chicago Press.

(1996). *When Work Disappears: The World of the New Urban Poor*. New York: Vintage.

Winfrey, O. (2006). Chappelle's Story – Oprah.com. *Oprah.com*. February 3. Retrieved July 24, 2013, from www.oprah.com/oprahshow/Chappelles-Story

Wodak, R., Cillia, R. d., Reisigl, M. and Liebhart, K. (1999). *The Discursive Construction of National Identity*. Edinburgh University Press.

Wolfram, W. (1969). *A Sociolinguistic Description of Detroit Negro Speech*. Washington, DC: Center for Applied Linguistics.

(1991). *Dialects and American English*. Englewood Cliffs, NJ: Prentice Hall and Center for Applied Linguistics.

Wolfram, W. and Schilling-Estes, N. (1998). *American English*. Oxford: Blackwell.

Woodson, C. G. (2011). *The Mis-Education of the Negro*. New York: Tribeca Books.

Woolard, K. (1985). Language Variation and Cultural Hegemony: Toward an Integration of Sociolinguistic and Social Theory. *American Ethnologist* 12: 738–749.

(1987). Codeswitching and Comedy in Catalonia. *IPRA Papers in Pragmatics* 1: 106–122.

(1998). Introduction: Language Ideology as a Field of Inquiry. In B. Schieffelin, K. Woolard and P. Kroskrity (eds.), *Language Ideologies: Practice and Theory* (pp. 3–47). New York: Oxford University Press.

(2008). Why *dat* Now? Linguistic Anthropological Contributions to the Explanation of Sociolinguistic Icons and Change. *Journal of Sociolinguistics* 12(4): 432–452.

Yankah, K. (1995). *Speaking for the Chief: Okyeame and the Politics of Akan Royal Oratory*. Bloomington: Indiana University Press.

Youssouf, I. A., Grimshaw, A. D. and Bird, C. S. (1976). Greetings in the Desert. *American Ethnologist* 3(4): 797–824.

Zentella, A. C. (1996). The "chiquitification" of US Latinos and Their Languages; Or, Why We Need an Anthropolitical Linguistics. In Ide, R., Parker, R. and Sunaoshi, Y. (eds.), *Proceedings of the Third Annual Symposium about Language and Society, Austin [SALSA]. Texas Linguistic Forum* 36: 1–18. Austin: University of Texas Department of Linguistics.

(1997). *Growing Up Bilingual: Puerto Rican Children in New York*. Malden, MA: Blackwell.

Zhu, J. and Harrell, F. (2008). Daydreaming with Intention: Scalable Blending-Based Imagining and Agency in Generative Interactive Narrative. *AAAI Press*: 156–162.

Index